P9-CDA-679

AMERICAN POETRY
The Puritans through Walt Whitman

Twayne's Critical History of Poetry Series
AMERICAN LITERATURE

Kenneth Eble, Editor
University of Utah

AMERICAN POETRY
The Puritans through Walt Whitman

ALAN SHUCARD
University of Wisconsin—Parkside

Twayne Publishers • Boston
A Division of G. K. Hall & Co.

To Maureen with more love than ever.

© 1988 by G. K. Hall & Co.
All rights reserved.

Published by Twayne Publishers
A Division of G. K. Hall & Co.
70 Lincoln Street
Boston, Massachusetts 02111

Copyediting supervised by Barbara Sutton.
Book design and production by Janet Zietowski.

Typeset in 10/12 pt. Palatino by
Williams Press, Inc., Albany, New York.

Printed on permanent/durable acid-free paper
and bound in the United States of America.

Library of Congress Cataloging-in-Publication Data

Shucard, Alan, 1935–
  American poetry.

(Twayne's critical history of poetry series.
American literature)
  Bibliography: p. 193
  Includes index.
  1. American poetry—History and criticism.
I. Title.   II. Series.
PS303.S58 1988   811'.009   88-1524
ISBN 0-8057-8450-0 (alk. paper)

· *Contents* ·

· *Preface* ·

This study was a joy for me to write, for the undertaking caused me to reevaluate and clarify ideas—the way the act of writing always does, bless it—that I had evolved over more than three decades as student and teacher. If the audience learns, relearns, unlearns in the reading of this volume about as much as I did in the writing, then will my reward be multiplied.

I hope that my decisions about the organization and content of the book do not seem unduly quirky. I ordered the mass of material in the only way that made sense to me—generally chronologically but with notable violations of chronology as aesthetic or cultural considerations dictated. Common sense is more attractive to me than a calendar. Thus, for example, the Puritans come first and Walt Whitman last, as one would surely expect, but Edgar Allan Poe, some half a dozen years Ralph Waldo Emerson's junior, precedes Emerson so that I could keep the Transcendentalists, and especially Emerson, grouped next to Whitman where they belong, and still come out with Whitman at the end of the volume.

The question of content alone caused me a certain amount of anguish. I was driven to make the study as wide and inclusive as possible and, at the same time, as deep and detailed as possible. As in the preparation of most literary histories, I had to compromise, reluctantly, on both width and depth. Still, I trust that common sense prevailed in the choice of content, too, and that all the American poets worth looking at have been appropriately covered and placed in a context that sheds light on literary relationships among poets and of the poets to the broader American culture.

Conscious of sexist language when I meet it, I tried to avoid it when I could without impairing the efficiency of communication. I resorted to grammatical gender when not to do so would have introduced awkwardness. Others might have done better, but I hope that no one takes offense; I intended none.

There are many to whom I owe thanks if the study is valuable, and none but myself to hold to account if there are any failings. The scholarly energy of my friends Ron Gottesman at the University of Southern California and Bill Shurr at the University of Tennessee is always an inspiration to me. Boosting me up to where I have what I hope is a clear and defensible view of American poetry are such fine teachers as Harold W. Blodgett, the Whitman scholar and gentleman, the professor who was my idol at Union College; a number of excellent writers of earlier books on American poetry, including Roy Harvey Pearce, Donald Barlow Stauffer, and Hyatt H. Waggoner, whose ideas have inevitably been absorbed into my own; and a great many American literature students— enough of them over so many years that I am beginning to feel like Mr. Chips—who seldom fail to show me things I did not realize were there. More immediately, I thank my colleagues in the English Department at the University of Wisconsin-Parkside, particularly Carl Lindner for reading the whole manuscript and Don Kummings for reading the Whitman chapter, both of whom made extremely useful suggestions; Marcy Ricciardi, who prepared the bulk of the manuscript, and Alice Hill for their patient creativity in using a word processor to transmute my barbaric script into a civilized manuscript an editor can deal with; the people on the Committee for Research and Creative Activity, the Sabbatical Committee, and the Library staff who supported the project; and Professor Fred Moramarco, at San Diego State University, one of my collaborators on the second two volumes of this study. Thanks, too, to Professor Ken Eble, at the University of Utah, who, when he is not being a distinguished scholar, teacher, and teacher of teachers, is an extraordinarily sensitive and helpful editor.

And, as ever, the greatest measure of my gratitude goes to my wife, Maureen, without whom I would be—give or take a little— half.

Alan Shucard

University of Wisconsin—Parkside

· *Acknowledgments* ·

Grateful acknowledgement is made to the following for permissions to use material as indicated:

The Boston Public Library for lines from "Battle of the Kegs" by Francis Hopkinson and "A Mournful Poem on the Death of John Ormsby."

Professor Pattie Cowell for quotations from John Winthrop, Sarah Morton, Bridget Fletcher, "The Lady's Complaint," and Judith S. Murray in *Women Poets in Pre-Revolutionary America, 1650–1775: An Anthology* (Troy, N.Y.: Whitston Publishing Co., 1981).

Doubleday & Co., Inc., for quotations from Perry Miller, Anne Bradstreet, and Samuel Sewall, in Miller, *The American Puritans, Their Prose and Poetry* (Garden City, N.J.: Doubleday & Co., 1956); Cotton Mather, in Daniel G. Hoffman, *American Poetry and Poetics* (Garden City, N.J.: Doubleday & Co., 1962); and John Saffin, John Steere, F. D. Pastorius, John Wilson, John Tulley, Nicholas Noyes, Urian Oakes, John Rogers, Michael Wigglesworth, William Bradford, and Nathaniel Ward, in Harrison T. Meserole, *Seventeenth-Century American Poetry* (New York: W. W. Norton & Co., 1968).

Farrar, Straus & Giroux, Inc., for lines from John Berryman, *Homage to Mistress Bradstreet*, copyright 1956 by John Berryman, copyright renewed 1984 by Kate Berryman. Reprinted by permission of Farrar, Straus & Giroux, Inc.

Harvard University Press for lines from Anne Bradstreet's poems quoted in Jane Eberwein, *Early American Poetry: Selections from Bradstreet, Taylor, Dwight, Freneau, and Bryant* (Madison: University of Wisconsin Press, 1978). Reprinted by permission.

The Historical Society of Pennsylvania for "A New Year's Wish, January 1766) and "Peter Jarvis, to His Friends and Patrons, . . ."

Macmillan Publishing Co. for quotations from William Penn, "Memo from the Letter-Book of S. Sewall," Benjamin Church, Mather Byles, "New England's Misery" (anon.), Benjamin Franklin,

Acknowledgments

The *New England Courant* of 5 November 1722 and 5 August 1723, Nicholas Scull, Joseph Breitnal, William Smith, Francis Hopkinson's "Il Penseroso," Nathaniel Evans, "Juba," Richard Lewis, Charles Woodmason, Lyrics "made by a Bostonian" (anon.), Ebenezer Cooke, William Byrd, James Blair, Governor Berkeley, Jonathan Boucher, "Misericordis," and Freneau and Brackenridge's "A Poem on the Rising Glory of America." Used by permission of Hafner Press, a division of Macmillan Publishing Co., from *Colonial American Poetry* edited by Kenneth Silverman (New York and London: Hafner Publishing Co., 1968). Copyright © 1970 by Hafner Press.

The Massachusetts Historical Society for lines from John Wilson's "Mr. Joseph Brisco."

The New York Public Library, Rare Books and Manuscripts Division, Astor, Lenox and Tilden Foundations for lines from "Earthquakes."

New York University for quotations from Walt Whitman, *The Early Poems and the Fiction*, edited by Thomas L. Brasher (New York: New York University Press, 1963); *Notebooks and Unpublished Manuscripts, Vol. I: Family Notes and Autobiography, Brooklyn and New York*, edited by Edward F. Grier (New York: New York University Press, 1984); and *Leaves of Grass: Comprehensive Reader's Edition*, edited by Harold W. Blodgett and Sculley Bradley (New York: New York University Press, 1965).

The North Carolina Collection, University of North Carolina Library, Chapel Hill, for William Byrd's "Upon a Fart."

Princeton University Press for lines from *The Poetical Works of Edward Taylor*, edited with an introduction and notes by Thomas H. Johnson. Copyright 1939 by Rockland, copyright 1943 by Princeton University Press. Scattered quotes reprinted with permission of Princeton University Press.

Professor Donald E. Stanford for lines from the "Prologue" to Edward Taylor's *Preparatory Meditations, First Series* and Taylor's "Meditation 56," quoted in Jane Donahue Eberwein, *Early American Poetry: Selections from Bradstreet, Taylor, Dwight, Freneau, and Bryant* (Madison: The University of Wisconsin Press, 1978), from Donald E. Stanford, *The Poems of Edward Taylor, edited by Donald E. Stanford with a Foreword by Louis L. Martz* (New Haven, Conn.: Yale University Press, 1960), copyright 1960 by Donald L. Stanford and reprinted by permission.

· *Chronology* ·

1687   Nicholas Scull born.

ca. 1690   Joseph Breitnal born.

1696   Francis Daniel Pastorius begins to put *The Beehive* together.

1705   Michael Wigglesworth dies.

1706   Benjamin Franklin born.

1707   Mather Byles born.

1708   Ebenezer Cooke's "The Sot-weed Factor." Jane Colman Turell born.

1710   John Saffin dies.

ca. 1720   Charles Woodmason born. Jupiter Hammon born. Francis Daniel Pastorius dies.

1721   Richard Steere dies.

1725   Richard Lewis born.

1727   William Smith born. Hannah Griffitts born.

1728   Mercy Otis Warren born.

1729   Edward Taylor dies.

1734   Benjamin Church born.

1735   Jane Colman Turell dies.

1736   Thomas Godfrey born. Annis Stockton born.

1737   Francis Hopkinson born. Elizabeth Graeme Fergusson born.

1742   Nathaniel Evans born.

1746   Richard Lewis dies.

1748   Hugh Henry Brackenridge born.

ca. 1750s   The "Pennsylvania Wits" of the Junto Club vs. the "Swains of the Schuylkil."

1750   John Trumbull born.

1751   Judith Sargent Murray born.

1752   Philip Freneau born. Timothy Dwight born.

ca. 1753   Phillis Wheatley born.

1754   Joel Barlow born.

1756   Anna Young Smith born.

1759   Sarah Morton born.

1761   Nicholas Scull dies.

1763   Thomas Godfrey dies.

1767   Nathaniel Evans dies.

1771   John Trumbull's Yale commencement poem "Prospect of our Future Glory."

1772   Philip Freneau and Hugh H. Brackenridge's Princeton commencement poem "The Rising Glory of America."

ca. 1776   Charles Woodmason dies. Benjamin Church dies.

1778   James Kirke Paulding born.

ca. 1780   Anna Young Smith dies.

1782   John Trumbull's *M'Fingal*.

1788   Mather Byles dies.

1790   Fitz-Greene Halleck born.

1791   Francis Hopkinson dies.

1794   William Cullen Bryant born.

1795   Joseph Rodman Drake born.

1796   Joel Barlow's *The Hasty Pudding*.

ca. 1800   Jupiter Hammon dies. George Moses Horton born.

1801   Elizabeth Graeme Fergusson dies. Annis Stockton dies.

1803   William Smith dies. Ralph Waldo Emerson born.

1806   Nathaniel Parker Willis born. William Gilmore Simms born.

1807   Joel Barlow's *Columbiad*. Henry Wadsworth Longfellow born. John Greenleaf Whittier born.

1809   Edgar Allan Poe born. Oliver Wendell Holmes born.

1812   Joel Barlow dies.

1813   Jones Very born.

1814   Mercy Otis Warren dies.

1816   Hugh Henry Brackenridge dies.

1817   Hannah Griffitts dies. Timothy Dwight dies. Henry David Thoreau born.

Chronology

1819   James Russell Lowell born. Herman Melville born. Walt Whitman born.

1820   Judith Sargent Murray dies. Joseph Rodman Drake dies.

1821   Frederick Goddard Tuckerman born.

1825   Frances Harper born.

1827   Poe's *Tamerlane and Other Poems.*

1828   Henry Timrod born.

1829   Poe's *Al Aaraaf, Tamerlane,* and *Minor Poems.*

1830   Emily Dickinson born. Paul H. Hayne born.

1831   John Trumbull dies. Poe's *Poems.*

1832   Philip Freneau dies. Ralph Waldo Emerson leaves the clergy.

1836   Emerson's *Nature.*

1841   Poe's "The Philosophy of Composition."

1842   Sidney Lanier born. Emerson edits *The Dial* (to 1844). Emerson lectures in New York on "Nature and the Poems of the Poet"; Whitman is in the audience.

1844   Emerson's essay "The Poet."

1845   Poe's *The Raven and Other Poems;* he lectures on poetry and gives readings.

1846   Sarah Morton dies.

1847   Emerson's *Poems.*

1849   Edgar Allan Poe dies.

1850   Poe's "The Poetic Principle."

1855   Whitman's *Leaves of Grass* published at his own expense.

1856   Whitman's *Leaves of Grass,* 2d ed.

1860   James Kirke Paulding dies. Whitman publishes 3d ed. of *Leaves of Grass;* Emerson fails to talk him out of including "Enfans d'Adam."

1866   Herman Melville's *Battle Pieces and Aspects of the War.*

1867   Fitz-Greene Halleck dies. Nathaniel Parker Willis dies. Henry Timrod dies. Whitman's *Leaves of Grass,* 4th ed.

1870 William Gilmore Simms dies. Whitman's *Democratic Vistas.*

1871 Whitman's *Leaves of Grass,* 5th ed.

1873 Frederick Goddard Tuckerman dies. Whitman suffers paralytic stroke.

1876 Melville's *Clarel.* Emerson's *Selected Poems.* Whitman's *Leaves of Grass,* 6th ed.

1878 William Cullen Bryant dies.

ca. 1880 George Moses Horton dies. Jones Very dies.

1881 Sidney Lanier dies. Whitman's *Leaves of Grass,* 7th (second Boston) ed. (1881–82).

1882 Ralph Waldo Emerson dies. Henry Wadsworth Longfellow dies. Whitman's *Specimen Days and Collect* (1882–83). Whitman's *Leaves of Grass,* 8th ed. published in Philadelphia after Society for the Prevention of Vice declares 2d Boston ed. immoral.

1886 Emily Dickinson dies. Paul H. Hayne dies.

1888 Melville's *John Marr and Other Sailors.* Whitman's *Leaves of Grass,* 9th ed.

1891 James Russell Lowell dies. Herman Melville dies. Melville's *Timoleon.*

1892 Walt Whitman dies. John Greenleaf Whittier dies. Whitman's 10th (deathbed) ed. of *Leaves of Grass.*

1894 Oliver Wendell Holmes dies.

1895 Thoreau's *Poems of Nature.*

1911 Frances Harper dies.

· ONE ·

The Puritan Beginnings of American Poetry

> . . . yet I cannot wish you a soul that
> shall be wholly unpoetical
>
> —Cotton Mather, *Manductio ad*
> *Ministerium*

Aesthetics According to The Puritans

In the beginning were the Puritans. The implications of that fact must be completely understood as the basis of any examination of American poetry until the colonies united to wrest their political independence from Britain a century and a half after the Puritans had established their base in the New World. Even more, their ideas continued to influence American poetry, and American culture generally, until Ralph Waldo Emerson in theory and Walt Whitman in practice declared and achieved poetic independence from the motherland the better part of a century later. Even more, when one takes into account the Puritan currents and countercurrents in modern American life and letters, their values still condition American mores and mythology, and the poetry that they spawn, to the present day. Other tributaries join American poetry in its flow to the present, but its headwaters are the values that fundamentally shape much of the reality and the mythology of America—the values that the Puritans carried with them in sailing ships to subdue the wilderness in the process of restoring God's earthly kingdom.

The Puritan Beginnings

Fathoming the New England Puritans is no easy proposition. They were, in many respects, a complex, paradoxical lot, holding sway over the entire Massachusetts Bay Colony with a willful twenty percent of the population. Contrary to long-held common belief, they did have aesthetic sensibilities. They were not merely drab little uncultured folk who wrapped themselves in gray cloth and ideas and uttered pieties to each other while the only passion that they permitted themselves bubbled from the persecution of dissenters. Lamentably, it is true that, like many of the oppressed in human history who turn on their tormentors with a cruelty of their own, they sometimes did ruthlessly abuse dissenters with a zeal that matched the malevolent enthusiasm of those who had oppressed them in England. It is also true that both the Calvinist tenets that drove them and the harsh conditions in which they lived fostered an austerity and often a certain dourness among them. But if they theoretically expected little from their life in this world and looked upon it as a regrettable way station en route to the holy life in the next—at least for the ones who were fortunate enough to have been foreordained membership on the list of the elect—in actuality, they put a great deal of stock in the here and now. As Calvinists, they were bound to believe that earthly deeds or possessions had nothing whatever to do with their election or damnation, since God had decided on one or the other alternative fates for everyone before and outside of time, but as humans they had to believe and did believe in what they could perceive with their senses. Common sense could hardly detach worldly success or failure from a reflection of God's favor or disfavor. Could God, after all, in His infinite wisdom and justice, really be imagined to have preordained the election of the village drunk or the witch burning in the hellfires lit by the pillars of the community? Would He really damn the successful in His earthly kingdom, the elders of His own church?

From the outset, the New England Puritans were not untutored louts but cultivated gentlefolk who left considerable wealth and position behind in the Lincolnshire countryside to accept their mission to the New World. Numbering only about a quarter of the people who took passage on the *Mayflower*, the Puritans, nonetheless, in part asserting the status that they had enjoyed in the old country, assumed ultimate leadership of the Massachusetts Bay Colony when they arrived in numbers in 1630 and thereafter.

Thomas Dudley, father of the most deservedly celebrated colonial poet Anne Bradstreet, had been steward to the Earl of Lincoln, while the poet's husband, Simon Bradstreet, as Dudley's assistant, had also been an administrator in the Earl's household, and therefore a member of the gentry. Both men served the colony as governor. Such people were zealous nonconformists in their enthusiasm to reform Christianity, to return the Anglican Church to the simplicity of the early Church, and to impose what they understood to be biblical structures of governance on the Church. But they knew Western culture, they knew seventeenth-century comfort, and they were not masochists. They had a rigid sense of proportion with respect to what part arts and luxuries should play in their lives, but life in the New World was, ipso facto, severe enough without the Puritans needing to abandon all of the humanizing entities that helped to make it worthwhile.

And so the Puritans eschewed neither learning nor delight, as long as the learning led to a greater appreciation of the power and glory of God, and the delight could be construed in some way as reflecting His gift of redemption. When, in 1650, Reverend John Woodbridge took a sheaf of his sister-in-law Anne Bradstreet's poems from North Andover, Massachusetts Bay Colony, to London and had them published—and, incidentally, well received—without her knowledge, he had the title of the collection declare her *The Tenth Muse Lately Sprung up in America;* more instructively, in one of the first advertising campaigns from America, the subtitle hawked *Severall Poems, compiled with a great variety of Wit and Learning, full of delight.* No, the New England Puritans had no aversion to education and gladness, of the proper kind. Sixteen years after the *Mayflower* had landed the Pilgrim separatists from the Church of England in 1620, the Puritan "purifiers" of Christianity founded Harvard College in their new Cambridge. Led by such men as John Winthrop, a lawyer and the first governor of the Massachusetts Bay Colony, and the theologian John Cotton, both educated at old Cambridge, as others among them had been, they had emigrated to New England in 1630 after gaining control of the Massachusetts Bay Company. True, they came to escape the arbitrary monarchy of Charles I and to establish a theocratic oligarchy under which cleansed and simplified Christianity could thrive (they had by then given up hope of cleansing the Anglican Church in England). But it must be borne in mind that those educated leaders also had mercantile ambitions when they rooted the Massachusetts Bay Company in the new soil and caused the charter of the corporation to serve also as the blueprint for government. They associated hard work with the notion of service to God, but there was no necessary contradiction between their hope for celestial reward and their insistence on a terrestrial one. Perry Miller explains the preoccupation with business as "a logical consequence of Puritan theology: man is put into this world, not to spend his life in profitless singing of hymns or in unfruitful monastic contemplation, but to do what the world requires, according to its terms . . . for the glory of God."[1]

Indeed, not only did the Puritans very quickly establish Harvard College, in 1636, to create their own clergy and thus ensure the propagation of their ideas, but in general they placed more emphasis on education than people did anywhere else in the colonies. Schools were instituted throughout New England—common schools for the basics, academies for both boys and girls, grammar schools to train boys for higher education. Boston had a school five years after its settlement, and by 1647 the colonial—which is to say the Puritan—government called for the founding of free schools wherever they could be sustained in the colony. The reason was simple enough and traceable to the all-pervasive religious motive: only an educated person could be guided correctly by the light of Scripture. There is no implication intended here that the New England Puritans adopted a policy of antinomian liberalism, encouraging individual thought that could lead to individual interpretation and faith that allowed salvation. On the contrary, although the Puritan establishment gave the parishioner the tools that could be used for individual thought, the theocrats strove to put down all intellectual deviation from the party line. In the eighteenth century Benjamin Franklin and others would tend to strip away the religious imperatives of the Puritans from their practical ones, and a hundred years further on Ralph Waldo Emerson, Walt Whitman, and Emily Dickinson would use the Puritan intellectual tools for their antinomian purposes. But in New England Puritan times, if the light that someone discovered in the Bible was at significant variance with the establishmentarian and enforced Puritan one, the dissenter would recant or could and would be subjected to the darkest ostracism. As Emily Dickinson put the issue some two centuries later but in much the same

The Puritan Beginnings

intellectual environment, "Assent—and you are sane— / Demur—you're straightway dangerous— / And handled with a Chain—." Such deviant thinkers as Roger Williams, Anne Hutchinson, and Samuel Gorton, who were exiled from the colony, and the nineteen "witches" who were executed in the name of Puritan orthodoxy at the end of the seventeenth century had that truth clearly confirmed for them. But that is another matter.

The Puritan theocracy used and promulgated Ramist logic[2] as a means of organizing the world on its terms. Peter Ramus, a sixteenth-century French "logician" provided the Puritans with a framework within which to argue ("reason," in an Aristotelian sense, is too strong a word), in effect, the existence of fire, of which they were already certain, from the presence of smoke. That is, they "proved" God's grandeur, grace, and providence, which were their givens, from natural and everyday phenomena, which they seized as their evidence. With their Ramist method, analysis and deduction became relegated to the cellar of the epistemological armory. What Ramus had called "invention"—the process of beginning with a concept and then looking for evidence in Scripture and in everyday events—was, for their purposes, the formidable intellectual weapon of the Puritans. Without presuppositions, of course, it would have been impossible to deduce the abstraction of Satan's malevolent scheming from a spider's entrapment of a fly, but if satanic machinations were bedrock certainties among the Puritans' theological assumptions, then the fate of the poor fly could provide graphic metaphorical evidence for such scheming, and that is exactly how Edward Taylor used the event in his poem "Upon a Spider Catching a Fly."

So the Puritans were educated, but their education taught them to arrange their perceptions within the context of their theological system. Lace, cloth of sundry colors, music, good food, natural beauty could in themselves delight the Puritans, as they could any sensitive human beings, but the Puritans were obliged always to go the extra step, to find in their joys the metaphorical evidence for their beliefs. Hence, for example, this passage from the entry for 1 October 1697 in Samuel Sewalls's diary:

Had first, Butter, Honey, Curds and Cream. For Diñer, very good Rost Lamb, Turkey, Fowls, Aplepy [apple pie]. After Diñer, sung the 121 Psalm. Note. A Glass of spirits my Wife sent stood upon a Joint-Stool which,

Simon W[illard] jogging, it fell down and broke all to shivers: I said 'twas a lively Emblem of our Fragility and Mortality.[3]

Further, Sewall could treat the death of his beloved mother as an indication of how "her infinitely gracious and bountiful master has promoted her to the honor of higher employments, fully and absolutely discharged from all manner of toil and sweat" (entry of 14 January 1701). Disasters and pleasures alike had to be subsumed under the Puritan system. He might rejoice in simple, natural things: "I saw six swallows together, flying and chippering very rapturously," Sewall rhapsodized on 11 April 1712. And on 15 October 1720 he noted with relish, "I dine on fish and oil at Mr. Stoddard's," and he alluded to attentions he was paying to a reluctant Madam Winthrop. The entry of the next day contained the Puritan connection, self-chastisement for enjoying, even momentarily, worldly things for themselves: "I upbraided myself that I could be so solicitous about earthly things, and so cold and indifferent as to the love of Christ, who is altogether lovely."

The Puritans' aesthetic was determined both by their theological responsibility to attribute all pleasure and all pain to their Redeemer and by the harsh conditions of their lives. Such dreadful hardships as disease, resentment on the part of Indians whose sense of outrage over their loss of territory and sovereignty would often well up into violence, frequent early death, a perverse climate that often enough ruined crops and brought ravening hunger to the door, a sense of isolation from civilization, were broadly seen as opportunities. God's servants could use them to prove themselves while they built His new "city on the hill" (Matt. 5.14) as an example for the purification of all Christendom. At the same time, those kinds of stern adversity surely militated against the notion of creating art for its own sake. That luxury, often scorned in lands as underdeveloped as the Massachusetts Bay Colony or the twentieth-century Third World, cannot really take hold until a society, or a sizable monied group within it, can indulge itself with the idea. Its time would not arrive in America until the early to middle nineteenth century, when nationhood and the standard of living could support it and Edgar Allan Poe could distill it from the intellectual atmosphere and champion it.

Thus the Puritans held that art, like all else, was a gift of God to be turned, finally, to God's service—a gift to God. Poetry, like all other intellectual and material pursuits, was to be made with that lucidly in mind. It was, in some way, to move poet and audience closer to the greatest Maker of all and shed light somehow into the mystery of His wondrous poem. To accomplish those high goals, their poems, like everything that the Puritans did, ideally had always to find an equilibrium between the temporal and the eternal. Balance was, after all, central to Puritan thought. As Anne Bradstreet wrote in her eighth meditation for her son (in her *"Meditations: For My Dear Son Simon Bradstreet,"* a collection of advice), "Downy beds make drowsy persons, but hard lodging keeps the eyes open. A prosperous state makes a secure Christian, but adversity makes him consider."[4] The following meditation, the ninth, may be taken as her insight into the necessity to balance all words, written and poetic as well as spoken and prosaic, between the felicitous and the moral: "Sweet words are like honey: a little may refresh, but too much gluts the stomach." Perhaps as well and as typically as anyone, Edward Taylor, born in England in about 1642, expressed the poet's particular mandate to apportion his verse between heaven and earth, with the scale tipped heavily on heaven's side. In the undated "Prologue" from *Preparatory Meditations, First Series,* Taylor, imaging himself as a crumb of dust, supplicated his Lord, through earthy figures of flowers and gems, to permit the poet to demonstrate both the existence of God and God's insuperable glory:

> Thy Crumb of Dust breaths two words from its breast,
>   That thou will guide its pen to write aright
> To Prove thou art, and that thou art the best
>   And shew thy Properties to shine most bright.
>   And then thy Works will shine as flowers on Stems
>   Or as in Jewellary Shops, do jems.[5]

The point is important because the Puritan aesthetic rests upon it. The intention of the Puritan poet was to use the evidence of the things of this world, à la Peter Ramus, to prove their theses concerning the existence and magnificence of almighty God— precisely the thrust of these lines by John Saffin, a minor poet born in England in 1626: "And Native Beauty doth most clearly Shine / When its own Ornaments makes it Divine."[6] Thus, poetry, to the Puritans, was nothing if not utilitarian, a device dedicated to understanding and praising God, and they regarded it as flawed in proportion as it failed to strike a mean between worldly matters and the putative divine plan. As Richard Steere, another minor poet, born in England in 1643, admonished poets and all good Puritans in his "Earth Felicities, Heavens Allowances. A Blank Poem"—in seemingly endless, mainly blank verse—people should have been:

> Looking through [Earth's Felicities]
>   up to those joys beyond,
> And so Enjoy them with a heav'nly mind,
> [So that] We may in them feel heav'nly joys below,
> That when our days shall Terminate, we may
> From Heav'n on Earth, to Heav'n in Heav'n ascend,
> Where our Felicities can know no End.
>
> (Meserole, 264–65)

When Francis Daniel Pastorius, born in Franconia, in what later became Germany, in 1651, came to set down a group of pieces that he titled *Epigrams*, he clearly exhibited the practical streak in Puritanism. Though Pastorius was Pennsylvania's first notable poet, his work fits naturally into the context of New England Puritan poetry. "He certainly is in the Right / Who mingles profit with delight" (Meserole, 301), he advised his readers half-humorously. For early American poets, the hardships that God provided as a test of faith were sufficient; there was no sense in going out of the way to find more. Pastorius the poet even argued that "From Poetry Poverty in all ages arose; / Therefore, my Children, content you with Prose" (Meserole, 301). Pastorius's untitled poem that begins, "When I solidly do ponder," in a more serious key, intones the dilemma of all of the early American poets, upon whom it was incumbent to find that proper proportion, that golden mean between nature and humanity on the one hand and God on the other—God, Who was forgiving and just, but demanding and capable of the direst punishment, God, to Whom humankind could never make payment comprehensive enough to wipe out the debt:

> When I solidly do ponder,
> How *Thoughts wander*; I must wonder,

And for shame exclaim, and own,
Mine are ranging up and down.
Now on Eagle's Wings ascending
Far above the Skies, there spending
Some good Minutes in a Song;
But, alas! this lasts not long.
Unawares they are departing,
And themselves (like Arrows,) darting
In the very Depth of Hell,
Where the Damned wail and yell.

(Meserole, 294)

Sources and Types of Puritan Poetry

As in the beginning of American poetry were the Puritans, so, to inform the composition of the early poets—as it illuminated all facets of life in New England—was the Bible. True, since the Puritan writers were Cambridge- and later Harvard-trained, they were versed in classical rhetoric, history, and poetry, that is, in the works of Demosthenes, Hesiod, Homer, Theocritus, Xenophon, and to a greater degree of Cicero, Horace, Juvenal, Livy, Ovid, Seneca, Tacitus, and Virgil. Allusions to, and echoes and paraphrases of, the classical writers thread through early New-World writing. But, of course, measured by quantity and importance, the influence of Scripture immeasurably outstripped that of any other source material.

Beyond the Bible and Greek and Roman classics, seventeenth-century American writers looked to literary sources according to their individual predilections.[7] Anne Bradstreet, for example, particularly in her early poetry, derived much from Joshua Sylvester's translation of the work of Guillaume de Salluste Sieur Du Bartas, a learned French Calvinist poet popular among other Calvinists in both the Old World and the New. In her "Prologue" to *The Tenth Muse*, in fact, she acknowledged her debt to Du Bartas and, too modestly, her inability to match his skill:

But when my wond'ring eyes and envious heart
Great Bartas' sugared lines do read o'er,
Fool I do grudge the Muses did not part
'Twixt him and me that overfluent store;

> A Bartas can what a Bartas will
> But simple I according to my skill.[8]

Sir Philip Sidney's poems attracted and influenced Anne Bradstreet as well, while Sidney, along with Michael Drayton and William Drummond, also caught the attention of New Englanders Cotton Mather, John James, and Richard Steere. Shakespeare's influence is detectable in echo; no direct allusion to his plays or poems has been found, but then Puritans on both sides of the Atlantic by and large scowled at theatrical people. However, references to lines by Samuel Daniel, Thomas Campion, Abraham Cowley, and Francis Bacon, and Puritan ownership of their books, have been established.

Because elements of the baroque were prominent in seventeenth-century European arts, not surprisingly English metaphysical verse, a branch of baroque, was distinctly influential on American poetry in the seventeenth century. As much as anything else, it was the wittiness of the baroque that attracted the Puritans, for they highly prized and strove repeatedly to achieve it in the multitude of anagrammatic, acrostic, and epigrammatic pieces that they loved to write. They admired the subtlety and sudden turns of powerfully compacted language in John Donne and the metaphysicals and, to a limited extent, the stagy oppositions, the overstatements, the elaborate analogy of conceits. Of course, the Puritans would have been, with their conservative sense of proportion, duly wary of the excesses of metaphysical poems, but found two English practitioners of the style, George Herbert and Francis Quarles, particularly congenial for their relative restraint. Quarles especially enjoyed approval because his imagery tended to be less sensuous than that of his peers, and his doctrine was generally acceptable.[9]

The esteem in which the Puritans held the witty use of language was no mere idle liking of cleverness. No, it arose from their belief that nothing in the world happened that was not part of the Creator's omniscient design, that man's frequent failure to understand the relationship between an event and the design was precisely that—*man's* failure owing to humans being so very much less than God. By exercising his wit, man could see a little further into the way God's world worked. Nothing occurred by chance, and a little cleverness could, perhaps, reveal why it did happen—could reveal, that is, something more of God. That is why, beyond their fondness for writing hymns, series of ballad stanzas, lyric verse, and regular elegies, they were positively addicted to composing anagrams and acrostics.

Like the form of the acrostic, that of the anagram called for the poet's use of the letters of a person's name in the belief that the lines thus controlled by the letters would, perforce, yield insight into the character of the person. The acrostic was formed, as acrostics are, by writing the person's name down the left margin of the poem and then causing each letter to become the opening letter of each succeeding line. John Saffin's "An Acrostick on Mrs Elizabeth Hull" shows the method:

> Elustrius Dame whose vertues rare do shine
> Like Phoebus faire in her Mirridian line
> I one doth thee favour for me think I see
> Zealous Dame Nature hath Adorned thee
> Above the Nimphs, in fair and comely feature
> Beautious-Sweet-Smileing and Heart-moveing Creature
> Ere you may prosper, may Great Juno pleasure
> Thee with High honour and with boundless Treasure
> Heavens give thee Sweet content, when heart and hands
> Hymen Shall Joyn in Sacred Nuptiall Bands
> Venus, and Vesta then shall with the Graces
> Lead hand in hand to Crown thy Dear Embraces.
>
> (Meserole, 195)

The unsettled spelling of the period certainly helped to make the acrostic writers' composition easier.

Anagrams, although sometimes mixed with acrostics, used the letters of a name differently from the acrostic. The anagram scrambled them to make a line that iterated the theme of the poem. The distance of time raises the suspicion that the Puritan poets exercised more selective control over their word games than they would admit to themselves. They did not, for example, use an anagram on G-O-D. However that may have been, probably the most famous Puritan example of the practice is John Wilson's attack on the Quaker Claudius Gilbert in which Wilson, who was born in England in about 1588 and educated at Cambridge, and who accompanied Winthrop and the other settlers of Massachusetts Bay in 1630, jumbled the letters of Gilbert's name and came up with "Tis Braul I Cudgel." A stretch of the imagination suggests the meaning of the tortured expression: Wilson intended to use a cudgel on spiritual brawlers, that is, on doctrinal deviates. The first six lines suffice to demonstrate the method and flavor of the piece "Claudius Gilbert Anagram. Tis Braul I Cudgel":

> [Tis Braul I Cudgel] Ranters, Quakers Braul,
> Divels, and Jesuites, Founders of them all.
> Their Brauling Questions whosoever reades
> May soone perceive, These are their proper heades.
> What better Cudgels, then Gods holy word
> (For Brauls so cursed,) and the Civil sword?
>
> (Meserole, 385–86)

Thus Wilson unravels the secret hidden in the letters of a name to discover God's antipathy toward Quakers, Jesuits, and other such "Divels." The art of anagrams and acrostics, of course, came in the attempt to make the lines flow smoothly despite the artificial pattern imposed on the verse by the letters of the name. The fact that the art was secondary to the revelation of God's mind is, as can be seen from Wilson's effort, often evident in the result.

The popularity in England of the ballad stanza, with its catchy, galloping rhythm, inevitably caught the ear of New World poets who employed it for all manner of verse, from secular doggerel to serious devotional. Michael Wigglesworth, the doctor and divine who had been born in Yorkshire in 1631, pounded out 224 such stanzas before reaching the *finis* of his hell-harrowing, heaven-praising, pietistic Puritan epic *The Day of Doom*.

Because of the misleading stereotype of Puritans as wholly tasteless, humorless, colorless people who smothered the intellectual atmosphere of New England, it is necessary to recall periodically that they were flesh-and-blood humans capable of a range of emotions. Their capacity for humor, for example, was reflected in such mock-epic poetry as Benjamin Tompson's "On A Fortification At Boston begun by Women." Tompson was a schoolmaster born in Massachusetts in 1642, and notable not only for the comedy in some of his verse, but for the fact that beyond the classical references in his lines, his work is quite distinctly American. His local subjects were treated from a local perspective. His Indians, for instance, were the real ones with whom the colonists often had to contend for survival, not the idealized, specious Indians of English and European literary works or American imitations of them. His book of verse on American subjects was really the first published in the colonies. Though Tompson was more highly regarded as a poet by his contemporaries than by posterity, his poems often have a gentle human quality and hardy vividness about them. The fun that he pokes at the women who start an earthen fortification around Boston Neck is gentle fun. He may compare the earthwork to a ruff (collar) and the women's handling of the mud to the making of pastry, he may mock the women's scolding of each other as they work, but through the mock-epic treatment of their labors emerges Tompson's respect for the pluck of the women.

Recognition of other human qualities, too, echoed through the poetry of the New England Puritans. They were, of course, susceptible to the spectrum of human emotion, not restricted to passion for their Savior. Genuine sorrow at times bled through the formal elegiac verse that attempted to reconcile their sense of loss with God's holy plan. Real love fleshed out their sense of duty to husband, wife, children, and friends. And they were aware of the potent magnetism of sex for the joy of it; it is not Nathaniel Hawthorne alone, two centuries later, who revealed a Puritan's capacity to earn a letter in amorous activities. Lighthearted—though didactic—almanac poetry registers the point: The "May" entry for John Tulley's almanac of 1688 good-humoredly observes:

> This is Love's month, else Poets lie, what then?
> Why then, young maids are apt to kiss young men:
> But for old maids unmarried, 'tis a sign,
> They either do want beauty, or else Coyn.
> (Meserole, 513)

By "July," matters have progressed two months further in more ways than one, especially for the young:

> Now wanton Lads and Lasses do make Hay,
> Which unto lewd temptation makes great way,
> With tumbling on the cocks, which acted duly
> Doth cause much mischief in this month of July.
> (Meserole, 514)

Not unexpectedly among a people in a wilderness society who lived constantly with the threat of premature death through either natural or unnatural causes, early American poetry disclosed an intense preoccupation with death. Musings on death, sometimes in the form of acrostic or anagrammatic wordplay, permeate the literature, elegies circulated as broadsides being the most common—and perishable—format.[10] A poem by Nicholas Noyes, a clergyman born in Massachusetts in 1647, hints at the frequency of funeral verse; even the title is telling. "May 28th. 1706., / To my Worthy Friend, / Mr. James Bayley, / Living (if Living) in Roxbury A POEM." Noyes offers the usual consolation of God's having taken the sting out of death by means of Christ's suffering and His Grace, but he also reminds the living or dead Bayley:

> Excuse me, though I Write in Verse,
> It's usual on a Dead mans Hearse:
> Thou many a Death hast under-gone
> And Elegies made of thine own.
> (Meserole, 278)

Apart from the omnipresence of death, though, and any personal needs to come to terms with fear or sorrow, Puritan poets had another, a religious motive for piling up mounds of elegies. Because death was the threshold over which a member of the congregation passed to join either the community of the elect or the legion of the damned, a major tenet of their Calvinist system, poets could scarcely resist the chance to use the occasion to cogitate more about God's ways to man. In other words, they used a person's death in their elegies in essentially the same way as they used the letters of a person's name in their acrostics and anagrams (which often were themselves elegies)—to probe the Maker's ordering of His Creation so that they could better comprehend it and so serve Him. Naturally, such apparent open-mindedness on the part of the poet was, up to a point, illusory, for the Puritans' doctrinal preconception of their world, not to mention the social pressure that it spawned, tended to determine the outcome of their investigations. The interpretation of evidence, that is, was mainly predetermined by orthodoxy through the application of Ramist logic. There was, however, in elegiac as in other verse, often—perhaps always, to an extent—the voice of the individual poet coming through the very doctrine that limited free rein for personal response even to death. The poet's tailoring of standard form to fit the circumstance, the poet's ordering of the events of the dead person's life, the poet's exercise of wit, the poet's utterance of grief even within permissible bounds inescapably told something of the poet. The fifty-second and final stanza of Urian Oakes's elegy on the death of the Reverend Thomas Shepard (verbosity was epidemic among Puritan poets, though it is not thought to have contributed to the high mortality rate) offers an example. In it, Oakes, born in England in 1831 and later a clergyman and president of Harvard College, sounds like a man dosing himself with doctrine to assuage very real bereavement. There is no reason to question the sincerity of the signature:

> My Dearest, In Most, Bosome-Friend is Gone!
> Gone is my sweet Companion, Soul's delight!
> Now in an huddling Croud I'm all alone
> And almost could bid all the world *Goodnight:*
> > Blest by my Rock! God lives: Oh let him be,
> > As He is All, so All in All to me.
> > > The Bereaved, Sorrowful
> > > URIAN OAKES
>
> > > (Meserole, 220)

The Puritan Legacy

The New England Puritans left a legacy whose exact dimensions are incalculable but whose effect on all America has been indisputably great from Puritan times to the present. Much in American life they would have reviled, but much—many of the subtleties of American life, the innuendoes of American mythologies, the undercurrents of American values—perhaps they would pride themselves on having instilled in the nation, insofar as they would keep any credit for themselves and not relinquish it all to God. The patrimony that they bequeathed is moral, political, economic, spiritual, and—in a perverse way—artistic.

Traceable to their Puritan forebears is Americans' belief in the need for moral justification for private, public, and governmental acts—their tendency, which others occasionally mock as being "naive," to insist that actions must be "right" actions. That belief operates frequently in tandem with the continuing existence of groups in the United States that practice that rigid "old-time religion," and, considering themselves guardians of moral standards, attack any aspect of life that seems to them tainted with a hint of promiscuity, excessive frivolity, or unorthodoxy.

America's heritage of questing for freedom and, once having obtained it, of working to safeguard it, is, in direct and indirect ways, an important part of the inheritance from the Puritans. They came to the New World, in the first instance, to be free to purify and live by Christianity according to their collective conscience. They were, in other words, dissenters who followed the instinct to cry "No! Enough!" when the exercise of their will was contravened by established authority, and if they turned and prosecuted, and sometimes persecuted, individuals who dissented from *their* regime—such people as Roger Williams and Anne Hutchinson—both they and their dissenters nonetheless provided America with indelible examples of freedom seekers.

Modern Americans may be most aware of the economic codicil in the Puritans' will to them—the belief in the possibility of attaining, indeed the cultural mandate to attain, a better corporeal life through hard work and thrift on the way to the more substantial insubstantial life hereafter. "The Puritan ethic" and "the American work ethic" are synonymous and essential in Americans' very definition of themselves. It is useful to keep in mind that while the primary impetus to the Puritans' crossing to the New World on the *Arabella* in 1630 was the pursuit of religious freedom, the venture and the colonial government that grew from it were both organized as a commercial as well as a religious enterprise.

The roots of nationhood may also be traceable to the Puritans. In their morbid fascination with death, as expressed in their endless elegiac verse—verse that passed increasingly out of favor and into ridicule of inane form in the eighteenth century—lay the roots of history, a caring for the past and national identity that contributed to the growing feeling of statehood.

The most nebulous but significant portion of the Puritan legacy must surely be America's characteristic belief in the necessity and possibility of approaching perfection. Part of the misleading stereotype of the Puritans is an overemphasis on gloom and doom, an absence of any future light but the flickering illumination from hellfires. Like many misconceptions, that one is based on incom-

plete comprehension. The fear of damnation did play an important
part in their worldly and spiritual thoughts, but that fear was not
at all the entire mind-set. It was an adjunct to a more central,
hopeful concept. Clergymen, parents, writers, the gatekeepers of
the culture used the potentiality for eternal damnation as a goad
to drive the community along the path of right living so the people
could perfect themselves for God and eternal life—even though,
paradoxically, as Calvinists convinced of predestination, they professed to think that nothing that people did in this life could alter
their pre-stamped ticket to heaven or hell. In other words, the
New England Puritans were, ultimately, optimists driven by an
overarching belief in the millenium that the New World represented to them. Because that belief was typically couched in their
hellfire poems and, especially, sermons, it has often been lost to
view in examinations of Puritan thought,[11] but their hope for and
expectation of a millenial future entered American culture and
language through those very jeremiads and became pervasive.
Humankind began in damnable sin, yes, their faith dictated, but
through God's gift of grace and the intensive striving for purification, it was also redeemable, perfectible. The ideal of the city
on the hill that the Puritans came to found made the doctrine of
progress extremely palatable in the nineteenth century, and could
readily be transmuted into the symbol of America as a light to
the world. On the voyage of the *Arabella* John Winthrop cried in
his sermon:

> . . . we must Consider that wee shall be
> as a Citty vpon a Hill, the eies of all
> people are vppon us; so that if we shall
> deale falsely with our god in this worke
> wee have vndertaken and soe cause him to
> withdrawe his present help from vs, wee
> shall be made story and a by-word
> through the world. . . .[12]

Warnings of the results of backsliding, of spiritual failure, are dire,
to be sure, but the hope, indeed the expectation, of success is
compelling to poets no less than to preachers (and they were
frequently the same people). Michael Wigglesworth in his *God's
Controversy with New-England* begins his verse jeremiad with a

galloping hymnal plea that the "Good christian Reader judge me not / As too censorious, / For pointing at those faults of thine / Which are notorious" (Meserole, 42), but by the time he finally reaches the fourth-from-last stanza of the long diatribe, he rings the positive note:

> Ah dear New-England! dearest land to me;
> Which unto God hast hitherto been dear,
> And mayest be still more dear than formerlie;
> If to his voice thou wilt incline thine ear.
> (Meserole, 54)

Like the Old Testament prophets, New England poets again and again blamed disaster on deviation from scriptural morality and exhorted their people to return to righteousness, but it is important to note that, at its coolest, the ember of optimism was never permitted to die out. Time never ran out for the realization of the dream. "O New England, thou canst not boast," William Bradford, governor of the Plymouth Colony for thirty-three years, railed in "A Word to New England," for "Fraud, drunkenness, whoredom and pride / . . . slay the poore, / But whimsic errors they kill more." However, Bradford reminded his readers,

> Repent, amend, and turn to God
> That we may prevent his sharp rod,
> Time yet thou hast, improve it well,
> That God's presence may with you dwell.
> (Meserole, 387–88)

All of their fundamental principles—moral, political, economic—including their paradoxical affirmation of the future, the Puritans poured into the foundations of America. They gave American poets forevermore the value system that they must reckon with. And if American poets should wholly or partially demur, the Puritans, ironically, set that up, too. Themselves exemplary dissenters, they prosecuted and sometimes persecuted antinomians, but by encouraging the use of the intellectual tools that could be used for independent thought and action, the Puritans inadvertently propagated antinomianism in America. Emerson in essays and verse, Melville in his poetry as well as his fiction, Whitman,

Emily Dickinson, E. A. Robinson, Robert Frost, T. S. Eliot, a host of American poets would resound with the themes of their Puritan forebears. Questions of ethics and morality, of self-exploration, of sin, of the individual's relationship to God and humanity would never stop reverberating through American poetry like distant bells tolling a beginning and an end—never stop because in every end is a beginning and the questioning could never stop.

That was in a future that the first American poets could not divine. They themselves tended to be doctrinally pure, naturally, for only doctrinaire verse was apt to be encouraged, circulated, and—let it be said—unpunished. Adherence to dogma, the smugness of fit within the Puritan schema, not artistic excellence, was the primary yardstick with which to measure the value of art. In that context, it is instructive to consider the poetry of the three major figures of the New England Puritan pantheon of poets—the most unambiguous portion of the Puritan legacy—Anne Bradstreet, Edward Taylor, and Michael Wigglesworth.

Anne Bradstreet

In 1956, after five years of grappling with the historical material of Anne Bradstreet's life and times, the American poet John Berryman published his tribute to her in the form of a long poem, *Homage to Mistress Bradstreet.* So much did her work move him, so intensely had he come to identify with her, that his voice, his being, merged with hers from the outset: "We are on each other's hands / who care," the narrator says; "Both of our worlds unhanded us."[13] The traits that seemed to attract Berryman to Bradstreet at the time he was composing his *Homage* were the sense of her humanity and her resilience in the face of the many calamities of her life, from "New World winters" to miscarriages, tragedies so daunting that "surely the English heart quails, stunned."[14]

Berryman was not the first American poet to be drawn to Anne Bradstreet. Her sensitivity to the human condition glinting through Puritan dogma always made her the most amiable and approachable of Puritan poets. Indeed, when her *Several Poems* (1678), an enlarged edition of the 1650 *Tenth Muse*, was posthumously published half a dozen years after her death in 1672, a number of poets contributed verse tributes to introduce the volume. Though the encomia are, for the most part, formal and stylized, drawing heavily on standard classical imagery, as seventeenth-century poetry was prone to do, such outpouring of admiration for a poet as poet (while many were eulogized for their clerical function) was unparalleled. Her brother-in-law Benjamin Woodbridge, for instance, brother of the Reverend John Woodbridge who had had her *Tenth Muse* published in London, proclaimed in "Upon the Author; by a known Friend" that "the Muses, Virtues, Graces," all females, formed "but one unity" in Anne Bradstreet. That feminine moon had "totally eclips'd the Sun"; men could no longer be said to "Monopolize perfection" (Meserole, 409). In "Upon Mrs. Anne Bradstreet Her Poems, &c" the physician John Rogers claimed to have "Twice drunk the Nectar of [Bradstreet's] lines" and, by the agency of her poems, walked "twice through the Muses Grove." So forceful, in fact, was the effect of her work on him that, in an image that was conspicuously unfelicitous even for the general run of Puritan poetry, he owned up to having been artistically debauched by her work: "Thus weltring in delight, my virgin mind / Admits a rape" (Meserole, 420–22). Despite the ungodly picture that he called to the reader's mind, Rogers had simply joined the ranks of readers who found themselves under Anne Bradstreet's spell.

Mistress Bradstreet's literary reputation has not been without its period of decline. Because the nineteenth century was, by and large, very much a man-centered time when poets and their audiences preferred nature and man's relationship to it painted in a rosy glow, that century was not an especially congenial one for her—or for Donne and the English metaphysical poets, for that matter—given her God-centered, baroque, puritanical seventeenth-century perspective. Esteem of her poetry was restored in the present century with the rising tide of interest in both metaphysical and Puritan work, but, for a time, critics found her Puritan didacticism unwelcome in light of the prevalent nineteenth-century belief in poetry as a sufficient end in itself. It was not that Bradstreet was insensitive to the beauty of nature. Her long "Contemplations," for example, reflected her delighted response to trees, and the sun, the green earth and its rocks and streams, the fish and birds, even "the merry cricket." But her master antenna was tuned to vibrations beyond the immediate sensations of pleasure that nature can induce. Those distant, intuited messages, orthodox antecedents of the personal impulses that the Transcendentalists would intuit from nature in the nineteenth century, signaled God's beneficence to her, as to other Puritans. In the penultimate stanza of "Contemplations" she remembered the punishment of those who lollygagged and pulled herself back from the seductive act of mere rejoicing at the loveliness of natural things—a spiritually dangerous temptation:

> . . . he that saileth in this world of pleasure,
> Feeding on sweets, that never bit of th' sour,
> That's full of friends, of honor, and of treasure,
> Fond Fool, he takes this earth ev'n for heav'n's bower.
> But sad affliction comes and makes him see
> Here's neither honour, wealth, nor safety;
> Only above is found all with security.[15]

All her life, from her early work, when she was under the retarding influence of Du Bartas's pedantry and theological didacticism until she later found more of her distinct voice, Bradstreet's concerns were, of course, ultimately Puritan concerns. Poem after poem dealt centrally or tangentially with humankind's original sin, human vanity and other follies, the coming of the Redeemer and the hope for triumph over sin, death, and hell in everlasting life with God. When her heart must have been nearly crushed by the death of grandchildren, by her husband's absence in England, by the burning down of her house, or by the prospect of her own death, her perceived certainty of Puritan doctrine saved her as surely as she yearned for Christ to save her soul. All that happened was attributable to God, only it was beyond human beings' puny capacity to reckon. She could only accept His perfection, and therefore the perfection of His unknowable reasons. It was "His hand alone that guides nature and fate" ("In Memory of My Dear Grandchild, Elizabeth Bradstreet, Who Deceased August, 1665, Being a Year and a Half Old," Eberwein, 55); ". . . yet He is good," she cried in the poem on the death of another grandchild, Simon Bradstreet, who died in November 1669 at the age of a month and a day. And always there was the Puritans' underlying hope: "Go pretty babe," she exhorted the dead Simon, "go rest with sisters twain; Among the blest in endless joys remain" (Eberwein, 56). After all, she remembered in that same poem, "Let's say He's merciful as well as just." And when Christ the Bridegroom came to call for her—even as Emily Dickinson would welcome death in the guise of a more secular gentleman caller two hundred years afterward—Bradstreet would gladly go with him:

> A corrupt carcass down it lays,
> > A glorious body it shall rise.
> In weakness and dishonour sown,
> > In power 'tis raised by Christ alone.
> Then soul and body shall unite
> > And of their Maker have the sight.
> Such lasting joys shall there behold
> > As ear ne'er heard nor tongue e'er told.
> ("As Weary Pilgrim," Eberwein, 60–61)

Such lines echo quite ordinary Puritan thinking. In a difficult situation (and when was the situation not difficult in her Massachusetts Bay Colony?) it was only human for Bradstreet, like her peers, to retreat to doctrine for solace. But her poetry has a human dimension beyond cant and deeper than that of her peers because she could never quite let doctrine take over for her personal sensibility. Finally, that is, she did not sound like a theocrat, but like a person living in the real and harsh world, loving and suffering and sometimes whistling in the New World dark. Beneath the catechistical phrases and before the prefabricated Puritan resolution, in her lyrics the beating of her heart could be heard.

It is for that reason that such a poem as "To My Dear and Loving Husband" has kept a place in the corpus of American poetry. A sanely compact piece—by any standard, and particularly measured by the Puritan predilection for excess verbiage—its twelve lines of heroic couplets exude genuine love and devotion. The eventual goal of her relationship with her husband was, of course, eternal happiness: "while we live, in love let's so persevere / That when we live no more, we may live ever." The intention, incidentally, hinted at the human difficulty that Bradstreet must have had in accepting absolutely the Calvinist notion that nothing that people did on earth could influence their predestined life after death—a tenet that seems to have been honored by Puritans largely in the breach. Meanwhile, the poem describes a marriage of fully requited love in which, on her part, "My love is such that rivers cannot quench, / Nor ought but love from thee, give recompense" (Eberwein, 41). Technically, these two lines even display a rare willingness to sacrifice perfect rhyme to perfect sense, an instinct that would not really take root in American poetry until the nineteenth century, notably in the very different work of Walt Whitman and Emily Dickinson.

The humanity of Bradstreet's familial emotions shines through repeatedly. "A Letter to Her Husband, Absent upon Public Employment" (Eberwein, 42) shows her mourning his temporary absence, for her sun was in its zodiac, and her limbs were numbed in the absence of his warmth—a figure of speech that may have contained a crystal of literal truth in that early New England winter. She presents the canonical resolution of her feeling about the burning of her house in 1666 in the realization that putting stock in earthly possessions is but vanity, since the only treasure truly worth having is in God's domain. But in that poem ("Upon the Burning of Our House," Eberwein, 59–60) she could not help but bare her sincere regret and nostalgia over the loss:

> Under thy roof no guest shall sit,
> Nor at thy table eat a bit.
> No pleasant tale shall e'er be told,
> Nor things recounted done of old.
> No candle e'er shall shine in thee,
> Nor bridegroom's voice e'er heard shall be.

She fitted the loving verse "In Reference to Her Children, 23 June, 1659" (Eberwein, 44–46) with vivacious bird imagery that unmistakably displayed the happiness that she derived from hatching and raising a brood of four females and four males. And "The Author to Her Book" (Eberwein, 43) suggests a trace of human vanity as well as humility over the surprise publication of *The Tenth Muse*, despite her frequent admonitions against vanity, in "The Vanity of All Worldly Things" (Eberwein, 39–40), for instance. Self-effacing as the author was in speaking of her book as "homespun cloth," yet she admitted that seeing her work in print caused her to edit the poems for a later edition (the posthumous *Several Poems*): "Yet being mine own, at length affection would / Thy blemishes amend, if so I could: / I washed thy face, but more defects I saw, . . ." This is homespun, indeed, and that in large measure is what has made her poetry live. But she was more sure of herself than her address to her book or her "Prologue" to her quaternions (four debates among the four elements, humors, ages of man, and seasons, standard Puritan and metaphysical fare) intimated. While she proved to her father and friends in her poems up to the publication of *The Tenth Muse* in 1650 that she had mastered the chiefly classical learning and conventions of her time, her work after 1650 tends to show her more at ease with her individual poetic powers, her own unpretentious poetic voice and sensibility.

Michael Wigglesworth

Reverend Michael Wigglesworth was born in 1631 in Yorkshire, England, and raised as the son of a New England Puritan farmer who shared the community belief in education in the service of God's church. Through great sacrifice, the senior Wigglesworth saw to it that his promising son was educated at Boston Latin School and Harvard. Devoting much of his clerical career to teaching, Wigglesworth repaid his father's generosity by willing the family name to posterity as the writer of the American poem that was, in its day and for some time afterward, the most popular and famous—some, in hindsight, have asserted infamous—American Puritan poem of all, *The Day of Doom*. A Puritan epic written in galloping "fourteeners" (iambic lines of fourteen syllables), "The Day of Doom" may seem utterly pernicious to a modern audience because of its unremitting insistence on the austere side of Christianity, the adamant, immutable justice of its punishment of the damned. Its significance to its own contemporary audience, however, was reflected in the extent of its readership: although the Puritan church could claim a membership of only some twenty percent of the total population of New England, the poem's first edition, nevertheless, provided a copy for every thirty-five people in the region.[16]

From the Puritan viewpoint—the one that counts—the poem was, in every respect, a success. It was tailored to fit the need that Wigglesworth perceived to return an already wayward flock back to the old-time religion from which it had strayed by 1662, a punishing drought year, the year of publication. He would, he clearly decided, compose an epic hellfire sermon in verse that would burn brighter than the others in an epoch of hellfire sermons. He would, like the Old Testament prophets, stop the backsliding by reminding the people of the clauses that they had broken in their contract with God and of the dreadful retribution that He would exact if they remained at sinful ease in the new Zion. All of this he accomplished. The "fourteeners" were an extremely effective mnemonic measure through which he could simplify the complex Calvinist theology for mass consumption and advance the story of Christ's judgment of humankind as rapidly as possible, given the 224 stanzas that Wigglesworth felt obliged to churn out. In addition to being solidly doctrinaire, so easy was "The Day of Doom" to commit to memory, in fact, that the church ordered it to be memorized with the Catechism. The poem's wide circulation in broadside format both attested and contributed to its vast popularity. Wigglesworth succeeded, moreover, in the difficult artistic job of depicting theological concepts—election, damnation, grace, judgment, and punishment of sinners—in homey, understandable figures. In so doing, he wrote such an accurate and comprehensible summary of American Puritanism that a modern reader who wanted to inquire into the nature of Puritan beliefs could do worse than read "The Day of Doom" as a source—and the inquirer would be doing a mild penance in the bargain.

An illustrative passage of *The Day of Doom*, treating the thorny problem of the judgment of infants, comprises stanzas 166 through 181. Following the standard Puritan line, Wigglesworth decided that he would have "Reprobate Infants plead for themselves," as he indicated in the marginal note to stanza 98. The procedure of having a class of sinner present its mitigating arguments to Christ sitting in judgment and then having Christ refute the plea was essentially Wigglesworth's blueprint for the poem. The "Reprobate Infants" advance two arguments on their own behalf. First, they point out, their damnation would be unjust because of their innocence of Adam's transgression: "Not we, but he, ate of the tree whose fruit was interdicted: / Yet on us all of his sad Fall, the punishment's inflicted" (Meserole, 99, stanza 168). Second, they assert, it would be unjust because it would be inequitable: how can Christ reasonably deny them grace "When he [Adam] finds grace before thy face, that was the chief offender?" (stanza 170).

The failure of such pleading was, of course, preordained by John Calvin and enforced by Wigglesworth's church. In his refutation, Christ, "the Judge most dread," declares that God forbids punishment of men (and babies, presumably) for what they did not do, "But what you call old *Adam's* Fall, and only his Trespass, / You call amiss to call it his, both his and yours it was" (stanza 171). This notion was a foundation stone of Puritan thought. Adam was not merely a man, but representative Man:

> He was design'd of all Mankind
> to be a publick Head,
> A common Root, whence all should shoot,
> and stood in all their stead.
> He stood and fell, did ill or well,
> not for himself alone,
> But for you all, who now his Fall,
> and trespass would disown.
>
> (stanza 172)

Christ will not permit the infants to play an inconsistent game. Quite simply, he reminds them, since they would have been glad to share in the reward of grace had Adam done right, they must accept the punishment resulting from his betrayal of God's trust. After all, the Judge tells them, although they think that had they been in Adam's place, they "to our cost would ne'er have lost all for a paltry Lust" (stanza 176), the fact is that they would have. Finally, Christ declares (stanza 177) that He may indeed deny the babies grace. He may withhold grace from anyone He chooses even if He did grant it to Adam, "the chief offender," for grace would not be grace without His freedom to choose those upon whom He will bestow it.

Though Wigglesworth could not conceive of Christ's forgiving the infants, since He would do that only for the Elect, the poet did cause Christ to recognize that the babies' crime was, after all, less than that of adults who had lived longer and so had the opportunity to sin more. Christ, therefore, consigned the infants to "the easiest room in Hell" (stanza 181), the poet's marginal note remarking tersely: "The wicked all convinced and put to silence." Wigglesworth was not a man without feeling and a certain generosity of spirit.

Actually, whatever the ominous rigidity of *The Day of Doom* may suggest to the contrary, Michael Wigglesworth was apparently not an unkindly soul, though his poetry obviously lacks the domestic warmth of Anne Bradstreet's. The community of Malden, in Massachusetts Bay Colony, which he served as minister and physician even as his health became increasingly poor, thought well of him. There is, furthermore, muted evidence of his kindliness in some of his poetry that is less dour, though not less serious, than *The Day of Doom*. In 1669, for example, he published a poem called *Meat out of the Eater*, a piece that provided the people with enough of a sense of meaning in their hardships, even in the frequent premature deaths among them, that they bought up four editions in a decade. The subtitle reveals his intention, and the poem's popularity shows his success; he called it "Meditations concerning the necessity, end, and usefulness of afflictions unto God's children, all tending to prepare them for and comfort them under the Cross."

God's Controversy With New England was a jeremiad poem that Wigglesworth composed during the drought of 1662, the year of the publication of *The Day of Doom*, though *God's Controversy* had to wait until 1873 for publication. The prologue, from Isaiah 5.3, establishes the tone of admonition concerning what he saw as the Lord's displeasure over New England's apostasy, its increasing propensity to substitute material for religious and moral values as the society prospered. As Isaiah had warned his hearers, "What could have been done more to my vineyard, that I have not done in it? wherefore, when I looked that it should bring forth grapes, brought it forth wild grapes?" Wigglesworth's God, acknowledging that "some there be that still retain / Their ancient vigour and sincerity," vows to chastise the reprobates who have exchanged hypocrisy, pride, luxury, false dealing, security, sloth, and other such sins for love of God and adherence to His convenant of peace. The inclusion of "luxury" and "security" among the transgressions (Meserole, 48, lines 215, 221) is particularly arresting for its underscoring of austere Puritan mores. But reflecting the Puritans' ultimate optimism, their final unwillingness to abandon hope for future perfectibility under God, Wigglesworth showed himself, in the end, to be a millenarian at heart. He exhorted his audience to repent, for there was still time to consider the rod with which sinners were punished, to return to the ways of God,

"Who wil not have his nurture be despized" (Meserole, 54, line 430). Because of the "many praying saints, / Of great account, and precious with the Lord," (Meserole, 54, lines 431–32) who interceded for the backsliders, the poet had not given up on his fellows and, in fact, anticipated the spiritual revival that would once again allow him to find his delight in New England.

In a word, Wigglesworth sometimes, as in *God's Controversy*, presumed more mercy for the wayward New Englanders than he did for irrevocably condemned infants and others in *The Day of Doom*. The inconsistency was inevitable, of course. Supporting and supported by the Puritan intellectual framework, he shared its contradictions. A structure of such rigidity cannot exist without some cracks.

Edward Taylor

A modern-day Puritan might contend that the current public knowledge of Edward Taylor's poetry—along with Anne Bradstreet's the most distinguished seventeenth-century poetry written in America—is a divine Providence. As a result of his own decision not to publish his poems, and his request that his family not publish them posthumously, they lay unknown in the manuscript collection of the Yale University Library until Thomas H. Johnson, the fine Emily Dickinson scholar, brought them to light in 1939, two years after he had come upon the poems at the Library.

When Parliament, after the Restoration of Charles II to the throne in 1660, passed the Act of Uniformity demanding the taking of communion in the Anglican Church each year to signify acceptance of the dogma and practices of the state church, thousands of Puritans who could not pretend to comply took ship to the Massachusetts Bay Colony. Among them, in 1668, was Taylor, twenty-six years old, born in Leicestershire in about 1642 and carried to New England on the new wave of Puritan immigration that followed the demise of Cromwell's Puritan Commonwealth.

Like many of his fellow Puritans, he did not arrive naked. He had been a schoolmaster in England, possibly educated at Cambridge, and he carried letters of introduction to Increase Mather, a leader of Boston's intellectual community. Mather, in turn, introduced Taylor to other influential people, including the president of Harvard, Charles Chauncy. Taylor was admitted to the college as an advanced student and did very well indeed, giving, alas, a graduation address in seemingly endless heroic couplets that argued the copiousness and excellence of English over the classics, thus fighting for a cause that George Puttenham and other early English linguists had taken up a century and more before.

Rejecting an inclination to stay on at Harvard for graduate work, Taylor went instead, in 1671, to the frontier settlement of Westfield, Massachusetts, in the Connecticut River Valley, and so to the Indian Wars raging in that region. As spiritual advisor, physician, community leader, farmer, and eventually fourteen times a father in two marriages, Taylor could neither really build a regular congregation for his ministry nor write poetry until King Philip's War, the worst of the Indian Wars, finally ended in 1682.

Mention of his ministry together with his poetry is not accidental, for he regarded the composition of his poems as a mechanism of support for his spiritual life. Taylor must have been aware of the aesthetic niceties in his poems, but his poetry was first of all utilitarian to him. He wrote his "Preparatory Meditations," for instance, every other month for forty-three years, each to prepare himself spiritually for the next Lord's Supper, or Eucharist. As the Puritans understood the covenant between God and humankind, His agreement to create saints of some people—that is, the elect— logically entailed His eternal condemnation of others—that is, the damned. That was the meaning of grace. The great preoccupation in the life of a Puritan was constant introspection, the search of his or her own soul to ascertain its condition, the quest for evidence that would divulge the secret of one's salvation or damnation. It would be difficult to overemphasize the everyday importance of the obsession that even though predestination effectively prevented a person from altering his or her doom by any act performed in mortal life, it was possible to make an educated guess at the disposition of the immortal soul. Weighing what one was and did in the flesh provided the clues.

Since the Lord's Supper was the time when the Puritans took special stock in the health of their souls, Taylor, like others, made special preparation for the event, and among the things he did was to write "Preparatory Meditations." The poems echoed the three themes that the occasion called up—the basic depravity of human beings; the immeasurable beneficence of God, which made the sinfulness of humankind all the more stark; and the hope for and wonder of God's grace. "Meditation Thirty-Eight" from his first series illustrates Taylor's method. Starting with the questions "Oh! What a thing is Man? Lord, Who am I?" he effectively employs an extended legal metaphor through the seven stanzas to urge Christ, not a bad advocate, to plead his unworthy case before God's Court of Justice. The reflexive use of juridical language makes for an aesthetically fine poem, as well as the spiritually satisfying one that was Taylor's main purpose. While he freely confesses that his "case is bad," he is confident that if Christ does accept it, "Although it's bad, thy Plea will make it best."[17] The Court, as one would expect, is archetypal, and yet Taylor presents it in fathomable social terms:

> God's Judge himselfe, and Christ Atturny is;
> The Holy Ghost Regesterer is founde.
> Angells the sergeants are, all Creatures kiss
> The booke, and doe as Evidence abounde.
> All cases pass according to the Law,
> And in the sentence is no Fret or flaw.

Taylor's considerable talent for giving abstruse religious concepts human dimensions through the use of commonplace imagery—including insects, food, spinning, gardening—marks him, with Anne Bradstreet, as an impressive Puritan poet. At times, his homiletic intention drove him to excess, as in "Meditation Thirty-Nine" of the first series, in which he cried out in the agony of his sins, "these Cursed Dregs, / Green, Yellow, Blew streak'd Poyson hellish, ranck, / Bubs [pustules] hatcht in natures nest on Serpents Eggs, . . ." (Meserole, 128). At times, his imagery may be deliberately inconsistent to focus attention on argument instead of art. And at times, the quality of his verse is simply uneven, as it is in his long "God's Determinations touching his Elect: and the Elects Combat in their Conversion and coming up to God in Christ together with the Comfortable Effects thereof." But the flaws are to be expected, given the frontier circumstance of his life, his didactic purpose, and the Puritans' utilitarian aesthetic context in which he composed. What is remarkable is his achievement, really the only body of poetry produced by an American Puritan that bears comparison to the best English metaphysical poets. Ironically, it is not unreasonable to suppose that his own suspicion of the artistic merit of his poetry drove him to cause its suppression for more than two hundred years after his death in 1729.

For himself and all the company of New England Puritan poets, Taylor summarizes at the beginning of "Meditation Fifty-Six" in the second series the underlying reason for the plain style in which he and they cast their verse. To have pretensions of aesthetic elegance would have been hubristic; no one can or should even aspire to fashion great beauty, for that is the province of God:

> Should I with silver tooles delve through the Hill
>   Of Cordilera for rich thoughts, that I
> My Lord, might weave with angelick skill
>   A Damask Web of Velvet Verse thereby
>   To deck thy Works up, all my Web would run
>   To rags, and jags: so snicksnarld to the thrum.
>
> Thine are so rich: Within, Without. Refin'd.
>   No workes like thine. No Fruits so sweete that grow
> On th'trees of righteousness, of Angell kinde
>   And Saints, whose limbs reev'd with them bow down low.
>   Should I search ore the Nutmeg Gardens shine
>   Its fruits in flourish are but skegs to thine.
>
> (Eberwein, 113–14)

The implied arrangement between God and poet is as plain and simple as the verse in which it is conveyed:

> Thou wilt me save, I will thee Celebrate.
> Thou'lt kill my Sins that cut my heart within:
> And my rough Feet shall thy smooth praises sing.
>
> (Eberwein, 107)

Yet by the time Edward Taylor died at the end of the third decade of the eighteenth century, a subtle loosening of the Puritan grip had been occurring in New England life and poetry. The witch trials of the 1690s were, at bottom, a reaction on the part of the theocratic establishment to unwelcome change, as would be the equally passionate but less bloody religious revival of the 1740s known as "The Great Awakening" and the revivals of the 1840s. Boston and other towns were growing and thriving commercially, and acquiring the periwigs and other fripperies of British society. Such poets as John Saffin were sometimes writing amorous or satirical pieces with little or no dogmatic content (for example, Saffin's "[Sweetly (my Dearest) I Left thee asleep]" and "A Charracteristicall Satyre on a proud upstart," dated March 4th Anno 1698 (both in Meserole, 198–99, 204–5). Sometimes they would compose a verse that was acceptable in human terms but dangerous Puritan theology, as in the case of Saffin's "A brief Elegie on my Dear Son John the second of that name of mine," in which the poet dared to *assume* that his dead sixteen-year-old son "is not but gone to take his Right / Of Heritance among the Saints in Light" (Meserole, 199).

The great orthodox leader Cotton Mather's *Manductio ad Ministerium,* issued in 1726, two years before his death, suggested the flux that characterized the New England intellectual climate. On the right hand, Mather decreed:

Be not so set upon poetry as to be always poring on the passionate and measured pages. Let not what should be sauce rather than food for you engross all your application. Beware of a boundless and sickly appetite for the reading of poems, which now the rickety Nation swarms withal: and let not the Circaean cup intoxicate you. But especially preserve the chastity of your soul from the dangers you may incur by a conversation with Muses that are no better than Harlots: among which are others besides Ovid's Epistles, which for their tendency to excite and foment impure flames and case coals into your bosom, deserve rather to be thrown into the fire, than to be laid before the eye which a covenant should be made withal. Indeed, not merely for the impurities which they convey, but also on some other accounts, the Powers of Darkness have won a Library among us, whereof the poets have been the most numerous as well as the most venomous authors.[18]

Mather reproved "the blades that set up for critics" for not agreeing on standards of perfection, and he chided writers who used the faddish *"Florid Style,"* who violated the old Puritan sense of purpose and proportion.[19] No enlightened liberal that Cotton Mather.

But, on the left hand, he showed surprising liberality in his 1726 tract in his limited defense of individual style:

. . . since every man will have his own style, I would pray that we would learn to treat one another with mutual civilities and considerations, and handsomely indulge one another in this as gentlemen do in other matters.

I wonder what ails people, that they can't let Cicero write in the style of Cicero, and Seneca write in the (much other!) style of Seneca; and own that both may please in their several ways.[20]

By the time Cotton Mather died in 1728, the fire that Puritanism had lit in America and its poetry was dying down. The eighteenth century would see not only the Great Awakening attempting to feed the flame again, but powerful clergymen, such as Jonathan Edwards, breathing hellfire to burn the secularism that was to flourish more and more under the guidance of such practical men as Benjamin Franklin—leaders whose preoccupation was life in this world, and to whom God was, more than ever, an extension of commerce and natural law. For good or ill, it was a struggle that the forces of the earth would win, but their victory would not quench the Puritan embers. They still glow.

Poetry Outside of New England

Because, for particular reasons, the Southern colonies produced very little verse before the eighteenth century, poetry of that region will be considered at some length in the next chapter, which treats colonial poetry of that era. Poetry was produced outside of New England, however, in the region that is often referred to as the "Middle Colonies," and especially in New York and Pennsylvania, but not in much quantity or quality except for some of the Dutch poetry written before the British annexed the territory of New Amsterdam.

The best and best known of the Dutch poets was Henricus Selijns, a Calvinist minister who had a way of combining classical allusion with the immediate life around him. Thus his "Bridal Torch," written in about 1636 after an Indian raid at Wiltwyck, nicely weds the danger of Indians, with their bows and arrows, to Cupid's hitting a man and woman with his armaments in the fort at New Amsterdam.

In general, the seventeenth-century Dutch poetry, since it was, like Puritan verse, Calvinist, shared with Puritan verse the paradox of focus on hardship as a manifestation of God's punishment along with a certain zest for gaming with language to see what words could reveal about God's ways to man.

The British settlers who came under British rule after New Amsterdam became New York in 1654 produced little poetry of any merit. Richard Steere may have been the most noteworthy, but he was a transplanted English Puritan who moved to Long Island from New England some time around the turn of the eighteenth century.

Nor did Pennsylvanians write much verse until the middle of the eighteenth century when the sway of German religious groups and the Quakers was broken. After all, William Penn himself helped to set the antipoetic tone of the colony by inquiring rhetorically: "How many plays did Jesus Christ and his apostles recreate themselves at? What poets, romances, comedies, and the like did the apostles and saints make or use to pass away their time withal?"[21]

Francis Daniel Pastorius comes closest to bring an exception in Pennsylvania, for Pastorius, in 1696, began to put together a voluminous manuscript in poetry and prose of instruction and information for the edification of his sons. The remarkable work, in half a dozen or so contemporary and classical languages, including English, covered most of what Pastorius had ever read, learned, thought, experienced, and observed; its poetry, sometimes humorous, comprised an astonishing range of forms. It shared the Puritans' emphasis on education, admonishing the boys to "Delight in Books from Evening / Till mid-night when the Cocks do sing; . . ." for in learning is "The Art of true Levelling: / Yea even how to please the king" (Meserole, 299–300). Yet Pastorius did not betray the regional attitude toward poetry. He did not publish his poems, and he warned young John and Henricus, "From Poetry Poverty in all ages arose; / Therefore, my Children, content you with Prose" (Meserole, 300). That was an alarm that American parents have often enough sounded for their offspring ever since.

· T W O ·

Poetry of the Eighteenth Century

> If any youngster cross the ocean,
> To sell his wares—may he with caution
> Before he pays, receive each hogshead,
> Lest he be cheated by some dogshead,
> Both of his goods and his tobacco;
> And then like me, he shall not lack-woe.
>
> —Ebenezer Cooke, "The Sot-Weed Factor:
> Or, a Voyage to Maryland"

The Age More of Reason than of Poetry

The reason why the soil of American poetry was relatively un-cultivated from about the time of Edward Taylor's death to roughly the end of the American Revolution cannot be declared with authority, but it is an interesting question that begs for speculation. The unavoidable supposition is that the vast and rapid changes that reordered American society and thought during the Enlightenment made the American intellectual climate generally less receptive to poetry than it had been during the intensely introspective, if rigidly pious, years of Puritan domination. Such perspicacious and influential writers as Benjamin Franklin consciously decided that they could best communicate what they had to say in prose.

Under the influence of such philosophers as John Locke and such scientists as Sir Isaac Newton, the world became a more reasonable and comfortable place than the Puritans had deemed it to be. No longer did people have to try to solve the mysteries of the universe through Scripture, self-exploration, and a restricted interpretation of daily events; they gained confidence in their ability to understand God and His creation through observation of the natural world and the rational application of the laws that they themselves induced. God became the aggregate total of careful perception and rational thought instead of the approximate substance of revealed word and inner groping. Newton showed that the universe operates harmoniously, systematically, and knowably; Locke argued powerfully that a person comes into the world with a mind like a *tabula rasa,* a blank slate, on which experience is to be recorded and added up. The human mind, that is to say, need not be encumbered by supposedly predetermined notions of evil and of good. Alexander Pope issued this proclamation in "An Essay on Man":

> All Nature is but art, unknown to thee;
> All chance, direction, which thou canst not see;
> All discord, harmony not understood;
> All partial evil, universal good:
> And, in spite of pride, in erring reason's spite,
> One truth is clear: Whatever IS, is RIGHT.[1]

Understanding of the harmonics of the universe brought with it an intimation of the overall benignity of that universe. Perhaps in an age of measurement, of scientific observation of natural laws, prose was the most appropriate mode of expression.

While the conceptual and spiritual ether was changing, so was the material world of the American colonies. A rollicking ditty circulated in 1701 that made reference to a number of contemporary clergymen, including Cotton and Increase Mather, John Cotton, and Thomas Hooker, alluded impishly to the colonies' religious and material flux. In part, the verse went:

> The old strait frate is now out of Date,
> The street it must be broad;
> And the Bridge must be wood, tho not half so good
> As firm Stone in the Road.
>
> Relations are Rattle with Brattle & Brattle
> Lord Brother mayn't command:

But Mather and Mather had rather & rather
The good old way should stand.

Saints Cotton & Hooker, o look down, & look here
Where's Platform, Way, & the Keys?
O Torey what story of Brattle Church Twattle
To have things as they please.

Our Merchants cum Mico do stand Sacro Vico;
Our Churches turn genteel:
Parsons grow trim and trigg with wealth wine & wigg
And their crowns are coverd with meal.[2]

European America was becoming more populous, less English, much larger, and a good deal richer. The colonial population jumped from something over one hundred thousand people in 1670 to over a million and a half by 1760. Many of those crossing the Atlantic were now German, Dutch, and French Huguenot—a demographic shift that would later be significant in encouraging the breaking away from England. In the two decades between 1700 and 1720 the population of Boston nearly doubled. The Jewish Diaspora reached Philadelphia and New York, the Jewish artisans and merchants who emigrated from Europe achieving influence through commerce rather than numbers.

The Puritans, although their quest had been partly a mercantile venture, had established the milieu of a commune in their colony, of everyone pulling together for the general good. Now, more and more as the colonies grew and prosperity increased, so did chances to make a fortune proliferate, and so did the profit motive flourish. England wanted more of what the New World could supply; shipping and ancillary industries thrived in New England, the tobacco, indigo, and rice suppliers in the South. There was money in land, too. In the ninety years between 1670 and 1760 when the colonial population was jumping some sixteenfold, the developed area trebled in size. With the demand by new settlers for land, by the early eighteenth-century entrepreneurs were buying and selling for high profits acreage of the kind that had been parceled out without charge to the earlier settlers. Like speculators in later generations of Americans, they saw their opportunities and they took them.

The energy of communication in such a time vented itself chiefly in the prose documents that bore in some way on the changing times: the religious tracts of the Great Awakening, notably of Jonathan Edwards, attempting once again to convince the citizens that they were sinners in the hands of an angry God; the worldly wisdom of Benjamin Franklin and others that would help people succeed in the increasingly competitive marketplace; the political and economic documents and satires that issued from the presses before and during the War for Independence and during the shaping of the newly free nation.

Why were such writings not in verse? As will be seen, some were. Why did the American Enlightenment not produce a poet of the stature of Alexander Pope? Such questions can never be answered satisfactorily, but perhaps as agreeable as any reply is another question: Why did England, with its ancient literary tradition and far more stable culture, produce only one Alexander Pope?

New England Poetry of The Mid-Eighteenth Century

The names of American poets writing from about the death of Edward Taylor to the Revolution are, for sufficient reason, not household words—not even, as a rule, in the households of professional critics of American literature. For the most part, their verse was both obviously imitative of their English betters, such as Pope and Dryden, and trivial. Benjamin Church, in "The Choice," published in 1757, in naming his intellectual godfathers, was almost obsequious to Pope ("Unequal'd Bard! Who durst thy Praise engage?"), only commendatory of "copious *Dryden*, glorious in defect" (Silverman, 245–46). At least in "The Choice" and in "The Times," published in 1765 and uttering a hope for reconciliation with King George, while indicting him for injustices against the colonies, Church showed himself to be a facile pupil of Pope in the use of heroic couplets. By the 1760s, indeed, there was a considerable outpouring of metrical outrage against abuses by the Crown.

Mather Byles's given name honored his Bible-thumping grandfather Increase Mather much more than Byles's verse did. His poetry tended to reflect the poetic gimcrackery of the mid-century (for example, his use of "scaly nation" for fish in the 1755 poem "The Conflagration") expressed in conventional prosody, usually the heroic couplet. Such a piece as his "Commencement" of 1744 is pleasant enough in its evocation of Harvard's jolly graduation day with, among other delights, its "tawny damsels, mixt with simple swains" (Silverman, 240). Occasionally, he went further. His "TO PICTORIO, on the Sight of his Pictures," in 1740, for instance, contrasted his contemporary America, in which the arts were beginning to flourish, with dowdy Puritan New England of the past, where the only artistic style had been the plain one:

> Rough horrid Verse, harsh, grated thro' the Ear,
> And jarring Discords tore the tortur'd Air;
> Solid, and grave, and plain the Country stood,
> Inelegant, and rigorously good.
> Each Year, succeeding the rude Rust devours,
> And softer Arts lead on the following Hours;
> The tuneful Nine begin to touch the Lyre,
> And flowing Pencils light the living Fire;
> In the fair Page new Beauties learn to shine,
> The Thoughts to brighten, and the Style refine, . . .
>   (Silverman, 235)

By 1740, not only could a poet call for elegance; he could even urge the artist to "call forth every Passion of the Soul."

Let it not be supposed, however, that all traces of Puritanism were eradicated in New England by mid-century. Puritanism was too ingrained in the region for that to have happened, and the Great Awakening stirred the instinct for the jeremiad. Indeed, while the Great Awakening promoted the writing of pietistic verse all through colonial America, the prophetic language and tonality of such pieces in New England continued to make much New England poetry regionally recognizable.[3] Signed and unsigned verse, elegiac verse, verse occasioned by natural and historical events alike continued to bear the mark of the Puritans. "New England's Misery, the procuring Cause and Remedy Proposed," published in Boston in 1758, illustrates the point:

> Behold and see how deeply we
> do feel divine Displeasure;

> Our land before has never bore
> of Wrath so great a measure.
>   (Silverman, 207)

Broadside poetry was rife with Ramist patterns of causation. Soon after an earthquake shook Boston in the spring of 1744, a broadside sheet appeared reminding the populace that the event had been a token of God's wrath, and warning that "Those flaming Magazines of God, / Have Fire enough in store."[4] Of course, other earthquakes, fires, hurricanes, drownings, murders, hangings, and other events and phenomena of equal cheer would elicit appropriate Puritan response.

Poetry of Eighteenth-Century Philadelphia

From about 1730 to the end of the century, with the pietistic grip of the Quakers and German fundamentalist sects loosened, the fulcrum of colonial life was unquestionably Philadelphia. Since secular pursuits were often confounded in New England, which was in the throes of the religious revivalism of the Great Awakening, the way was clear for Philadelphia to become the center of intellectual life.

A few years earlier Benjamin Franklin, never backward in recognizing an opportunity or bashful about seizing it, had come to Philadelphia with the famous loaf of bread under his arm but questing for another kind of sustenance. He had felt stultified in New England, where, to him, possibilities had become circumscribed by outward forms that had become silly and empty, subject, as with the Puritan elegy, to parody. In 1722, in his seventh Dogood Paper in the *New-England Courant*, he ridiculed standard elegiac verse not only by supplying a do-it-yourself "RECEIPT to make a New England Funeral ELEGY," but by singing these lines of comic demolition on the death of one Mehitebell Kitel:

> Some little Time *before she yielded up her Breath*,
> *She said, "I ne'er shall hear one Sermon more on Earth,*
> *She kist her Husband* some little Time *before she expir'd,*
> *Then lean'd her Head the Pillow on, just out of*
> *Breath and tir'd."*[5]

Poetry of the Eighteenth Century

The recipe for cooking up an elegy, the New England-born Franklin observed in his Dogood essay, was uncomplicated: "Take one of your Neighbors who has lately departed this Life; it is no great matter at what Age the Party dy'd, but it will be best if he went away suddenly, being Kill'ed, Drown'd, or Froze to Death." Toss in some *"Virtues, Excellencies* [of which more are needed if the corpse is female], *Last Words,"* perhaps some *"Melancholly Expressions."* A dash of Latin would be nice to "garnish it mightily."

What Franklin saw was the irony that the Puritan poetry that had started out as primarily utilitarian, to clarify the Calvinist God and His works, had become merely hollow ornamentation—an absurd and provincial bauble to the intensely practical Franklin. It was not that he deprecated poetry in all of its manifestations, but only, as he perceived them, their meaningless, formulaic ones. In that, at least, Franklin was quite puritanical. He himself did work with poetry, but only when he labored to improve his writing skills, depending on verse to sharpen his sense of syllabics and rhythm. In years to come he was to argue directly against functionless poetry and other arts:

All things have their season, and with young countries as with young men, you must curb their fancy to strengthen their judgment. . . . To America, one school master is worth a dozen poets, and the invention of a machine or the improvement of an implement is of more importance than a masterpiece of Raphael. . . . Nothing is good or beautiful but in the measure that it is useful; yet all things have a utility under particular circumstances. Thus poetry, painting, music (and the stage as their embodiment) are all necessary and proper gratifications of a refined state of society but objectionable at an earlier period, since their cultivation would make a taste for their enjoyment precede its means.[6]

How very enlightened—in the eighteenth-century meaning of that word—and how very American is the statement's modification of the Puritan belief in usefulness to serve anew the pragmatic needs of Franklin's time. His quarrel, after all, with Puritan elegiac verse was that it had become unmodern, had failed to become an element of current values but had instead, in the Enlightenment, become a cultural dinosaur.

Reactions to Franklin's piece in the *New-England Courant* suggest that he was not alone in his feeling that the elegy had been transmogrified into a hump on the back of society. Comments on what came to be called "Kitelick" verse (after Franklin's absurd satiric elegy on Mehitebell Kitel) range from that of one exasperated urban reader who wailed that there was "scarce a Plow-Jogger or Country-Cobler that has read our Psalms, and can make two lines jingle, who has not once in his Life, at least, exercised his Talent in this way," to a wag who asserted that New Englanders had to refrain from good-doing in order not to be dubiously honored with elegies at their deaths.[7] As for Franklin, having assaulted the traditional New England elegiac form with laughter, he continued to print them. He was not a man to violate his own conviction about the importance of practicality over theory.

As eighteenth-century American cities went—an important qualification—Franklin's Philadelphia was literarily exciting. It harbored literary circles, such as that of Elizabeth Graeme Fergusson at Graeme Park, and enough presses, with over forty in the decades around mid-century, to churn out the verses of their members, as well as the outpouring of occasional and topical poems in various formats, including broadsides. Franklin attracted intellectual activity the way his kite drew lightning. In a city that reflected the eminence of such scientists and mathematicians as James Logan, John Bartram, and David Rittenhouse, Franklin's Junto was among the most interesting cultural cliques. With a clear conscience, he could encourage its production and discussion of verse primarily because the poetry of the Junto was intended for the betterment of its members. Moreover, their poems frequently took the form of more or less witty statements of scientific observation or treated the "Queerys in Philosophy . . . / Gravely considered & at length Discust" at the club, as Nicholas Scull, a member, described the business of the group in his poem "The Junto." The poem went on to describe such topical matters as the perversion of Britannia's basically just laws, and such scientific ones as "How tender twigs by art are taught to bear / On the same stock the apple and the pear." Using pseudonyms for fellow Junto members, Scull both chided one whose "Numbers flowd Confusdly on / And Faultring Accents shewd his muse was gone," and flattered another called "Denham" (perhaps Franklin himself) on his telling about New England's plight and plucky refusal to yield her freedom to the King (Silverman, 372–73). Franklin was sufficiently taken with another poem on the Junto, this one by member Joseph Breintnal, that Franklin wanted—presumably with tongue in cheek—the poem to "be read once a Month, and hum'd in Consort, by as many as can hum it."[8]

In one respect at least, Breintnal is the most singular of the Junto group because of the marriage in his verse of poetic form, chiefly the heroic couplet, with the most dead-level prosaic subject matter imaginable. "A plain Description of one single Street in this City" (Silverman, 374), for example, is exactly that, a laboriously detailed description of what one would see walking from the Delaware River through the city: brick buildings, judicial institutions, food stalls, a Friends' meeting house, an industrial neighborhood of wheelwrights and smithies, tenements, a tavern, finally gardens and orchards—the lot. His "July 1740. On the lately discover'd Wild Raspberries" is scarcely more aesthetically pleasing; he simply describes that plant with all of the artistic skill of a rhyming botanic taxonomist, a Linnaeus with a verbal tic. Yet Breintnal was not alone in celebrating the local scene. Chauvinism toward Philadelphia and the Pennsylvania colony was a hallmark of the club's Wits, including Titan Leeds and Jacob Taylor.

Better poets than the "Pennsylvania Wits" of the Junto club were the "Swains of the Schuylkil," a less formally organized group to which William Smith played preceptor.[9] There was some overlapping between Pennsylvania Wits and Schuylkil Swains despite the fact that the latter group ran about two decades younger than the former, but, partly because of the difference in age, there was also some animosity. For one thing, the two leaders, Franklin and Smith did not much care for each other, and the factors that triggered their ill will tended to separate their cohorts into two very distinct camps. The Swains were, generally, college-educated, conservative, Anglican, elitist, young Turks with British sympathies and a spot of scorn for those who were not as educated as they were; the Wits self-made, generally more nationalistic, and deistic in their religious leanings.

Smith, having himself attended Oxford University and Lincoln's Inn, came to Philadelphia as a member of the British Royal Society and an Episcopal clergyman in the 1750s after the sun of the Junto had gone well past its zenith. He established two important institutions in short order that were significant to the poetry of that time and place, the College of Philadelphia (which would become the University of Pennsylvania), at which he could train acceptable young men, and the *American Magazine*, in which he could publish their work and his own. With a far less parochial literary view than that of the Junto members, he also sometimes helped his students to place their verse in other organs in Britain and America.

There was a theoretical strain in Smith that Franklin's sensitive antennae picked up and led him to mock. In a note on a pamphlet that Smith put out in 1759 Franklin gibed, "For all mankind, unknown, his bosom heaves, / He only injures those with whom he lives."[10] Franklin was quite correct about Smith's impracticality. As Franklin understood, the fondness of Smith and the Swains for classical education, for instance, hardly served the improvement of life in the colonies or moved them closer to independence.

On the other hand, Smith, like Franklin, did advocate a utilitarian purpose for literature, wishing that it be used as a tool to promote a sense of community among writers and their audiences. In this, Smith anticipated, broadly speaking, the leaders of the Harlem Renaissance in the 1920s who, like the poet Countee Cullen, argued that poetry, and other art forms, should be used to bridge gaps between American blacks and American whites. Smith's school, indeed, was the only one in America to encourage the study and creation of imaginative literature to the extent that it did. In so doing, his College of Philadelphia put into practice the essence of what Smith postulated in a utopian tract called "Proposal for the College of Mirania." In that essay he reckoned that literature both "renders Life comfortable to ourselves" and "contributes highly to the cement of society, and the tranquility of the state." Training in the arts, he supposed, militated against the learner's ever becoming "a boisterous subject, an undutiful son, a rough husband, an unnatural parent, a cruel master, a treacherous friend, or an unruly and turbulent man."[11] Miranian students, accelerated by ample training, would spend two months in an intensive study of poetry, consisting of about two weeks each for "the drama and pastoral," and the remaining month for work on the epic.[12] Such an education, thought Smith, would determine whether or not the cultural epicenter of the Western world would be translated from the Old World to the "Infant-State."[13] Belief in that "Translation," as it came to be called—that perception of a shift in the world's cultural center of gravity from Europe, particularly England, to

America, with a concomitant heightening of pride in the New World and a denigration of the Old—was another characteristic of Smith and his Swain disciples. This qualification must be made: gripped as he was by Anglophile sentiments that later caused his imprisonment, Smith could only look forward to the movement, the augmentation of the arts across America to California, not to the diminution of the arts in Britain. The translation was a theme that had been struck in American poetry since Cotton Mather, and would be played into the decades after the Revolution, when intellectuals craved an artistic independence that would match the political independence from Britain that had been accomplished in war.

The Swains of the Schuylkil—among them Francis Hopkinson, Thomas Godfrey, and Nathaniel Evans—themselves attest, by word if not always by example, to the excellence of the literary education that they received from Smith. Hopkinson, for example, in his "Il Penseroso," conjures a "shining Throng" of poets who "ascribe their Birth" to William Smith's "Blest Institution," while Smith himself is invited to "hear the muse thou taught'st to sing" (Silverman, 359). Beyond such references in poems, the best testimonial to Smith and his program is the range and sometimes the quality of the poetry that his group produced. Francis Hopkinson went on to become a public official of the emerging nation and composed more and more rousing anti-British verse potboilers; his became the most popular—because the most public—poetry of the Swains, though not the best. The members of the group felt as free to go their own artistic ways and to experiment with form and feeling as Franklin felt with lenses, kite string, and women. Thomas Godfrey tried the style of English cavalier poets. Nathaniel Evans, artistically the most interesting of the clique, began, as virtually all Enlightenment poets did, with the mannerisms of Alexander Pope, but he succumbed to the preromantic breezes that were starting to stir the world of letters, and he moved in the direction of Thomas Gray and the churchyard elegy.[14] "The Soul, alas! has fled to endless day," he mourned on the death of Godfrey, "And left its house a mould'ring mass of clay" (Silverman, 405).

In all, the fact that poetry in Philadelphia did not radiate more heat and light was determined, perhaps, less by lack of talent than by the rapidly changing political, economic, and social conditions of late eighteenth-century America. No less was it limited by the early deaths of the best of the poets, Godfrey at twenty-seven, Evans at only twenty-five. But Philadelphia's sparking was a welcome and attractive sight in the night of eighteenth-century American poetry.

Poetry of The Southern Colonies

It is appropriate to begin a consideration of southern poetry in the eighteenth century for a very uncomplicated reason: there was little poetry, especially published poetry, in the southern colonies to speak of in the seventeenth century.[15] While seventeenth-century Puritans used verse as a key to partially unlock the secrets of the individual's and community's relationship to the Deity, southerners, without Calvinist doctrine to absorb almost their every waking thought and endeavor, were free to treat poetry as a bagatelle, an amusement for gentlemen that the unwritten rules of gentility in the region held should not normally be published. In the North the writing of poetry was a matter of high seriousness to be duly respected; in the South it was the occasion for a display of wit, often enough of ennui, of dissatisfaction with the less-than-genteel conditions of life in the New World and especially of isolation from England.

Far more than in the North, where poets tended to accept life's severities as part of God's design and to reconcile them as part of the expectation of the millenium, in the South, what poets there were, lacking a pervasive structure of such belief, were inclined to grumble about the rough circumstances, or even to dissolve the hardships in fantasy. The author of "To the LADIES OF MARYLAND," for example, published in the *Maryland Gazette*, 14 June 1745 by one "Juba," warns the ladies to "scorn the *Foppling Flutters* of the Town" as if there were any; "Juba" apparently imagined himself in mannered and sophisticated London rather than in colonial Maryland.

Poems that did meet the New World situation head-on leave small wonder as to why southern poets at times transported themselves telepathically to the civilization of mother England and father Europe. Often they exhibited a regretful ambivalence of feeling. Thus did Richard Lewis lament in 1728:

There [i.e., "on fair ITALIAN PLAINS"], PAINTURE breathes,
There, STATUARY lives,
And MUSIC most delightful Rapture gives:
There pompous piles of Building pierce the Skies,
And endless Scenes of Pleasure court the Eyes.
While Here, rough Woods embrown the Hills and Plains,
Mean are the Buildings, artless are the *Swains:*
"To raise the Genius," WE no Time can spare,
A bare Subsistence claims our utmost care.
                    ("To His Excellency BENEDICT LEONARD CALVERT . . . ,"
                                                   Silverman, 302–3)

In yet another poem, "CARMEN SECULARE, For the Year, M, DCC, XXXII," the same Lewis owned that "Industry and rolling Years" had made Maryland habitable.

The ambivalence is perhaps best expressed by Charles Woodmason in his "C. W. *in* Carolina *to* E. J. *at* Gosport," published in the *Gentleman's Magazine* of July 1753; the language of the poem and its place of publication echo the superior gentleman-to-gentleman tone of most southern poetry, which was often recited at clubs and when printed at all was usually printed in such supercilious outlets. Woodmason both acknowledges "How has kind heav'n adorn'd this happy land, / And scatter'd blessings with a lib'ral hand!" and bemoans the purposelessness of those blessings in a wasteland where noxious reptiles and stinging insects reign, and droughts and hurricanes ruin the crops. Woodmason's breast is wounded with pain when he recollects the old country in contrast: "O Britain! Queen of isles, serenely bright" (Silverman, 333–36).

So did southern colonial poets, Woodmason, George Seagood, and others tend to bewail both the physical and cultural deprivation—as they saw it—of the New World in favor of the Old. For the most part, that is to say, they denied the Translation that northern writers from the Puritans to William Smith to Joel Barlow anticipated with relish. Lyrics "made by a Bostonian," for example, sang out in 1774:

That Seat of Science, Athens, and Earth's proud Mistress, Rome,
Where now are all their Glories? We scarce can find their Tomb.
Then guard your Rights, Americans, nor stoop to lawless Sway,
Oppose, oppose, oppose, oppose for North America.[16]

But Richard Lewis mourned that colonists, while eking out bare subsistence, could spare no time "To raise the Genius." Ebenezer Cooke's 1708 version of "The Sot-Weed Factor," a long poem that claims public attention more for John Barth's use of the title in his comic novel of 1960 and for its vituperative view of life in colonial Maryland than for its artistic merit, was a strong but not untypical statement of the southern position on Translation. With others, Cooke shared a loathing for the place with its wolves; surly peasants; disgusting dishes unfit for a hungry dog; and plagues of frogs, rattlesnakes, mosquitoes, heathen Indians, drunks, lawyers, and chinch bugs, to name a few unpleasantnesses. Far from looking forward to the colonies' supplanting England as a light to the world, Cooke shed his venom on "that Shoar, where no good Sense is found, / But Conversation's lost, and Manners drown'd" (Silverman, 282–301). Rejecting the idea of Translation, numerous poems such as "The Sot-Weed Factor" and Jonathan Boucher's "ABSENCE, a Pastoral: drawn from the life, from the manners, customs and phraseology of planters (or, to speak more pastorally, of the rural swains) inhabiting the Banks of the Potomac, in Maryland" disparaged, with aristocratic posturing, both the country as an irremediable cultural swamp and the bumpkins who inhabited it and were well bred to its artlessness.

The plain style of New England that was intended and suitable for an audience of the entire community was, naturally, foreign to the southern poets with their haughty pretensions. This is not to say that southern poets could not stoop to the common in subject matter, however, especially in a display of wit to their peers—at times, in fact, stoop to a level scarcely imaginable in the North. Thus, the southerner William Byrd, who wrote the *Dividing Line Histories* and was probably neither Scots nor Welsh, composed a brief disquisition "Upon a Fart," which began (and ended) without much northern seriousness of purpose or loftiness of insight:

> Gentlest Blast of ill concoction,
> Reverse of high-ascending Belch:
> Th' only Stink abhorr'd by Scotsman,
> Beloved and practic'd by the Welch.
> (Silverman, 273)

Such frivolousness, to some extent, suggests the South's understandable lack of commitment to a demanding, single-minded, religious ideal and to an educational system that could underpin the effort to fulfill that ideal. The region just happened not to be settled by Puritans, who were dedicated to education because learning served their understanding of God and their mission to establish a New Jerusalem in preparation for His Doomsday. In the North young poets could congregate at four institutions that gained importance quickly, Harvard, then Yale, William Smith's College of Philadelphia (later the University of Pennsylvania), and King's College (later Columbia University). There were systems of public and private schools to encourage learning and participation in the arts—of course, within the Calvinist framework, two activities that the New England culture valued. The story of education in the South, however, was vastly different. Though the College of William and Mary, in Virginia, received its charter in 1693, the attorney general of the colony admonished the founder of the school, James Blair, not to concern himself with educating a ministry, but "to forget about souls and make tobacco."[17] The official's attitude was not more enlightened than that of Virginia's Governor Berkeley, who a couple of decades before had thanked God that *"there are no free schools* nor *printing"* in the colony, for education "has brought disobedience, and heresy, and sects into the world, and *printing* has divulged them. . . . God keep us from both" (Silverman, 260). It is not surprising that printing was a rarity in the South, and that, in the opinion of Jonathan Boucher at any rate, in 1769, those with an appreciation of literature were no "nearer than the country I had just left [England]: nor were literary attainments beyond merely reading or writing at all in vogue or repute"; as for poetry, it "may yet be considered only as an exotic" (Silverman, 261). The dichotomy between the North's insistence on education and the South's aversion to it helps to explain the competing strains ever after in American culture of admiration for learning and the arts on the one hand and anti-intellectualism on the other.

Women's Poetry

Women poets, northern and southern in America, did not have an easy time, but if the practice of their avocation was difficult in the North, where printing and at least a truncated education, unequal to the education of males, were available to them, it was well nigh impossible in the South. Of the thirty-nine "frequent" and "infrequent" poets included in the comprehensive anthology *Women Poets in Pre-Revolutionary America, 1650–1775,*[18] not a single one was born or lived in the South, except for Bathsheba Bowers, and even she late in her life moved to South Carolina from Philadelphia as a Quaker preacher.

The only notable periodical outlets for poetry in the South were the *Maryland Gazette,* founded by William Parks a few years before he founded his *Virginia Gazette* in 1736, and the *South Carolina Gazette,* first published in 1732 as one of Benjamin Franklin's myriad business ventures. All three printed poems to fill otherwise dead space, and in the southern as in the northern periodicals poems by women were occasionally accepted as a device to increase female readership.

In the New World as well as the Old women's artistic aspirations from the beginning had been suppressed by patriarchal male attitudes. There were, to be sure, limited exceptions. Anne Bradstreet's family esteemed her poetic accomplishments, for instance, as Jane Colman Turell's father prized hers, the slave Phillis Wheatley's owners encouraged hers, and Mercy Otis Warren's father assisted her by allowing her to share her brother's tutor. Even in Bradstreet's case, John Woodbridge, the brother-in-law who had gone to the trouble of getting her *Tenth Muse* published, felt constrained to cover her for any possible charge of neglect of wifely duties that the public, to protect one of its fundamental mores, might have leveled at her. Her poems, Woodbridge soothed, cost merely "some few hours, curtailed from her sleep and other refreshments";[19] society could rest easy, assured that its Tenth Muse had not pilfered any of her laundry time to write a poem. Various men expressed their ethic in this matter variously: after Anne Yale Hopkins, the author of several missing book manuscripts and wife of the Governor of Connecticut, visited John Winthrop with her husband in 1645, Winthrop noted in his diary:

. . . if she had attended her household affairs, and such things as belong to women, and not gone out of her way and calling to meddle in such things as are proper for men [i.e., reading, writing, producing many books], whose minds are stronger, etc., she had kept her wits, and might have improved them usefully and honorably in the place God had set her.[20]

Few New Englanders—believing as they usually did in the right of women to write, as long as the task did not violate the communally- (i.e., male-) established priorities of their lives—would have been as extreme, perhaps, as the Reverend Thomas Parker of Newbury, Massachusetts, a model of simple, elegant peremptoriness. Coming to the point in a letter to his sister in England in the mid-seventeenth century, Parker said ". . . your printing of a book, beyond the custom of your sex, doth rankly smell."[21]

When it came, recognition of the accomplishments of female poets could be tainted with condescension; when Nathaniel Ward applauded Anne Bradstreet as "a right *Du Bartas* Girle," he qualified the compliment by archly joking: "It half revives my chil frostbitten blood, / To see a woman once do, ought, that's good; / . . . Let Men look to't, least Women wear the Spurrs," Ward smugly quipped (*M*, 367). The same "Juba" who, in "To the LADIES OF MARYLAND" in the *Maryland Gazette* of 14 June 1745, affected a warning to women to avoid imaginary "*Foppling Flutters* of the Town," enjoined the ladies to "Fly Books; they'll turn your Head, and spoil your Charms; / Philosophy your ev'ry Grace disarms" (Silverman, 325).

The result of such pressure on female poets was threefold. First, a number of them accepted, or pretended to accept, America's jaundiced male view of them. Second, they often published their regrets over the supposed affront that they committed in daring to go into print with their poems. The instances were numerous, but a representative one follows: in the preface to her first volume, *Ouâbi: or the Virtues of Nature. An Indian Tale in Four Cantos*, in 1790, Sarah Morton begged her audience to "make many allowances for the various imperfections of the work, from a consideration of sex and situation; the one by education incident to weakness, the other from duty to domestic avocations."[22] The anonymous editor of Bridget Fletcher's 1773 *Hymns and Spiritual Songs* articulated society's attitude with unfortunate clarity in declaring the inevitable—because sex-related—inferiority of the collection:

In as much as this small collection of hymns and spiritual songs is to appear in public, it is expected that every candid reader will be ready to make allowances for the many inaccuracies of a female pen, when he considers that the advantages of females in general are but small, in comparison to those of the other sex, in point of polite learning.[23]

If female poets were frequently apologetic, however, the third result—equally predictable—of society's snide reception of their work was their publicly speaking out against it. Whatever other themes of private experience and public occasion ran through the women's work, one theme that recurred often was a feminist one, beginning as early as Anne Bradstreet, who remonstrated in "The Prologue":

> I am obnoxious to each carping tongue
> Who says my hand a needle better fits,
> A poet's pen all scorn I should thus wrong,
> For such despite they cast on Female wits:
> They say it's stolen, or else it was by chance.
> (Silverman, 57)

Sometimes the women's anger welled up in a political way, as in this 1736 protest in the *Virginia Gazette:*

> Then equal laws let custom find,
>   And neither sex oppress;
> More freedom give to womankind,
>   Or give to mankind less.[24]

At other times the complaint was more general: "They rob us of the power t'improve" Judith Sargent Murray wrote in 1779, "And then declare we only trifles love."[25]

Without much support from men, women poets looked for support of their avocation from each other, and they found it. It is clear from letters; from references in poems of such women as Jane Colman Turell and Mercy Otis Warren; from a list of American, British, and European female poets in Judith Sargent Murray's article "Observations on Female Abilities," published in 1798; and from other extant documents, including a commonplace book that Elizabeth Graeme Fergusson wrote for Annis Stockton, that women supplied needed fortification to other women, sometimes on a transatlantic and often on an intercolonial basis. They sometimes addressed poems to one another, as Sarah Wentworth Morton did to Mercy Otis Warren in the *Massachusetts Magazine* of July 1790 for Warren's "matchless worth" and "fame-embellish'd lays." Apart from written encouragement, there was occasional personal contact among the female poets, as in the literary circle established by Elizabeth Graeme Fergusson at Graeme Park outside of Philadelphia. Her salon entertained both men and women poets, among the latter, her niece Anna Young Smith, Annis Stockton, and Hannah Griffitts. The welter of poetic activity among women in the Philadelphia area, in fact, moved a columnist, "Misericordis," in the *Pennsylvania Chronicle*, to comment superciliously that the women were "more eager to mix the ingredients of a little piece of this manufacture [i.e., poetry], than to mix the ingredients for a pudding."[26] Women, poets among them, still had a long way to come in American society.

The almost complete omission of American female poets from anthologies[27] is remarkable. The women's output was continual, at least in the North, from Anne Bradstreet on. They wrote of the blisses and exigencies of domestic life and of death and religion; they reflected the imposing intellectual forces of their times—Puritanism, the Great Awakening, the forms and themes of the Enlightenment, the growth of national feeling and rebellion against an oppressive Crown. Sometimes, as in the case of Sarah Wentworth Morton's "The African Chief," they were in the forefront of such sociopolitical movements as the push for the abolition of slavery. It does the women poets no extravagant service to assert that in the slack period between Edward Taylor and the Revolutionary War, the work of such poets as Morton, Jane Colman Turell, Hannah Griffitts, Mercy Otis Warren, Elizabeth Graeme Fergusson, Judith Sargent Murray, Phillis Wheatley, and Anna Young Smith was, by and large, at least as good as that of their male counterparts. The pity is that that still has to be said.

Broadsides

Broadside verse in America, as elsewhere, did not aspire to high literary achievement. Furthermore, as in the case of the first American example, the "Freeman's Oath," an official public document printed in 1639 by Stephen Daye's press in Cambridge, Massachusetts,[28] broadside material was frequently in prose, in the form of public reports or announcements. The broadside, however, is important to examine in the context of American poetry because it was a supremely important manifestation of popular literature. As prose or poetry, it was a cheap source of information and—for a while, pious—entertainment. Since its nature was to treat matters of immediate concern, broadside verse, for much of the seventeenth century, focused mainly on that most passionate interest of the Puritan colonists—death. Much of the funeral verse that the Puritans composed, which is to say, much of the total bulk of the poetry that they produced, including the eulogistic wordplay of anagrams and acrostics, was published as broadside. At the outset, in the mid-seventeenth century, the elegiac broadsides were simple, unmemorable memorials that were, at least, imbued with a sense of honest grief. They were immediate expressions of the genuine sorrow of a small community over the loss of a valued member, and they reconciled the ancient human questions concerning life and death with the religious system to which they all subscribed. But the folk were fruitful and multiplied, and more settlers came—many from places other than Mother England—and towns and villages grew as the Puritan grip relaxed. Yet the habit of cranking out and running off funereal sentiments as broadsides did not abate for a surprisingly long time. More of them than ever appeared toward the end of the seventeenth century and for the first thirty years of the next century. By now the paltry work of death versifiers that moved Cotton Mather to observe in his elegy on Urian Oakes that "Grief never made good poet" had become worse than mediocre. It was almost always a depthless, stylized, formulaic expression of unfelt sentimentality—mere prepackaged form. The Puritan obsession with the Old Testament suzerain contract between God and his human vassals had become larely fin de siècle poetic ornamentation. That is the situation that Benjamin Franklin spoofed so tellingly as Dogood in his Kitelic elegy and "Receipt to make a New-England Funeral Elegy."

Not quite all broadside verse was elegiac. In 1675 half of a broadside account of a battle in King Philip's War was rhymed in ballad form; it is impossible to say how many other such broadside pieces were printed, for many broadsides did not long outlast their timely appearances on cheap throwaway sheets. Without doubt, others were published. The 1675 verse, for example, "Some Meditations Concerning our Honourable Gentlemen and

Fellow-Souldiers, in Pursuit of those Barbarous Natives in the Narragansit-Country, December 28, 1675" survived, not in the original broadside form, but through a 1721 reprint run off in New London, Connecticut. What is certain is that by the 1720s, ballads of the Indian wars were popular, some, in their use of dialogue, standing in the venerable line of British balladry. A couple of decades later the French and Indian War was the subject of popular broadside ballads that dramatized in particular the exploits of the New England units fighting patriotically for the Crown in Canada, and the romantic circumstances of the death of General Wolfe at Quebec in 1759.

There were other current events besides warfare that inspired the production and purchase of broadside ballads in the seventeenth century—reports of and admonitory reactions to such catastrophes as the Merrimac River's going dry; various earthquakes, floods, and tornados; and accounts of such disasters as shipwrecks and crimes, that always ended with standard moralizing about the wages of sin. When, for example, John Ormsby was hanged on Boston Neck, 17 October 1734 for slaying a fellow inmate of the jail in which he had been incarcerated for assault, and Mathew Cushing with him for having stolen some clothing from a shoemaker, the ensuing broadside exhorted one and all to:

> . . . let this Warning loud and shrill
>   be heard by ev'ry one,
> *O do no more such wickedness*
>   *as has of late been done.*
> Lament and wail his [i.e., Cushing's] woeful Case,
>   and by him Warning take;
> A sight I think enough to make
> A Heart of Stone to ake.
>
>   (Winslow, 85)

The quality of such lines as these goes far toward explaining why most broadsides were published anonymously. It also helps to explain why broadsides depended considerably on art work— usually about as crude as the verse—to illustrate the occasion and to take some of the burden off the poetry. Typically, the accompanying drawings were simple and obviously symbolic—coffins, death's heads, headstone-shaped frames for elegies, gallows for death-sentence sermons.

Occasionally, some versifier was less shy than the verses warranted, and did admit to authorship, as in the case of one Molly Gutridge of Marblehead, Massachusetts, who confessed to writing a rough-hewn prosodic report in 1779 of the plight of the people in towns like hers during the Revolution, "A New Touch on the Times, Well Adapted to the Distressing Situation of Every Sea-Port Town." Even more rarely could authorship be acknowledged of a broadside whose display of wit could redound to the credit of the author, as was Francis Hopkinson's burlesque "Battle of the Kegs," although, after a time, Hopkinson chafed at the notoriety that "Kegs" brought him. That ballad, which could be sung to the tune of "Yankee Doodle," mocked the shooting up by British soldiers of kegs of rum that the rebels floated down the Delaware at Philadelphia in 1778. The British, made to think mistakenly that the kegs were floating bombs, tried to explode them in midstream before they could do damage along the shores. Hopkinson paid the redcoats mock heroic homage for their successful attack on the harmless kegs:

> An hundred men with each a pen,
> Or more upon my word, sir,
> It is most true, would be too few,
> Their valour to record, sir.
> Such feats did they perform that day
> Upon these wicked kegs, sir,
> That years to come, if they get home,
> They'll make their boasts and brags, sir.
> (Winslow, 153)

The "Battle of the Kegs," welcome as a rare example of revolutionary broadside humor, was reprinted, as were many other broadsides, as a broadside either simultaneously with or after original publication in a newspaper. In the absence of concern about copyright infringements, and with many newspaper printers also putting out broadsheets, many a newspaper ballad was reprinted by its original or some other printer as a broadside. Newspaper stories often formed the bases of broadside issues. The connection between broadsheets and newspapers led, in the 1760s and afterward, to the circulation of numerous broadsides of New Year's greetings, which almost always reviewed some history and expressed the community's wishes for the future, then solicited money for the paper boy. "January 1776. The Carrier of the *Boston Gazette*, to his Customers. A New-Year's Wish," for instance, declared the day to be gone "When *Tyrants* wish'd to strike fair FREEDOM dead," and, without the clear vision of hindsight, still dared to hope that ". . . *GEORGE* the Great, with open'd *Ears* and *Eyes*, / Observe our *Injuries*, and hear our *Cries*." Politics may come and politics may go, but the need to eat goes on regardless; the carrier proceeded to request from his customers "some Trifle for my past Reward" (Winslow, 207).

The New Year's broadsheets are not as trivial as they may at first seem. They mark the application of poetic devices—rhyme, metrical patterning, and the yoking together of such disparate elements as the emotional catchword "freedom" with a plea for donation and continued patronage—to advertising. The value of the technique was not lost on eighteenth-century tradesmen other than publishers, and it was never to disappear from the American scene. Peter Jarvis, a Boston cabinetmaker, for example, issued a series of New Year's broadsides beginning in 1787 that advertised his artifacts and sometimes his own misfortunes, picturing the pleasures of family life while portraying himself as honest, caring, even affectionate—at least as far as his friends and patrons were concerned (Winslow, 213). And an 1832 broadsheet circulated by a Boston trash collector ended:

> Now hand us out a little cash,
> And we will come and take your trash—
> And wish you free from ev'ry pain,
> Till a NEW YEAR comes round again.
>
> (Winslow, 212)

It is instructive to compare the driving force of that nineteenth-century conclusion with the end of any of the seventeenth-century Puritan elegiac broadsides, such as that of Pastor John Wilson on the death of Joseph Brisco in 1657, Wilson reminding his audience and himself:

No matter how or where the Lord doth bring
Us to our end, in Christ who live and die
And sure to live with Christ eternally.

(Winslow, 5)

In the intervening years, a part of America's poetry, and the spirit that made it, had become—and would henceforth be—commercial.

· THREE ·

Poetry of "The Future Glory of America"

This is thy praise American thy pow'r
Thou best of climes by science visited
By freedom blest and richly stor'd with all
The luxuries of life. Hail happy land
The seat of empire the abode of king, . . .

—Philip Freneau and
Hugh Henry Brackenridge
"A Poem, on the Rising Glory of America"

By mid-eighteenth century the allegiance of the colonies to England was fast eroding. They felt intensely the results of oppressive British colonial policy. Immigration from nations other than Britain increasingly loosened the ties that bound. In defense, education, religion, commerce, and other matters, intercourse increased rapidly among the colonies. The sense that such forces gave the colonials that they were not British but American grew stronger, though, of course, as in the case of the Schuylkil Swains, important pockets of Toryism remained through the Revolutionary War. In general, if Europeans and Britons writing about American manners and language were contemptuous of them, so were Americans who visited the Old World disenchanted with what they perceived as the jaded quality of life there. Where in Europe were the boundless possibilities of the New World? Not only the Translation motif, but the full range of nationalistic sentiments and complaints against British rule were expressed more and more openly in broadsides and newspapers. As the feeling of nationhood grew and became rampant, poets sought markets for their verse in regions other than their own. Mather Byles, for example, was published in Franklin's *General Magazine* and Joseph Dumbleton in *Gazettes* in Maryland, Virginia, and South Carolina.[1]

The Nationalistic Pastoral

The most interesting and important phenomenon in American poetry from mid-century to the Revolutionary War and beyond was the mythologizing of America in nationalistic pastoral verse. At first the pastorals, whose popularity derived from the breezes of romanticism that were freshening in Britain and Europe, were a focus for the expression of the Translation, the shift of the Western cultural center of gravity from the Old World to the New, but increasingly they reflected an intensification of political nationalism. Whatever their emphases, they contained a remarkable element of fantasy. By 1771 the versified Princeton commencement oration "A Poem, on the Rising Glory of America" by Philip Freneau and Hugh Henry Brackenridge sang of and to an America that did not and never would exist. Their jingoism equated America with the great empires of history and extended her boundaries "From Baffin's Bay to Del Fuego south, / From California to the Oronoque" (Silverman, 429). The young poets, to be sure, did not call for separation from the Crown, yet they did envision America, not Britain, as the new world empire to be reckoned with, and they artistically, if not politically, turned their backs on the motherland: "No more of Britain, and her kings renoun'd, . . ." (Silverman, 424). For Freneau and Brackenridge, the present—and especially the future—were in America, where shines

> The rising glory of the western world,
> Where now the dawning light of science spreads
> Her orient ray, and wakes the muse's song;
> Where freedom holds her sacred standard high,
> And commerce rolls her golden tides profuse
> Of elegance and ev'ry joy of life.
>
> (Silverman, 424)

To their chauvinistic imaginations, still four years away from the Revolution, colonial cities had gone beyond being mere Athenian models of culture and morality; America had become the chief empire of the world, from which freedom would be spread. Freneau and Brackenridge were declaiming a vision that was so strong and so readily nourished in the millenial soil that the Puritans had prepared that it was to become and has been a major theme of American poetry ever since—has been because it became the salient feature of America's self-image.

The extent to which a national mythology coincides with actuality is always open to debate, but what is certain is that the poets of "The Rising Glory of America" like those of other tendentious pastoral verses—including John Trumbull's "Prospect of Our Future Glory," Timothy Dwight's "America, or a Poem on the Settlement of the British Colonies," and Joel Barlow's interminable *The Vision of Columbus* and *The Columbiad*—outrageously exaggerated the intellectual and political condition of America in their own time. It is almost impossible to recognize the territory from the verbal map that the poets drew with so little correspondence between symbol and reality. Freneau and Brackenridge, like the others, raised the anchor of time and space and sailed the seas of dream, wishful thinking, high-level abstraction, but that is quite what they intended to do, to lead the cheer, to assert the magnificence of America's political and commercial and cultural future. For America to distance herself from Britain was not enough; the pastoral poets had to show America under full sail pulling ahead of her motherland and leaving a wondrous wake on the race course of nations.

The Puritan Influence

The significant American poets of the late eighteenth century, especially Dwight, Barlow, Trumbull, and, to an extent, Freneau were much more under the spell of their Puritan antecedents than one may at first suppose. First, they wrote allegorically and symbolically for an audience that was used to reading allegorically and symbolically, an audience that was capable of perceiving allegory even when none was intended (as in the case of Dwight's *The Conquest of Canaan* (1771–73), an account of the biblical Joshua's exploits in Exodus, which his American audience chose to take as an allegory of George Washington and the Revolution). The poets tended to indulge the allegorical expectation. After all, they, too, were members of that same audience. Thus Dwight consciously did oblige his readers in 1780 with the deliberate allegory "America: Or a Poem on the Settlement of the British Colonies," a chauvinistic history that concludes, in good patriotic pastoral form, with a personification of freedom celebrating the new nation's glorious future.

Second, the poets of the period echoed the Puritans' relish of allegory because they also shared their propensity to view the world millenially. To be sure, by the late eighteenth century the millenial vision was, for the most part, political, cultural, and economic rather than religious, but it was no less optimistically ecstatic for all that. Not only Freneau and Brackenridge's "The Rising Glory of America," but numerous other examples reflect the nationalistic delirium of a golden age of humankind dominated by a heavenly America. The end of Dwight's complacent paean to Connecticut and America, *Greenfield Hill* (1794), and Barlow's New World epic *The Columbiad* (1807) are examples.

Third, the late eighteenth-century poets retained the Puritans' propensity for heavy-handed moralizing about the way in which humanity can approach closer to perfection by dint of the individual's effort toward moral self-improvement. Dwight's highly Calvinistic, sententious *Greenfield Hill* provides as clear an example as any.

The Connecticut Wits

Together, Timothy Dwight, Joel Barlow, and John Trumbull, all educated at Yale, came to be known as the "Connecticut Wits," an epithet that from a late twentieth-century perspective may have been giving them credit for too much. Their work is mainly of antique interest now, a curious conglomeration of eclectic philosophy, Calvinist cant, classical epic and allusion, and a variety of traditional English verse forms including blank verse, Spenserian stanzas, and ubiquitous couplets.

BARLOW'S COLUMBIAD. Probably the most attractive poems published by the Connecticut Wits are Barlow's *Columbiad*, because it is as heroic, though badly flawed, as any they produced, and

Trumbull's well-known satirical pieces *The Progress of Dulness* (1772–73) and, especially, *M'Fingal* (1782), because they were effective in their time and are still reasonably stinging and funny even if many of the topical references are lost on a modern audience. Barlow based *The Columbiad* on his earlier unsuccessful try at an American visionary epic, *The Vision of Columbus* (1787). He was, of course, joining a line of composers of American epics that reached back at least as far as Cotton Mather's *Magnalia Christi Americana* in prose. In the Barlow effort, an infelicitous, meandering trek through philosophy and narrative in soporific couplets, Columbus, at the onset, is led by an angel to a mountaintop, much in the manner of Milton's Adam, from which he can see that quite standard late eighteenth-century phenomenon, the future glory of America. But if the conservative *Vision of Columbus* was poor, its revision, published two decades later, after Barlow had been tenderized by the humanism of the two great revolutions of the time, the American and the French, was even weaker. As if he realized that *The Vision* had been lumbered with bits of unoriginal philosophy, Barlow determined to strengthen the narrative line in *The Columbiad* and write a proper epic, but he doomed his own effort from the start by failing to lend the figure of Columbus the stature or interest that befits an epic hero. As Pearce says, "Barlow's actual hero is what he and his contemporaries liked to call the republican institution, toward which all history, natural and human, progressed. . . . [Columbus's] passion is that of a voyeur, since he does not participate in the vision."[2] What Barlow was ultimately attempting to do, which made his creation of an engaging human actor in the person of Columbus unimportant, was to project a utopian vision of the New World in which God had deferred to nature and science (since *The Vision* of twenty years before) and perfection was palpably possible. Even that passionate vision he framed, paradoxically, in verse that rings mechanically, even as the vision itself reverberates extravagantly. Yet while Barlow's try at an epic is less successful than his more controlled "The Hasty Pudding"—a sound mock-heroic poem that he wrote in France in 1793 when the taste of a food, like Proust's *madeleine*, triggered recollections of his blessed Yankee life—*The Columbiad* is, at least, like Gatsby, a grand failure. It is ironic, though, that Barlow and his fellows were at their best, as in "The Hasty Pudding," when they essayed the least profundity.

John Trumbull's Satires

As is expected, Alexander Pope loomed large in the estimation of his late nineteenth-century American cousins, and not infrequently they paid him homage by imitation. Barlow's "The Hasty Pudding," in octosyllabic couplets, is an example of a mock-heroic verse in the manner of *The Rape of the Lock*, right down to its division into cantos (though there are fewer cantos in the Barlow piece than in Pope's). John Trumbull's *The Progress of Dulness* and *M'Fingal* are satires reminiscent of Pope's *Dunciad*, with undertones of Jonathan Swift, Samuel Butler, and Joseph Addison. *The Progress of Dulness* is divided into three parts issued sequentially, the first of which called Trumbull's gall to public notice. In tracking young Tom Brainless from the farm through Yale and into the ministry, in section one, Trumbull attacks the shallowness of academe and the ministry—in his day, for practical purposes, about the same thing. The second section is too gentle and derivative. Trumbull clearly goes out of his way to avoid being offensive here, though he was in the first section with its lampooning of specific clerics and their practices. He creates a highly generalized and derivative English dandy, Dick Hairbrain, as the target of his satire. Restraint is not a helpful handmaiden of satire. Miss Harriet Simper, the heroine of the final section, is a standard satirical flirt. Though Trumbull's endeavor to reconcile the three parts of *The Progress of Dulness* collapses into slapstick, the poem remains, through considerable passages, more readable and even more clever than much eighteenth-century satire produced on both sides of the Atlantic.

There are problems with Trumbull's *M'Fingal*, too, but it is more successful overall and was in its time more popular than *The Progress of Dulness*. *M'Fingal* was, in fact, the most popular poem by an American since Michael Wigglesworth's *Day of Doom* (1662).[3] The many topical allusions that have long since been lost on readers necessarily limit modern interest in *M'Fingal*—a fate that comes, alas, to much good satire. But Trumbull's wit often glows through the murk, indeed too brightly for many of his readers. In the years following the Revolution, many readers lost the satirical point and took the gaseous speeches of the character Honorius, the Whig counterpart of the rampant Tory M'Fingal, to be serious—and even soberly recited them.[4] Roused to write the poem by General Gates's strutting declaration of martial law in Boston in 1775, Trumbull managed to be impressively impartial in his carving up of both Tories and Whigs and to achieve a universality in *M'Fingal* that exceeded the political situation in America. But these qualities were largely unappreciated by a zealously patriotic audience that found much in the poem that Trumbull did not intend. He discovered, as have other satirists before and since, that once written, the satire sometimes has an embarrassing life of its own.

The Wish to Create a National Literature

Perhaps the most arresting thing about the Connecticut Wits is less their actual poetic achievement than their drive to create a literature independent of English literature that would mirror the political independence that obsessed their compatriots. They filled their lines with American objects, events, and sentiments—from hasty pudding to a New England village green to musket fire in the name of liberty, but, in the end, they lacked the genius to speak of American things in a *voice* that was distinctly American. Even their most flag-waving verse could have been uttered by a newly converted Englishman; the prosody was entirely and the diction almost entirely English. But they could at least begin to conceive of what was required for a new national literature. In Book 10 of *The Columbiad* Joel Barlow articulated, though haltingly, the relationship between new language and his utopian vision:

> At this blest period, when the total race
> Shall speak one language and all truths embrace,
> Instruction clear a speedier course shall find,
> And open earlier on the infant mind.
> No foreign terms shall crowd with barbarous rules
> The dull unmeaning pageantry of schools;
> Nor dark authorities nor names unknown
> Fill the learnt head with ignorance not its own;
> But wisdom's eye with beams unclouded shine,
> And simplest rules her native charms define;
> One living language, one unborrowed dress
> Her boldest flights with fullest force express;
> Triumphant virtue, in the garb of truth,
> Win a pure passage to the heart of youth,

> Pervades all climes where suns or oceans roll,
> And warm the world with one great moral soul,
> To see, facilitate, attain the scope
> Of all their labor and their hope.[5]

At one level the passage, with its contorted syntax, yearns for a kind of generalized language that would express the oneness of all the human race. At another, in the context of the utopian vision of America, Barlow is apparently calling for new skin to hold the sublime new American wine, a new, simple "living language." Such a language would be purified of "foreign terms" and authorities filling the heads of Americans with irrelevant ideas that have not sprung from native soil—"ignorance not its own." Ironically, while *The Columbiad* contains Barlow's hope for a new language that would express the new land, he was not capable of achieving it. Ralph Waldo Emerson would unmuddle the idea some thirty-five years later in his essay "The Poet," and Walt Whitman would build his poetry with it forty-eight years later: "A new language: a new soul: a new world."[6]

Philip Freneau

The efforts of the Connecticut Wits to establish an American literature and Barlow's fuzzy insight into what was needed notwithstanding, the most important American poet of the eighteenth century was Philip Freneau. He was two poets in one, really. One was the political animal who collaborated with Hugh Henry Brackenridge on "The Rising Glory of America." Freneau's politicization was later intensified when he was captured aboard a blockade runner and spent six weeks on a British prison ship during the Revolution. After his release in a prisoner exchange, he wrote patriotic and anti-British pieces for the *Freeman's Journal* in Philadelphia, and later he earned the enmity of Washington and the Federalists for training his vituperative guns on them. This was the fervid revolutionary Freneau, the propagandist Freneau, who wrote neoclassical essays in both verse and prose lampooning, satirizing, sometimes reasoning on behalf of whatever democratic political cause he burned with at the moment. At the beginning of the Revolutionary War, for example, in 1775 he cried in "A Political Litany":

From a kingdom that bullies, and hectors, and swears,
We send up to heaven our wishes and prayers
That we, disunited, may freemen be still,
And Britain go on—to be damned if she will.[7]

After the war, in 1784, in the poem "To Sir Toby," he deplored Jamaican slavery under which "whips on whips excite perpetual fears, / And mingled howlings vibrate on my ears." Nor was Freneau blind to the affront to human rights in his own country after white people had won their liberty from an oppressor. Anything less than perfect democracy was abhorrent to him, as he implied in the 1785 call for settlement of the West "On the Emigration to America and Peopling the Western Country." Through migration, Reason would yet come to rule, and slavery could not stand in the presence of Reason:

> O come the time, and haste the day,
> When man shall man no longer crush,
> When Reason shall enforce her sway,
> Nor these fair regions raise our blush,
> Where still the African complains,
> And mourns his yet unbroken chains.[8]

Freneau sanctioned the breaking of chains everywhere. In 1791 he ratified Tom Paine's essay in defense of the French Revolution with the poem "To a Republican With Mr. Paine's Rights of Man." In that piece Freneau assented again to a position that has been at the center of American culture and policy ever since and intimates a romantic view of the American citizen that would be developed by Emerson and Whitman:

> Without a king, the laws maintain their sway,
> While honor bids each generous heart obey.
> Be ours the task the ambitious to restrain,
> And this great lesson teach—that kings are vain;
> That warring realms to certain ruin haste,
> That kings subsist by war, and wars are waste;
> So shall our nation, form'd on Virtue's plan,
> Remain the guardian of the Rights of Man,
> A vast Republic, fam'd through every clime,
> Without a king, to see the end of time.[9]

"The Future Glory of America"

The other Philip Freneau was a prototypical romantic nature poet several of whose works anticipated the qualities of nineteenth-century romantic verse. Sometimes they contain sensuous lyricism exulting in the primitive and natural, sometimes delightfully simple nature imagery reminiscent of that of the Puritans, though—insofar as it might be religious at all—more deistic than Calvinistic. Of course, the two Freneaus are not unrelated. While it is true that his work does frequently ring neoclassically, his political and nationalistic poems are, after all, not really far removed from his nature poems; his insistence upon freedom is the Jeffersonian political side of the romantic coin, the other side of which is the individual's unfettered appreciation of nature. Both sides are stamped by the romantic impulse to celebrate the private consciousness, the freedom to be free imaginatively, emotionally, artistically, and politically. It is mainly because of his frequent deference to Reason that Freneau is a transitional figure between neoclassicism and romanticism.

But in spirit Freneau was quite clearly more romantic than otherwise. "The House of Night," published in the shorter of two versions in 1779 and later expanded in a 1786 edition, is deeply romantic in its abstraction of death—the first American poem of its kind, although it is a homegrown fruit of the English graveyard variety. In it, the narrator recollects with standard trembling his nightmare of "the horrors of the House of Night," made possible, it is critical to note, when the very Reason that the neoclassical side of Freneau adulates elsewhere deserts him here ("when Reason holds no sway"). Part of the vision is of an eight-foot tombstone whose unusual size is, presumably, necessitated by the epitaph of five quatrains that is inscribed on it. The inscription resounds with the political thrust of Freneau's romanticism, for he notes the ultimate banishment of all to Death's democratic nation: " 'Even mighty Julius died beneath my hand, / For slaves and Caesars were the same to me!' "

Luckily, Freneau did not spend much time in the visionary cemetery of "The House of Night." His imagination ran the romantic gamut from acknowledging "The Power of Fancy" as early as 1770, when he was still a Princeton undergraduate, to whimsically contemplating nature in "On a Honey Bee Drinking from a Glass of Wine and Drowning Therein" (1797), to foreshadowing the cult of the noble savage in "The Indian Burying Ground." At his worst, he could be strikingly unoriginal or unpolished or merely argumentative. He had not the power to be innovative in voice. No more than his American contemporaries, the Connecticut Wits and others, could he make his American subjects (Indians, for example in "The Indian Burying Ground") sound un-British in treatment. But at his best he could free himself sufficiently from ideological constraint and speak with sufficient power to earn, in the estimation of many, the encomium the Father of American poetry. Passages such as the penultimate stanza of "The Indian Burying Ground" show his genuine gift:

> By midnight moons, o'er moistening dews;
> In habit for the chase arrayed.
> The hunter still the deer pursues,
> The hunter and the deer, a shade![10]

Phillis Wheatley

All too few poets joined Freneau in his condemnation of slavery. Perhaps noteworthy among those who did not inveigh against that "Peculiar Institution" was America's first Afro-American poet of any import, Phillis Wheatley. The circumstances of her life explain both her reticence to denounce the system that brought her in shackles to America and the conservatism of her poetic substance and style. Phillis Wheatley was shipped to Boston in 1761 from west Africa as an appallingly young slave. " 'She is supposed to have been about seven years old, at this time, . . . from the circumstance of shedding her front teeth.' "[11] Bought by John Wheatley, a Boston tailor, as a house slave for his wife Susannah, the youngster grew up in a comfortable and not un-kindly household. She was even taught, mainly by the Wheatley's daughter, to read and write, skills that would have been criminal offenses had she chanced to be enslaved in the South. She read the Bible, studied sciences and history, learned Latin to read Latin classics in the original (she translated Ovid into heroic couplets at some point between her twelfth and fourteenth years), and began to compose verse under the influence of hymnal literature and the English neoclassical writers, chiefly Pope. Small wonder that by the time she published her first poem at about thirteen and a number of broadside poems thereafter, she was taken both by the Wheatley family and at large as a child prodigy. A collection of thirty-nine of her poems was published in London in 1773 while she was there with the Wheatleys on a visit. But, though celebrated by the Lord Mayor and others in London and by admirers in Boston, she could not ignore her bonds, velvet though they may have been. When she sat with the family coachman on a drive, her owner Mrs. Wheatley sharply rebuked him—and, by implication, her for the familiarity. With the insecurity that resulted from such episodes, when she accepted invitations to dinner in Boston society, she felt obliged to ask to be seated at a separate table.[12]

If she was made to fear that sitting with whites at private dinner parties could bring her genteel Boston life down around her ears, she certainly could not and did not seek to upset the social order in her verse. Had she tried, her career as a poet would, doubtless, have been unceremoniously stopped and her work could hardly have found outlets for publication. The abolitionist press would not be cranked up for some time, though when it was, in the nineteenth century, it used her lines to demonstrate that blacks could possess human sensibility in abundance. Abolitionists were to invoke the mild rebuke and assurance of intelligence from her poem "On Being Brought from Africa to America":

> Some view our sable race with scournful eye,
> "Their color is a diabolic dye."
> Remember, *Christians, Negroes,* black as *Cain,*
> May be refined, and join the angelic train.[13]

There is, in fact, little overt reason to suggest that Phillis Wheatley thought that there was much wrong with the social order. A child when she was wrenched from her African home, she was thoroughly indoctrinated with the Christian rationalization for slavery, and she seems to have subscribed to it. In the same "On Being Brought from Africa to America" she makes the standard case for what may be called the paradox of "the fortunate enslavement," the casuistic belief, cherished by pious slaveholders and inculcated into slaves, that had blacks not been enslaved and brought to America, they could not have been Christianized, and, hence, their souls could not have been favored with the possibility of salvation:

"The Future Glory of America"

'Twas mercy brought me from my *Pagan* land,
Taught my benighted soul to understand
That there's a God, that there's a *Savior* too:
Once I redemption neither sought nor knew.[14]

Unable to rock the artistic boat any more than the social, Wheatley wrote fluent but generally undistinguished verse that, nevertheless, compares not unfavorably with much of the derivative verse of many late eighteenth-century American poets. Her work, like most of that of the period, was in couplets, blank verse, and other traditional cadences, frequently rife with classical allusions that could do little to support an illusion of originality. That is what the readers in the society expected, including George Washington, who, boosted toward his superhuman stature by her poem "To His Excellency George Washington," invited her to visit him at Cambridge in February 1776. Thus, for a time, for her intelligence, her extraordinary accomplishment in the face of her being a slave, and her ability to play the game by the rules, it seemed that she was to be rewarded in this life. In the end, though, her reward was held back for the next, or at least for posterity, through the place that came to be recognized for her in American literary history. She was released from her servitude upon the death of her owners and married another freed slave, John Peters, who may have been an early spokesman for black rights, but she died in 1784 ill and bereft of her children, who had died, and of her husband, who was possibly serving a prison sentence for debt at the time.

One further observation about Phillis Wheatley must be made. It has been made all too seldom. Among her best lines are ones that she sent in 1772 "To the Right Honorable William, Earl of Dartmouth, His Majesty's Principal Secretary of State for North-America, &C." that betray a fire burning beneath her dead-level conservatism. Writing, before open hostilities broke out, to ask the Secretary of State to intercede for the colonies lest the King further yoke his people, she anticipated the earl's curiosity about her love of freedom and explained it to him:

I, young in life, by seeming cruel fate
Was snatch'd from *Afric's* fancy'd happy seat:
What pangs excruciating must molest

> What sorrows labor in my parent's breast?
> Steel'd was that soul and by no misery mov'd
> That from a father seiz'd his babe belov'd:
> Such, such my case. And can I then but pray
> Others may never feel tyrannic sway?[15]

Perhaps no American poet of the late eighteenth century could understand that revolutionary time as Phillis Wheatley could.

Hammon, Horton, Harper

As unremarkable as her poetry was, except insofar as the conditions of her life made it extraordinary, Phillis Wheatley was to be not only the first, but the best black American poet for about a century, until Paul Laurence Dunbar donned the mask that whites looked for on a black poet and published his verse at the end of the nineteenth century. The surviving work of her contemporary, the Long Island slave poet Jupiter Hammon (ca. 1720–1800) is, pretty much, rhymed pastoral moralizing. The only verse of his that attracts attention is "An Address to Miss Phillis Wheatley," and that only because it is a tribute to her, though it is sanctimonious and quite vapid.

George Moses Horton (ca. 1800–80) was rather better than Hammon because he was less annoyingly pious, but Horton, a North Carolina slave who came to writing through access to the Library at the University of North Carolina at Chapel Hill, churned out slick, vacant love poems for students. In fact, he tried unsuccessfully to buy his liberty by selling his versified wares. He sometimes wrote more seriously, however, and the effectiveness of his poems on the plight of the slave cannot help but be touching, although their prosodic conventionality tends to trivialize them. In "Slavery," for example, while he goes far beyond Hammon and Wheatley in indicting the dreadful system, he yearns for the grave as a refuge where "Drudg'ry and pain and toil are o'er, / Yes! there I shall be blest!" As one commentator observes, "There is not much thought in most of his work, his best pieces being those that plead for his freedom with a sincerity that is believable, despite the conventionally stilted syntax and the abstract language."[16]

Considerably more effective than Horton as an abolitionist poet was Frances Harper (1825–1911), a freeborn firebrand who turned to the temperance cause after emancipation finally came. Her poems are highly oratorical, but their imagery is often concrete enough to bring home the degradation of slavery with notable force. "Heard you that shriek?" she demands, for example, in "The Slave Mother," and Frances Harper goes on to show in that poem the mother's boy clinging to her while she vainly tries to hide him so that he will not be taken from her. Frances Harper could certainly muster an immediate power, but her value as a poet was restricted, finally, by the patent propagandist in her, however proficient her propaganda verse was.

The surprising thing about Afro-American poetry before emancipation is not the limitation on its quantity or quality, but that black poets overcame the unconscionable odds against them to produce even as much and as good poetry as they did manage to write. The potential for good black poetry, however, could not be fulfilled until freedom was gained, and especially until a black urban consciousness made the Harlem Renaissance possible in the 1920s.

· FOUR ·

The Nineteenth Century: Romanticism in American Poetry

> To him who in the love of Nature holds
> Communion with her visible forms, she speaks
> A various language . . .
> —William Cullen Bryant, "Thanatopsis"

Energized by the force of the great political and social revolutions of the late eighteenth century, and, to an extent, by the increasing power of science and technology, nineteenth-century culture tended to yield itself to the romantic impulse pervasive in the Western world. The period between the introduction of Andrew Jackson's egalitarian democracy in the late 1820s and the conclusion of the Civil War and reestablishment of a Union dedicated to that ideal was, in America's poetry as in its fiction, a period of enormous creative vitality. The romanticism that dominated the literature was rooted in the belief in the individual that had been asserted by the American Revolution. While such a vexing range of political, economic, social, and religious issues—slavery and its expansion or abolition, territorial aggrandizement, the rivalry between industrialism and agrarianism, North and South, and questions of reform—were being settled with prose tracts, speeches, laws, and eventually bullets, in some cases, poets were rehearsing these and concomitant matters in their, chiefly, romantic verse.

Among others, William Cullen Bryant, Ralph Waldo Emerson, Henry David Thoreau, Henry Wadsworth Longfellow, Oliver Wendell Holmes, John Greenleaf Whittier, and James Russell Lowell focused largely and in a variety of ways on spiritual and moral questions. They often sought in nature—as the Puritans had but now in a far more anthropocentric world—patterns for the relationship between God and mortals. Some wrote as northern regional poets, counterbalancing the work of such southerners as Sidney Lanier, Henry Timrod, William Gilmore Simms, and Paul H. Hayne. The period produced at least four American poets of extreme importance: Herman Melville, less poet than novelist, who still produced some of the best war poetry of the Civil War and perhaps any other; Ralph Waldo Emerson, who by theory and occasional example was the precursor of Walt Whitman; Whitman, the nonpareil poet of American egalitarianism and the forerunner of many twentieth-century poets; and Edgar Allan Poe, the highly ethereal, symbolic romantic, whose poems and criticism were to become more influential decades after his death than many have liked to admit. Because of their stature, Emerson, Poe, and Whitman are not to be examined in depth in this chapter; Emerson is accorded a chapter in the company of his fellow Transcendentalist poets, and Poe and Whitman chapters of their own.

William Cullen Bryant

The romantic trickle in American poetry that came from England and touched Philip Freneau at the end of the eighteenth century turned into a flood in the nineteenth. That swell of romanticism was funneled, at first, through the criticism and highly popular verse of William Cullen Bryant. In retrospect, Bryant seems to have been the ideal conduit through which the outpouring of the British romantic poets could flow and be absorbed by the emerging American nation. A citizen of rural Massachusetts by his birth in 1794, and of bustling New York City by choice, the lawyer-essayist-editor-poet Bryant came to poetry armed with traditional conservative Calvinist religious presumptions and attendant Federalist political views. Such ideas were his heritage from his old New England family (although his father, a physician, exhibited liberal tendencies) and the result of his education at the hands of clergymen in his native Berkshires. But while the formality of Alexander Pope and the other British Augustan poets was congenial to him under those early conservative influences, when he began to read Wordsworth, Coleridge, and Byron, they spoke to him poignantly. Some tropism in him responded, and he opened like a spring flower.

The disarmed Bryant soon became measurably Jacksonian democratic in his politics and, eventually, Unitarian in his religion. Acceptance of Unitarianism implied in Bryant a compromise, characteristic of many northeasterners of his time, between the Puritan God of his fathers and the consummate faith that, as a young poet, he had begun to place in an essentially benign nature as mentor to a fundamentally perfectible humanity. Hawthorne, Melville, and others might continue to "say no, in thunder," and Emily Dickinson, later in the century, would not be the last to "see New Englandly," but by Bryant's time the romantic light was fading the shadows of the constricted optimism of the Puritans.

An interesting point about William Cullen Bryant's poetry, however, is that the best of it, all written by the time he was about forty, reflects none of the liberalism that he brought later to his influential half-century editorship of the *New York Post*. His early and best poems echo the morbidity of British graveyard verse and Gothicism. In fact, inspired not only by Wordsworth, but by the graveyard poets and perhaps by Philip Freneau's "The House of Night," he composed the first draft of his most famous poem, the meditation on death that he called "Thanatopsis," when he was yet a teenager. In it, the young Bryant achieved excellent control over the blank verse iambic pentameter to convey a great loftiness of tone well suited to the subject—a remarkable accomplishment for a poet at any age. The poem presents the common nineteenth-century view of nature as a universal teacher speaking "A various language" to the individual consciousness; it does not give the reader much to look forward to, though; in the end, there are only the roots of the oak tree to "pierce thy mould," and "long train / Of ages" gliding generation after generation to the inevitable terminal of death. So depressing was the initial version that in later revisions Bryant offered the mitigating advice[1] that one should "go not, like the quarry slave at night, / Scourged to his dungeon, but, sustained and soothed / By an unfaltering trust, approach thy grave," and think of death as a sleep of "pleasant dreams." The expression "unfaltering trust" is an arresting one because of its ambivalence. Trust in what? The answer is not necessarily the Christian notion of immortality that was at the core of Puritan thought. It might be that, but it might also be a far fuzzier Unitarian idea, a secular hope, anything that could alleviate the gloom of dead-ended death. That "Thanatopsis"—a poem that, in a sense, substituted reflection for prayer—was widely memorized by nineteenth-century schoolchildren says something about the extent to which the American spiritual climate had changed, despite the lingering effect that Puritanism had, and would continue to have, on the nation's culture. Bryant's faith, though not less mystical than that of his forebears, and still necessary to overcome the gloom of a strictly objective view of the world, was far more nature-driven.

Not that Bryant had entirely forsaken God. But whereas the Puritan poets had filtered nature through their Ramist logic to justify their formal theology, Bryant, like many good romantic poets on both sides of the Atlantic, tended to use nature to reassure himself, as his own priest, of God's importance to human beings. "To a Waterfowl" (1821), for example, gives a name, God, to the more nebulous "unfaltering trust" of "Thanatopsis." And in "To a Waterfowl" Bryant extrapolates from God the guide of the bird to places it must go, to God the guide of the individual man who, Bryant romantically notes, "Must tread alone." The relationships among God, nature, and man are shifting and fascinating in Bryant, as in other romantic poets. Sometimes God and nature share the role of tutor or inspirer of humankind, in "A Forest Hymn" (1832), for instance, in which man is depicted as having learned to worship God first in nature ("The groves were God's first temples"), and which ends with a plea that man be permitted to return to the "calm shades" of nature in order to "Learn to conform the order of our lives." There are other poems, such as "Green River" (1821), in which God seems to fade completely and nature assumes the necessary tutorial and reassuring functions; in that poem, which echoes such Wordsworth verses as "The Tables Turned," the speaker rhapsodizes on the serene insight that he acquires every time he revisits the banks of the green river, that beautiful spot where in the "lonely and lovely stream / An image of that calm life appears / That won my heart in my greener years." The "Silent dream" in which he gazes on the green river is, of course, the romantic and moral dream of harmonious inner serenity that comes of tuning in to the natural order.

A wholly secular poem of Bryant, and the one that most obviously derives from Wordsworth is "Oh Fairest of the Rural

Maids," which stands in the shadow of Wordsworth's Lucy poems and fails to shed as much light. The piece reinforces a romantic theme that still persists in American literature, as difficult as its truth would be for social science to prove: that the pastoral setting and the human being in it are somehow purer, "more sinless," as Bryant puts it, than the urban scene and urban dweller. Long since a New Yorker by the time he composed the poem, he is clearly yearning for the simpler days of his Berkshires boyhood, here invested in the rural maid—for "The holy peace, that fills the air / Of those calm solitudes." At the same time, the *sinlessness* of the maid suggests the moral force exerted by nature; in that form, American romanticism reveals the haunting hold of Puritanism.

Quite naturally, in view of Brackenridge, Freneau, Barlow, and his other recent predecessors in American poetry, Bryant's romanticism frequently has a peculiarly American coloration: its patriotic optimism, its continuation of the advertising of America that began with the Puritans, persisted throughout the eighteenth century, and rose to a crescendo after the Revolution in such poems as *The Columbiad*. When his close friend Thomas Cole, founder of the Hudson River school of landscape artists, sailed for Europe, Bryant was moved to versify some advice for him in "To Cole, The Painter, Departing for Europe" (1832). The poem makes a halting attempt to capture some of Cole's highly romanticized American landscapes, referring to "Lone lakes— . . . / Rocks rich with summer garlands—solemn streams— . . ." and the like; thus it stands in a line of American poems that are based, in one way or another, on paintings, including, in the twentieth century, works by Wallace Stevens, William Carlos Williams, John Ashbery, and others. Bryant conjures up Cole's landscapes to admonish the painter not to forget that however fair the views of Europe, they are "different" from scenes of America; Coles must "keep that earlier, wilder image bright." And Bryant's impassioned ode to the wide open spaces, "The Prairies" (1834), occasioned by a visit to his brother in Illinois in 1832, is scarcely more controlled than the chauvinistic outpourings of his eighteenth-century forerunners; he even manages to work in a modicum of classical allusion, imagining the civilization of prairie moundbuilders as contemporaneous with the Attic Greek civilization. Fortunately, a "wind sweeps by" and breaks his reverie, which involves the flora, fauna, and geographical features of the plains, and he romantically fancies himself "in the wilderness alone."

By the 1850s, and afterward, Bryant was publishing mainly such undistinguished poems as the patriotic "Oh Mother of a Mighty Race" (1854), rather Whitmanesque in its patriotism, but in the English mannered style, and "The Death of Lincoln," which is hopelessly pedestrian compared to Whitman's "When Lilacs Last in the Dooryard Bloom'd" elegy or even the lesser Lincoln elegy "O Captain! My Captain." Even Wordsworth's influence was not salutary. "The Poet" (1864), for example, is a heavily didactic verse, a recipe calling for would-be poets to use both inspiration and experience in their work. Alas, Wordsworth's golden lines are transmuted into something closer to lead; the "flash upon that inward eye / Which is the bliss of solitude" becomes the warning, "Before thine inner gaze / Let all that beauty in clear vision lie."

So much for Bryant's limitations as a practitioner of poetry. Despite them, his work was moralistic enough to be extremely popular with Americans; to many his employment of nature in the service of morality was positively exemplary. One of his audience, expressing a widely held view, wrote Bryant in 1864 to tell him he was not only America's "first poet," but her "first citizen," possessed of a "sweet, tender, thoughtful, and majestic spirit."[2] In *Specimen Days* Walt Whitman, five years after Bryant's death in 1878, gushed that in Bryant had been "pulsing the first verse throbs of a mighty world—bard of the river and of the wood, ever conveying a taste of open air."[3] Whitman was recalling the romantic nature poetry that Bryant had popularized and was finding more of himself in Bryant than was there.

No doubt, Bryant's significance to American poetry was real; it lay in his notable influence as a man of letters, editor, critic, and friend to poets and other artists, in his defense of America as a place for poetry even before Emerson and Whitman came along, and then as their ally in the defense. His prose pronouncements comforted Americans—poets, would-be poets, and their audience—by refuting arguments that a worthy "American" poetry could not be. The doubts had grown as the decades had passed since the Revolution and Americans listened in vain for the birth cry of a national poetry. The artificial attempts by the Connecticut Wits and the rest to produce one had been fruitless, and none had been organically begotten. In such declarations as "On Poetry in Its Relation to Our Age and Country"[4] Bryant cited the arguments: paucity of traditions; a people "too much in love with peace and gain"; a material, unromantic culture; a suspicion that humanity had "degenerated in . . . mental powers and moral temperament"; a disheartening fear that Americans could not equal the "immortal poems of the old [world]"; even difficulty with using a "transplanted" language with "force, effect and grace." One by one and again and again, Bryant could counter the naysaying, usually sagaciously, on rare occasion naively, as when he suggested that if American poets did lack native material, they could find what they needed elsewhere. After all, he speculated, "the best English poets have done this. . . . Shakespeare has laid the scene of many of his finest tragedies in foreign countries. Milton went out of the world for the subject of his two epic poems. Byron has taken the incidents of all his poems from outside of England." Believing in his exhortation, Bryant exhorted, "If . . . our poetry should fail of rivalling that of Europe, it will be because Genius sits idle in the midst of its treasures."

Bryant's greatest contribution to American poetry has been widely overlooked.[5] Before him there was really no significant critic of American poetry. Perhaps influenced by the prosodic intentions of Wordsworth and Coleridge in *Lyrical Ballads*, Bryant attacked rigid metricality, as early as 1819, as detracting from the beauty of poetry. Though he was something of a virtuoso in the use of standard metrical forms in considerable variety, he really started critics of American poetry on the path toward form that grew organically from meaning; in other words, he modestly anticipated such advocates of organic poetry and use of vernacular rhythms as Emerson, Whitman, William Carlos Williams, and Charles Olson.

The Knickerbocker Poets

Bryant is not the only poet of his time associated with New York. Along with Boston, one of the two major centers of nineteenth-century American poetry was New York, the artistic home of such other popular poets as Fitz-Greene Halleck, Joseph Rodman Drake, James Kirke Paulding, and Nathaniel Parker Willis. A reasonable generalization can be made about an essential difference between the New York and the Boston-based poets: whereas the latter, living within the shadows of their Puritan forebears, tended to compose with serious, didactic purposes, the New Yorkers, by and large, seemed to regard letters as a slightly eccentric avocation. The New York group, in fact, earned the appellation "Knicker-bocker" poets because of the perceived resemblance of their attitude to that of Washington Irving's bemused Diedrich Knickerbocker in the delightful *History of New York*. The truth of the observation is, naturally, mitigated by a certain amount of cross-fertilization between the two centers through such figures as Bryant who were raised in one region and worked in the other, but the generalization does stand.

The thirty-odd verses that Drake and Halleck published pseud-onymously as Croaker and Croaker, Jr., were popular satires and lampoons that had no pretensions to greatness, or even, in Hal-leck's own estimation, to longevity. Both poets, however, achieved a certain modest distinction beyond creating simple fun. Essentially a gifted amateur in the Byronic manner, Halleck composed at least three poems of some importance: "On the Death of Joseph Rodman Drake" (1820), a beautifully controlled elegy, justly praised by Poe and outstanding still among the elegies written in America; "Marco Bozzaris" (1825), a rousing account of the Greek hero's adventures in the war between the Greeks and Turks; and "Alnwick Castle" (1827), which projects an effective seriocomic tension be-tween the medieval romance of the castle and the starker reality of the nineteenth-century world. If Mark Twain read "Alnwick Castle," it must have tickled him.

Drake was best known for his fairy-tale poem *The Culprit Fay* (1816), a rather mechanical poor relation to Shelley's "Queen Mab." In 1836 Poe wittily demolished the poem as a piece of puerile stuff unworthy of the lofty human mind, but it is never-theless absorbing on three counts. First, the vast popularity of *The Culprit Fay* says much about American public taste in the heyday of Jacksonian democracy. Second, the poem reveals Drake's fas-cination with the palisade landscape of New York's Hudson River valley, which was transformed into a sometimes misty and cliffy romantic dreamscape on the canvases of the Hudson River school of painters. It was a fixation that he shared with others, including the poet-painter Washington Allston, which puts Drake in the long line of American poets (including Bryant, Stevens, Williams, and Ashbery) who have been at home on the border between poetry and painting. The particular landscape that preoccupied

Drake, of course, is the one that provided local settings for the fictions of Washington Irving and James Fenimore Cooper. And third, following the lead of Coleridge in *Christabel*, Drake's use of a kind of syllabic verse in *The Culprit Fay* (four heavy stresses to a line without regard for the total number of syllables in the line)—called by Gay Wilson Allen "This adaptation of Coleridge's principle"[6]—did make a noteworthy contribution to American prosody by helping to loosen the grip of traditional, rigid verse forms.

James Kirke Paulding is somewhat better known as a playwright and novelist, and especially as coauthor, with Washington Irving, of the urbane *Salmagundi Papers*, than as a poet. As poet and critic, however, his importance lies in his furthering the view of America as light to the world and his echoing the call for a national literature that would reflect the political independence wrested from the Old World (as in the second *Salmagundi Papers*, 1819–20). He anticipates Emerson and Whitman in his insistence upon the use of the material of America—her people, her geography and flora and fauna, her history and ideas—as the stuff of American literature, though he is not as sensitive as they to the need for a new language through which to convey the material. Nor does he have the capacity to break with traditional forms (although he does eschew such contemporary British models as Byron in favor of such earlier eighteenth-century ones as Pope). Thus, for example, in his seemingly endless narrative poem *The Backwoodsman* (1818) he creates the character of a tenant farmer from New York who hears and heeds the call of the frontier. Telling Basil's story affords Paulding the chance to run through some American history and the geography of the Hudson River valley and Alleghenies, as well as to reiterate Crèvecoeur's romantic belief in the ability of the American frontier to ennoble its settlers. All this, Paulding couches in hundreds of heroic couplets that demonstrate a knack, but certainly not the talent or wit of an Alexander Pope.

A fourth Knickerbocker poet, N. P. Willis, cannot be ignored because of his wide popularity, probably owing to his moralizing and sentimentality, and his inclusion by Poe in a ranking of American poets in 1846 as fourth after Longfellow, Bryant, and Halleck.[7] Willis can be rapidly dismissed, though (one assumes that Poe's judgment was influenced by personal favors that Willis had done for him), for when modern standards and tastes are applied to his verse, he comes out only a small cut above such pious sentimentalizers of his day as Mrs. Lydia Sigourney, "The Sweet Singer of Hartford," who enjoyed the largest audience in America before Longfellow edged her out in the 1850s.[8] James Russell Lowell's comment on Willis in *A Fable for Critics* (1848), to the effect that Willis "ought to let Scripture alone . . . / For nobody likes inspiration-and-water," summarizes what needs to be said of Willis's poetry.

Henry Wadsworth Longfellow and "Frogpondia"

Of the other American poets of roughly the middle half of the nineteenth century, Henry Wadsworth Longfellow rivaled Bryant for popular esteem. Born in Maine in 1807, some thirteen years after Bryant, Longfellow remained in New England almost all of his life. The child of a middle-class family, he attended Bowdoin College while Nathaniel Hawthorne was there; he later became a professor at Harvard. He became, if anyone was, the leader of the poetic land that Poe mockingly called "Frogpondia," the chief "Frogponder." Poe was, of course, referring to New England generally, the Boston area in particular, the region that, to Poe's dismay, had assumed again, from such other urban centers as New York and Philadelphia, intellectual leadership of the nation. And one cause of Poe's dejection must have been, in light of his own identity problems and lack of popularity, the potent self-confidence and enormous popularity of what to him were those croaking Brahmins—Longfellow, Oliver Wendell Holmes, James Russell Lowell, and John Greenleaf Whittier. The audience, with the nineteenth-century emphasis on literacy and culture, was enormous for these so-called Fireside, or Schoolroom Poets, and through such organs as the *North American Review* and Lowell's *Atlantic Monthly* their influence was pervasive. It is difficult to know whether or not his New Englandness is what engendered the pervasive darkness of Longfellow's vision, but gloomy it was, in spite of the esteem he shared with his Fireside Poet friends. The romantic Bryant could touch the back of his hand to his wrinkled brow and wonder what could cleanse the world's bosom "from its painful memories of guilt" (in the poem "Earth"), but there is always a heavenly, often patriotic, glow behind his clouds—a hope that with the New World comes "a newer page / In the great record of the world" which may be "fairer," which may need the natural order, the voices from the streams and woods, and so learn not to make a hash of the Earth. Longfellow, though, when he is closest to his true self, imparts a sense of sad, gentle, cosmic abandonment that anticipates the brutal isolation of the naturalists at the end of the century.

The public loved the didactic public figure, the declaimer of public issues as in "The Arsenal of Springfield" (1846), the narrator and mythologizer of "Paul Revere's Ride" or "Hiawatha," the paternal, fireside storyteller and purveyor of warm familiarity as in "The Village Blacksmith." But from early to late in Longfellow's work, there are looks into the abyss. "Hymn to the Night" (1839), a kind of standard gothic breath of night air, welcomes night—sleep or death?—as the only means of surcease from the oppressiveness of life: "Thou layest thy finger on the lips of Care, / And they complain no more." In the flames of "The Fire of Drift-Wood" (1850) is no more brightness, albeit the poem is set in a cozy room before a fire where friends reminisce. There is no America, no nature, no God here, though, to soften the sorrow of their contemplation "of what had been, and might have been, / And who was changed, and who was dead." No wonder the burning of the driftwood is like the burning of their hearts as they rue "The long-lost ventures of the heart, / That send no answers back again." If anything, Longfellow became more estranged from real hope after the tragic death of his second wife in 1861 (his young first wife had died on a trip abroad in 1835). His sonnet "Nature" (1878) represents man as a child at bedtime, leaving his broken toys behind as he is led off to bed; the mother is nature, but not the benign nature from whom Wordsworth and Bryant and many of the romantics intuit moral truths that will help in the spiritual progress of the species. Longfellow's nature is the firm parent whose ways, like those of the God of the Puritans, defy understanding because the child's capacity to understand is minute; "How far," the sonnet concludes, "the unknown transcends the what we know."

Longfellow tends to be remembered for the wrong things, somewhat like Robert Frost. Longfellow is really pedestrian in his prose defenses of poetry and his calls for literary nationalism, both of which appear, for example, in his essay *"The Defence [sic] of Poetry"*;[9] he is mellifluous but not awfully convincing in the nostalgic, homey sops to morale that he provides in such poems as "My Lost Youth" (1858): "A boy's will is the wind's will, /And the thoughts of youth are long, long thoughts." His real strength is in the brooding quality of "The Jewish Cemetery at Newport" and his other best poems—a quality that holds up well against the habit of the happier romantics, like that of Bryant and the Transcendentalists, of conjuring bright answers to dismal and complex human problems. Furthermore, one of the best-kept secrets of American poetry is that Longfellow is among the most effective sonneteers that America has produced. The "Divina Commedia" cycle (1867) that he composed in association with his translation of Dante; his sonnet tributes to Chaucer, Milton, and Keats (1875), each reflecting its subject in its diction, rhythm, and imagery; and assorted others, including "The Harvest Moon" (1875) and "Nature," would be sufficient to mark Longfellow's place in American poetry. The praise that he received from the public and from such friends as Oliver Wendell Holmes (who named Longfellow America's "Chief Singer"), who admired him for their own reasons, was largely misdirected.

Or was it? Longfellow, Holmes, and their fellow "Schoolroom Poets" James Russell Lowell and John Greenleaf Whittier clearly had the pulse of that American public, though, except for Whittier, the poets were far better educated. Indeed their readers made their poetry a paying profession to a considerable extent, and, in return, the group of poets edged the national poetry closer to being "American" than English.

Oliver Wendell Holmes

Perhaps Holmes himself is the most personally absorbing of the Fireside Poets. Like Longfellow, he had a large following, probably more for his public face than for the resonance of his poetry. Born in 1809 and trained as a medical doctor at Harvard and in Paris, he became a well-known raconteur, avidly sought after for both after-dinner speeches and poems celebrating public events and issues. A better poet than novelist (he published three novels), the excellent physician, teacher of physicians, and dean of the

Harvard Medical School from 1847 to 1853 was immensely erudite and self-assured, given to the clever satire of ideas but not to embarrassing lampoon. He was, by nature or social commitment or both, not contemplative very often, and when he was in his poems—as in "The Chambered Nautilus" (1858)—even there, there was something far more mental and quick than passionate. The poem is characteristically well wrought, using the cephalopod's movement through a series of larger chambers within its shell to symbolize what the poet accepts as the laudable human urge to strive, to expand. On the way, there are striking images, of reefs "Where the cold sea-maids rise to sun their streaming hair," and of the shell's "frail tenant" as it "Stole with soft step its shining archway through" while it enlarges its miniscule domain. But then, rather suddenly, comes a tidy conclusion: "Through the deep caves of thought" the speaker *thinks* that he hears "a voice that sings," and the message is that it is fine to live the life of an achiever, to "Let each new temple, nobler than the last, / Shut thee from heaven with a dome more vast." In the end, it is the building of the larger and larger—presumably the better and better—building, always "a dome more vast" than its predecessor, that leads to a spiritual liberation, a kind of heaven, when the shell is finally outgrown and left "by life's unresting sea!"

Dr. Holmes had a penchant for connecting the quasi-scientific, the physical, to the romantically incorporeal, though he did not do it as well anywhere else as he did in "The Chambered Nautilus," even with its contrived tidiness. "The Living Temple" (1858) is, more than anything, an overwritten Augustan exercise in versification that glories in the parts of the human anatomy. Yet it is more overtly spiritual than "The Chambered Nautilus," calling finally on God the Father to make His the "mystic temples" of the body, and when "the last tottering pillars fall," to mold their dust "into heavenly forms"; whether those forms represent a physical reconstruction of matter or a spiritual regeneration is uncertain.

"The Living Temple" reflects Holmes's frequent weakness as a rhymer of ideas, but also his exuberant fundamental romanticism. He is a celebrant of humanity in all of its manifestations—body, mind, and spirit. "Dorothy" (1875) is a delightful piece that, in bringing his great-grandmother to life, is surprisingly open sexually. He is most assuredly not an atheist, but any system of thought—

religious or secular—that inhibits the potential for human realization is unwarrantable. Nowhere is that plainer than in his well-known "The Deacon's Masterpiece, or The Wonderful 'One-Hoss Shay,' a Logical Story" (1858), which satirizes Calvinism in particular and, by extension, any tightly reasoned system that impinges on human potential. Holmes uses gentle dialectal humor to chide the clergyman who so solidly and *logically* engineers a carriage out of its component parts so that it can last forever, whereas it suddenly crumbles after a hundred years. The builder's logic may have been impeccable, but the construct was, nevertheless, erroneous. That was precisely the problem that Holmes had with Calvinism, which he saw as impeccable, but cold and in error. "I reject . . . the mechanical doctrine which makes me the slave of outside influences," he once declared, "whether it work with the logic of [Jonathan] Edwards, or the averages of Buckle; whether it come in the shape of the Greek's destiny, or the Mahometan's fatalism; or in that other aspect, dear to the band of believers . . . 'election.' "[10]

There is sufficient merit in the urbane wit, calm good humor, and core of ideas in Holmes's body of poetry to make one wonder how great his achievement might have been had literature not been an avocation subordinate to his distinguished medical career and had he not given so much of himself to his defense of ideas (such as a place for women in medical schools and the use of anesthesia). As it is, this liberal patrician is best known as the author of *The Autocrat of the Breakfast-Table* and as the poet of such felicitous occasional poems as "Old Ironsides," which is credited with saving the historic vessel from demolition, and a number of Harvard poems that do warm credit to that institution.

James Russell Lowell

Like those of Holmes, many of the romantic instincts of James Russell Lowell that might have been fashioned into lovely poetry were dissipated among secondary activities and causes—like those of Holmes, too, all of them worthy. Not as lofty as Holmes, Lowell, born in 1819, was still very much the patrician; he played out his social responsibility in party politics and advocacy of reform, most notably the eradication of slavery. Though he graduated from Harvard Law School in 1840, from 1855 to 1872 he held the chair in modern languages at Harvard that had been Longfellow's, and he was simultaneously an editor and, as editor, a critic. With his Fireside friends, he helped to establish the *Atlantic Monthly* in 1857, acting as its first editor for five years. Then, from 1864 to 1872, before he became ambassador first to Spain and then to Great Britain, the many-faceted Lowell coedited with Charles Eliot Norton the important *North American Review*.

Not only were his psychic energies about as dispersed as those of Holmes, but, like Holmes, he was both a public figure and a poetic corporation with three directors, a light-verse one, a meditative one, and an occasional one. He is generally best recalled— when he is—for the poems with the light and witty touch, especially *A Fable for Critics* (1848) and the character Hosea Bigelow's untutored vernacular observations in *The Bigelow Papers* (1848). *A Fable for Critics* remains for modern readers a wonderful, insightful series of sketches of American writers presented in deft, amusing couplets to Phoebus Apollo by a critic. Emerson, for instance, the critic ventures, has "A Greek head on right Yankee shoulders, whose range / Has Olympus for one pole, for t' other the Exchange"; Bryant comes off as less than congenial: "He may rank . . . first bard of your nation / (There's no doubt that he stands in supreme iceolation)." In his evaluation of James Fenimore Cooper, he is kinder than Mark Twain, but he anticipates Twain's criticism; "His Indians," says Lowell's spokesman, "with proper respect be it said, / Are just Natty Bumppo daubed over with red." He is defensive of his friend Longfellow and mild in his critique of his friend Whittier, whose failings, the *Fable* points out, have the same cause as Whittier's determination to be a poet: "A failure of mind which knows no separation / 'Twixt simple excitement and pure inspiration." Characteristically, Lowell does not spare himself just self-evaluation: as a poet, he says of himself, "The top of the hill he will ne'er come nigh reaching / Till he learns the distinction 'twixt singing and preaching."

With Hosea Bigelow, Lowell created the first significant comic, vernacular-speaking character in American poetry. Indeed, the unlettered Yankee anticipates the frontier humorists, the post-Civil War local-color writers, and certainly Mark Twain; among poets, Walt Whitman, in a way, E. A. Robinson, Robert Frost, William Carlos Williams, John Berryman, and others would follow James Russell Lowell's lead. And Hosea Bigelow's Yankee dialect rings a good deal truer than the written dialect of many an American writer to follow.

There is more to be said for *The Bigelow Papers.* Lowell's motivation for writing the pieces was commendable; he wrote them to attack the Mexican War, which he abhorred for dividing American society and occasioning the spread of slavery to conquered territory. And Lowell created two other effective characters in the work to play off against Bigelow's simple honesty, one Birdofredum Sawin, who serves Lowell's purpose by ineffectively opposing Bigelow, and the Reverend Homer Wilbur, a silly pedant, who, with Sawin, serves as a foil to underscore Bigelow's down-home virtue. When another conflict, the Civil War, came along to rend the American social fabric, Lowell produced a sequel, *The Bigelow Papers, Second Series* (1862). But, ultimately, the resurrection of *The Bigelow Papers* is symptomatic of one of Lowell's weaknesses, a frequent inability to sense when he had come to an end. As does an attempt to read his *Complete Poetical Works,* even the First Series alone becomes tedious. Hosea Bigelow's words sparkle at times, but both series taken together are quite intolerable. A further flaw in both sets of *Bigelow Papers* is the tiresome peripheral apparatus, the introduction and glossary, the notes and notices meant to unify the parts.

A romantic, meditative vein runs through the corpus of Lowell's work, leaving the reader with a sense of aloof abstraction. Even in love poems, Lowell could not connect to everyday humanity even as far as Bryant or Lowell's fellow Hearthside Poets could. Two of his best-known contemplative poems, *The Vision of Sir Launfal* (1848) and "Ode Recited at the Harvard Commemoration, July 21, 1865," come early and late in his career. *The Vision of Sir Launfal* (1848) is a romance, based on the King Arthur cycle, laced with moralism; virtue, the poem purports to show, is not an object, the Grail, acquired by an external quest, but an internal matter within the human spirit. "The Cathedral" (1869), while suffering from Lowell's sin of discursiveness, is somehow tonally correct, a serious contemplation of the mid-nineteenth-century *spiritus mundi.* Like Tennyson and Henry Adams, Lowell was often a great admirer of new ideas but at times wished that they had never been born. The Dynamo is a mighty force to be reckoned with, but it is no Virgin. "This is no age to get cathedrals built," Lowell regrets, sounding much like the Tennyson of "In Memoriam" or the Matthew Arnold of "Dover Beach." This is the same Lowell who in his best occasional poem, the "Ode Recited at the Harvard Commemoration, July 21, 1865" (the best of a number of impressive, if overbearing odes), praised the Harvard men, living and dead, who had fought in the Civil War in order that "We sit here in the Promised Land / That flows with Freedom's honey and milk." To Lowell, as to many of his sensitive contemporaries on both sides of the ocean, the possibilities of progress warred with the loss of the old verities through the Darwinian upheaval, the ugliness that accompanied the scientific and industrial revolution (with its infinite promise), the disillusionment resulting from the American Civil War. To them, the events through which they lived—like events in all ages—made their years the best of times and the worst of times. But it was not Lowell's ambivalent worldview that flawed his work; it was mainly the tendency that he smiled at in himself in *A Fable for Critics:* "he'd rather by half make a drum of the shell, / And rattle away till he's old as Methusalem, / At the head of a march to the last new Jerusalem."

John Greenleaf Whittier

The scion of an old Haverhill, Massachusetts, Quaker farming family, John Greenleaf Whittier, born in 1807, was called to poetry as a boy when his teacher gave him a volume of Robert Burns's poems. It is always a little sad when a pupil cannot grow larger than his mentor, as Whittier always fell short of Burns's piquancy and musical facility, but Burns's treatment of common Scottish life was a comfortable model for Whittier to follow.

Much of his creative energy during his early years he spent in various editorial jobs and in the writing of a number of antislavery tracts—abolition remained a cornerstone of his personal values—that his powerful Quaker conscience compelled him to write. Typical of the amateurish sentimental poems that he composed during that period is "Moll Pitcher" (1832), a piece not without narrative appeal, but marred by enough sentimental bombast to lead Whittier to retire the poem after his 1840 collection.

By the mid-1840s, however, he had developed a quite distinctive poetic style, familiar, simple, clear—akin to the ideal of the Puritan aesthetic (though with a certain mawkish force, as in "Memories"

[1843])—that attracted him to public attention and the company of his Fireside peers (with whom he joined in founding the *Atlantic Monthly* in 1857).

An odd Frogponder because he was probably the least a Brahmin of all the members of the Saturday Club (a conclave of like-minded men who, from 1855 or 1856, met at the Parker House in Boston), including Longfellow, Holmes, Lowell, Emerson, and others, it may or may not be to Whittier's credit that his poems are not high poetry. They seldom lose their common touch, and his strength is in that limitation, a fact of which he was perfectly aware. In "Proem" (1849) he confidently admitted that to him belong "Nor mighty Milton's gift divine, / Nor Marvell's wit and graceful song," but, he proclaims to Freedom, "I lay, like them, my best gifts upon thy shrine!" To the romantic in him, nature was, of course, the center of the individual's learning experience ("Nature never hints in vain, / Nor prophesies amiss," Whittier asserts in "The Old Burying-Ground" [1860]). But recognizing his inability to sing of it in "The songs of Spenser's golden days" or in "Arcadian Sidney's silvery phrase," he describes in "Proem" what he can do well: "Unskilled the subtle lines to trace, / Or softer shades of Nature's face, / I view her common forms with unanointed eyes." Anne Bradstreet would have been pleased.

His plain style is what made him a public favorite, even before publication of *Snow-Bound* (1866) eased the financial strain in his life through heavy sales. With his familiar form goes a soothing gentleness. Even in his well-known "Ichabod" (1850), written in the wake of Daniel Webster's speech of March 1850 in support of the Fugitive Slave Law, which was abominable to Whittier, the poet does not excoriate the senator; on the contrary, he admonishes his readers to not revile or insult Webster, who has dishonored himself by his stand on the fugitive slave issue when he "might / Have lighted up and led his age." No, the Christian humanist implores with simple decency, "Walk backward, with averted gaze, / And hide the shame!"

In his attitudes, in many of his essential values, in his poetic style and diction, Whittier expressed and romantically idealized the common American life of the mid-century as much as anyone. That was the secret of *Snow-Bound*'s popular success. Small matter that the poem is technically the best that Whittier ever wrote, that dark-light, storm-fire, life-death images are skillfully woven through it and give it a fine unity and texture. What must have been attractive to its nineteenth-century audience was the warm familiarity of the extended family that peoples the poem; the homey, intimate sketches of the family members that make up most of it; and, perhaps above all, the comforting reassurance that storms pass and, meanwhile, that whatever the uncertainties of an external world that may be becoming more complex to understand and more uncaring about the human condition, there are still values and relationships and memories that offer sanctuary from the storm. The speaker rejoices in the recollection of more than surviving, or thriving in the flow of fire and family all the while "No church-bell lent its Christian tone to the savage air, . . ." when "solitude [was] made more intense / By dreary-voiced elements, The shrieking of the mindless wind." The setting suggests the cold aloofness of a naturalistic universe, but Whittier's conclusion is poles apart from that of the naturalist author. Under the aegis of the "Angel of the backward look," there comes "Some Truce of God," that is, a retreat for spiritual resupply represented by the gathering of the family by the fireside against the snowstorm, that works its wonder, permitting the traveler to move on, now owning "the grateful sense / Of sweetness near, he knows not whence," now able to take on his "forehead bare / The benediction of the air."

With Darwin and science and all of their ramifications, as well as the Civil War, Whittier's age was a time of greater uncertainty than any that had come before, and no one expressed the essence of American life more plainly and simply than he. If he was hopelessly sentimental, as in "Telling the Bees" and "Abraham Davenport," that was part of the basis of his mass appeal; that was how lines like " 'Shoot, if you must, this old gray head, / But spare your country's flag,' she said," from "Barbara Frietchie" (1864), became absorbed by the culture to be repeated even by people who did not know where they came from. Knowing that, a who's who of American writers from Bryant to Twain honored Whittier on his seventieth birthday in 1877 with a magnificent party; and knowing that something was disappearing from American life and that Whittier must soon stop capturing that life in his work, the entire nation celebrated his eightieth birthday.

Yet a not-so-celebratory note must be struck in a reasonable consideration of Whittier and his companion poets of the hearthside—and their audience. While their British romantic counterparts were able to deal with matters of innocence and the claims of the ego in grown-up poetry, there is a jejune quality about much of the work of the American Fireside Poets that is surprising in such mainly learned men. That is part of the paradox that attaches to them: they produced some good poetry, but, with some notable exceptions such as Whitman and Dickinson, the childishness in their poetry seems to have slowed the development of American poetry until the next century.

A New England "Independent": Frederick Goddard Tuckerman

A fair assessment of Frederick Goddard Tuckerman has been elusive, though the essential facts of his life are not. The poet and naturalist was a scion of a wealthy Boston family and had the kind of Brahmin upbringing that that fact normally entailed, including attending Harvard, where the transcendentalist mystic Jones Very was his tutor for a time. He obtained the credentials to practice law but never did. Instead he married Hannah Lucinda Jones, whom he idolized, and withdrew to Greenfield, Massachusetts, to enjoy her company and to indulge his other favorite avocations—poetry, astronomy, and botany, which, curiously, he sometimes combined in poems replete with abstruse botanic references. The world of his comfortable isolation was shattered by Hannah's death in 1857, however, when Tuckerman was thirty-six years old. The blow intensified his innate scientific skepticism and reverberated through his poetry until his death in 1873.

In the depression triggered by his wife's death Tuckerman produced a string of crepuscular sonnets divided into several series, the last of which, comprising sixteen sonnets, he did not complete until 1872, the year before he died. Since sonnets are easy to anthologize, mainly they have represented him, though he also wrote a variety of poems in other forms on conventional subjects and an excessively praised contemplative poem called "The Cricket," which went unpublished until 1950. Although the sonnets contain numerous fine passages and are sometimes excellent whole poems, the effect of reading many of them, particularly those in the first series, is one of having bathed in self-pity in a rather elaborate tub. No wonder some commentators have seen Tuckerman as pretty much a Johnny-one-note.[11] And because the sonnets come in groups whose numbers illuminate one another, they draw the masochistic reader on. But as the tragedy fell away in time, more positive notes graced the monotone of the early sonnets. Tuckerman did not escape the grip of the event; the maudlin tone persisted, but it was relieved by a reconciliation with death that is the end of all good elegiac verse, and, in Tuckerman's work, by the happier prospect of reunion with Hannah after death. Thus by the time he worked his way through "Sonnets: Second Series" (1860), he was still asking in "IX" whether "spring could return . . . a brother's face, / Or bring my darling back to me—to me" and concluding that neither spring nor any season could. Yet by "XXVII" he was able to say, "And yet I know the splendour of the light / Will break anon: Lo! where the gray is white!" and in "XXXIV" he affirms that although he shall never again see his beloved Anne, "I would not hide my face from light, nor shun / The full completion of this worldly day."

If the claim of Tuckerman's limitation has sometimes been inaccurate, so has that of his greatness, the latter proclaimed chiefly by Ivor Winters. Tuckerman's reputation had evaporated by the time he died in 1873, and it was resuscitated by W. P. Eaton in 1909 and Witter Bynner in 1931 (through Bynner's publication of the complete sonnets). Then Winters came along and publicly declared that Tuckerman's "The Cricket" was merely "the greatest poem in English of the [nineteenth] century"—and, even more, outshone one of the twentieth century's finest poems, Wallace Stevens's "Sunday Morning,"[12] This is hardly true. "The Cricket" is a good poem, especially in its description of a summer day, in its meditative rhythm, and in its achieving an almost mythical dimension for the cricket. Part 2 is notably effective for establishing the soft summery setting:

> Let the dead fragrance round our temples beat,
> Sunning the senses to slumber, whilst between
> The falling water and fluttering wing
>   Mingle and meet
>   Murmur and mix,
> No faint pipings from the glades behind,
>   Or alder-thicks: . . .[13]

And the end is effective both on its own and in the context of the poem. Tuckerman remembers the great lesson of his life that "Even while we stop to wrangle or repine, / Our lives are gone— / Like thinnest mist," but he has learned, too, that we must live; for we can only "Rejoice! rejoice! whilst yet the hours exist— / Rejoice or mourn, and let the world swing on / Unmoved by cricket song or me."

But for all that one can say of its virtues, the poem is too long, has a formulaic classical section that is out of date in the present and may well have been even in Tuckerman's time, and suffers from an obvious comparison with two other poems that contain spirits kindred to its cricket. Walt Whitman's thrush in "When Lilacs Last in the Dooryard Bloom'd" reconciles powerful musical motifs in a powerful crescendo, and Emily Dickinson's cricket nation in "Further in Summer than the Birds" (J 1068) thrives in an ecology far more whimsical than that of Tuckerman's cricket, but also blessedly compressed.

Ultimately, two facets of Tuckerman's intellectual stance and prosody are of greater consequence than any of his poems. First, he was rooted in Emersonian romanticism but pretty much pulled clear of it. Having searched nature and death for clues to cosmic meaning and finding none, except the ineluctable need to go on, he became much more a kind of Victorian stoic than a romantic. And second, he really was a master prosodist, starting with traditional English forms and loosening them, working them by breaking lines, varying line length, and rearranging patterns of rhyme to control meaning and pace. He was no Walt Whitman; his voice was not notably American, but he would let no one else beat the slow drum of lament for him, and he was one of the nineteenth-century poets who tried not to let the exigencies of verse dictate meaning.

Poetry in the South

The cultural forces that militated against the writing and publishing of poetry in the South during the eighteenth century— including widespread anti-intellectualism and a dearth of outlets for publication outside of the North—with some exceptions continued through the nineteenth. At all events, but for Edgar Allan Poe during the first half of the nineteenth century, there were, arguably, no southern poets who had much merit in their craft except that which becomes magnified by comparing them with each other.

SIDNEY LANIER. The Georgia-born poet Sidney Lanier, who wrote during the second half of the century, is minimally conspicuous, and that much only by default. He is, to say the most, among the best of his southern peers, more often anthologized, but more, alas, as a curiosity or out of a wish for regional balance than for the quality of his work. Like the Fireside Poets in the North, Lanier combined several ambitions and careers; unlike them, he had interests that tended to fill his poetry with static that made much of it impenetrable. A graduate of Oglethorpe College, which later became defunct, he was at least as taken with music as with literature, later playing first flute with Baltimore's Peabody Symphony and accepting a lectureship at Johns Hopkins University.

His music and the strong southern sense of chivalry that he absorbed from his old-time Virginia family roots were the factors in his experience that combined, strange to say, to defeat his verse. So taken was he with Poe's insistence on the fusion of music and poetry, especially in Poe's essay "The Rationale of Verse," that Lanier carried the relationship to excess in his tract *The Science of English Verse* (1880), as well as in his poems, especially those written in the last few years of his life after publication of *Poems* in 1877. He evolved and then tried to write by rigid musical formulas of prosody that caused him to subjugate sense to sound to the point where sense was essentially lost. *The Science of English Verse* is utterly derailed by Lanier's confusion of "music" in its usual meaning with the term as it is applied, in a specialized and partly metaphorical sense, to poetry. If Poe and Swinburne were not extreme enough, Lanier often sounds like them but he is far more excessive. And he used such measures to romantically defend the ideal of southern agrarianism and chivalry against what he apprehended as a corrosive invasion by commerce, science, and social degradation. In "The Symphony" (1877) he claimed to hold his "Full powers from Nature manifold" to "Demand of Science whence and why / Man's tender pain, man's inward cry"; meanwhile, Trade perverts courtly love by wooing a distraught, gentle lady, saying, "*Here, you, Lady*, if you'll sell, I'll buy: / Come, heart for heart—a trade? What! weeping? why? / Shame on such wooers' dapper mercery!" Thus he brings virtually his whole arsenal to bear at once—music (including obtrusive alliteration), chivalry (or at least a lament for its being sold out), the works.

Lanier is best known for "The Marshes of Glynn"; it may also be his best poem, though one winces to say so. It is a relatively mindless, flowery, romantic fantasy, a statement of the speaker's determination to betake himself into the "Beautiful glooms" of the marsh to build for himself—like the marsh-hen—"a nest on the greatness of God" and to soar, like that bird, "In the freedom that fills all the space 'twixt the marsh and the skies." The reader must take the transition to belief on faith.[14] In Wordsworth nature acts as moral tutor, teaching principles through its examples and the inspiration that it promotes; in Emerson nature produces sudden revelation and an intuitive harmony in its beholder; in Lanier it is unclear what nature does, other than provide a wildlife refuge for a speaker who sees himself as a marsh hen. He loses the reader in sonorous syllables that yield neither the pure musical pleasure of Poe in his stride nor the intellectual pleasure of comprehensible, sensible language.

Lanier died in 1881 before his fortieth birthday; there is nothing in even his latest poems to suggest that he had the talent to redeem himself as a poet had his life been longer. It is, nonetheless, true that he had a following in his day. Thomas Wentworth Higginson, for example, dubbed him the Sir Galahad of contemporary poets. That is the same Higginson who tried to get Emily Dickinson to make her poems more regular.

HENRY TIMROD. Of the handful of southern poets of any interest, the South Carolina-born Henry Timrod may have had the most talent and potential. But they were first channeled into chauvinism and bombast by his zealous advocacy of the Confederacy and then cut short in 1867, when he was in his late thirties, by death from malnutrition and tuberculosis, which he had contracted as a Confederate soldier. His poems appeared from 1849 on in the *Southern Literary Messenger*; tellingly, he felt obliged to use a pseudonym, "Aglaus," for them. Taking a leaf from the Fireside Poets' book, he founded *Russell's Magazine* as a kind of southern counterweight to the *Atlantic Monthly*, but in the intellectual and economic climate of the South the venture was doomed. He turned to a northern publisher, Boston's Ticknor and Fields in 1860, for the publication of his only volume of poems. Then war broke out, and he succumbed to the southern strain of war fever, with its flush of nationalism and heat of hatred. "[W]e are a nation among nations," he declaimed in the broadside piece "Ethnogenesis" (1861), "and the world / Shall soon behold in many a distant port / Another flag unfurled!" The title of the poem clearly intimates the establishment of a whole new race of humans to undergird the new secessionist nation.

Timrod did compose some verses of worth. After venting his initial fervor, he began to write some more thoughtful war poems that compare not badly with most written on both sides of the line, except for those of Herman Melville and Walt Whitman. "Spring" (1873) ends with spring calling the hills "To fall and crush the tyrants and the slaves / Who turn her meads to graves," but the poem creates a nice sense of calm before battle through the tension between the softness of the newly arrived spring and the war that is about to interrupt it. Like many of the World War I poets who went off to fight full of high ideals and romantic notions of glory, Timrod underwent the sobering change that being witness to rampant sickness and death is bound to bring. "The Unknown Dead" (1873), for all its purple tint and patriotism, focuses on the death that is the cost of battle. Here nature is less the benevolent nurturer of the romantics than the unheeding nature of Stephen Crane and the turn-of-the-century naturalists: "with eyes unwet," she is "Oblivious of the crimson debt / To which she owes her April grace," as she "Laughs gayly o'er their burial-place." And there may be no nineteenth-century martial ode, not even Emerson's "Concord Hymn," more effective for its simple dignity than Timrod's "Ode Sung on the Occasion of Decorating the Graves of the Confederate Dead, at Magnolia Cemetery, Charleston, S. C., 1867."[15]

WILLIAM GILMORE SIMMS AND PAUL H. HAYNE. William Gilmore Simms and Paul H. Hayne sometimes come up in recollections of nineteenth-century southern poetry when the discussants rack their brains for names of poets. They can hardly be remembered for the value of their poems. Simms spread himself through a variety of literary forms, at his best, if anywhere, in historical romances. As a poet, he was attractive to Poe; they had in common the southern penchant for strong, and often strange, dominance of sound over sense.

Paul H. Haynes may be most interesting for his belief that he owed his status as merely a minor poet to his southernness. True, it was hard for a southern poet to secure a northern audience and outlets for publication (like other southern poets, he paid for publication of his books in the North), but Haynes was blind to the primary obstacle to greatness—his own acutely limited poetic gifts.[16]

Herman Melville

A survey of nineteenth-century American romantic poetry, exclusive of Edgar Allan Poe, Ralph Waldo Emerson, and Walt Whitman, who command separate chapters of their own, reasonably concludes with the New Yorker Herman Melville.

After he had ceased to be a writer of fiction—but for some sketches and the manuscript of *Billy Budd*, which were unpublished before his death—what was left of Melville became a poet. His public acclaim really went down with the *Pequod*. In the story "Bartleby the Scrivener," Bartleby lived shut in—or out—by a vacant society and blank walls, preferring not to participate in a world with which he could reach no understanding, an alien "handled with a chain" and content to die before an empty wall in a prison courtyard. When Melville met Hawthorne in England in 1856, on Melville's way to Constantinople and Palestine, Hawthorne realized that his old friend had "not been well of late; he has been affected with neuralgic complaints in his head and limbs, and no doubt has suffered from too constant literary occupation, pursued without much success latterly; and his writings, for a long while past, have indicated a morbid state of mind. . . . He can never believe nor be uncomfortable in his unbelief; and he is too honest and courageous not to try to do one or the other." Hawthorne further reported that during that visit Melville confessed "that he had pretty much made up his mind to be annihilated."[17] That was the period of Melville's life and his state of mind when he pretty much abandoned prose and turned to poetry.

By and large, the personal passion that sparked his fiction, the hallmark of his genius that caused him to fashion White Jacket and Ahab and Ishmael and Starbuck and Queequeg and Bartleby and Delano and the others (he still had Billy Budd, Captain Vere, and Claggart left in him, but they would remain dormant for years) out of facets of his own psyche, would be absent from his poems. In them, the dancing fire would become room-temperature dispassion. He would write many a good line and passage and some very good poems, but he was no longer the man he had been, could never match in his poems the poetry of his fiction. Except for the Civil War poems published in 1866 as *Battle-Pieces and Aspects of the War*, there would always be a question as to whether the poems shed light of their own or were noticed only in the reflected light of Melville's superb novels and stories.

The question is readily answered with regard to Melville's painfully long philosophical and historical verse tract *Clarel*, published in two volumes in 1876. The work has occasionally been called "ambitious"; that is like calling the cosmos "large." It runs to some 187,000 octosyllabic lines, most of them turgid. With the concurrence of Robert Penn Warren, Walter Bezanson has defended it as an important contribution to intellectual and literary history,[18] ranking it with the works of Henry Adams, William James, and others. Another view, that as a poem *Clarel* is hopelessly flawed, at best narcotic, at worst punishing, may well be prevalent and more accurate. Melville himself shared the latter, harsher judgment, calling his poem "a metrical affair, a pilgrimage or what not . . . eminently adapted for unpopularity."[19] Even its detractors, however, find it as hard to ignore as a three-hundred-pound figure hulking at the dinner table.

In part 1 of the four-part work, *Jerusalem*, the fallen-away divinity student Clarel, on a spiritual quest to the Holy Land, tours the Jerusalem area, meeting and falling in love with one Ruth, daughter of an American who has converted to Judaism. The lovers are separated when her father is killed on his farm near the city and Ruth must observe the traditional mourning period. Clarel agrees to travel about with a group of pilgrims at their invitation. In part 2, *The Wilderness*, the group travels to the Jordan and the Dead Sea, meeting assorted characters and moving south. Part 3, *Mar Saba*, mainly covers a visit to a fifth-century Greek Orthodox monastery, and part 4, *Bethlehem*, the return to Jerusalem via Bethlehem. Once back in the Holy City, Clarel discovers that Ruth, too, is dead.

For Melville lovers, perhaps the most arresting feature of *Clarel* is its autobiographical dimension, notably the interplay between Clarel and Rolfe (one of the pilgrims with whom Clarel joins up) on the one hand, both aspects of Melville's own personality, and Vine (who is very much based on Melville's sense of Nathaniel Hawthorne) on the other. While the subjects about which Rolfe expostulates are mainly postbellum, Vine's low-key responses to Rolfe are distinctly reminiscent of Mrs. Hawthorne's descriptions of her husband's stolid reactions to the earlier Melville's enthusiasms. The cantos of *Clarel* also reveal much of Melville's worldview during the so-called posthumous decades after the demise of Melville's literary following. For example, in part 4 it becomes clear that Rolfe rejects the notion that the New World is any better than the Old and can serve as a light to it, while Ungar, a Confederate veteran among the pilgrims, offers a forecast of "the Dark Ages of Democracy."

Notwithstanding any assertions of *Clarel*'s value, there are major flaws in the work that, in justice, cannot be overlooked. One is that the appearance of Rolfe, from which the poem draws much of its energy, is far too long delayed. A second is that the images of renewal with which the poem ends are so sudden and contrary to the overriding dismal tone of almost all that precedes them that they ring false. Faced with the death of his fiancée, Clarel is urged to be "like the crocus budding through the snow— / . . . like a swimmer rising from the deep—"; he now can "prove that death but routs life into victory." The poetry of the Epilogue is the most aesthetically effective in the whole work, but it is tonally inconsistent with the rest. The third fault is that much of the poem is simply couched in bad verse. Below is a passage that shows why many a reader's good intentions have turned to exasperation since Scribner's first published the poem in 1876 (with the help of a subvention left for the purpose in the will of Melville's uncle, Peter Gansevoort). Since the lines are mainly syllabic, with irregular rhyme (often in couplets, often alternating), Melville had ample opportunity for flowing, natural verse or a comprehensible elegance where that was his goal. But through much of *Clarel* the syntax is pointlessly askew, and few of the characters would be taken for native English speakers, including Derwent, the pleasant Anglican clergyman, who figures in the following example from part 2, Canto 21:

"No, no," cried Derwent gay,
Who late, upon acquaintance more,
Took no mislike to Rolfe at core,
And fain would make his knell a chime—
Being pledged to hold the palmy time
Of hope—at least, not to admit
That serious check might come to it:
"No, sun doubt's root—'twill fade, 'twill fade!
And for thy picture of the Prime,
Green Christianity in glade—
Why, let it pass; 'tis good, in sooth:
Who summons poets to the truth?"[20]

At least the characters seem to speak the same language even if the reader does not. Following Derwent's remarks, Vine regards him "sidelong . . . / . . . in envy of his gift / For light disposings: so to skim!"

Another well-known Melville poem, "Billy in the Darbies," was almost certainly meant for the *John Marr* collection until the prose introduction to it grew into *Billy Budd* and Melville decided to use the poem as a postscript to that novella. "Billy in the Darbies" would stand upright alone, but it brings an exceptionally fine closure to the story.

Melville privately published in small editions two other collections of his poems, *John Marr and Other Sailors* (1888) and *Timoleon, Etc.* (1891). There are some very good poems in them, such as "The Maldive Shark" (in *John Marr*), a strong exploration of one of Melville's favorite themes from his early fiction through *Moby-Dick* to *Billy Budd:* the delicate and often deceptive relationship between good and evil. Here there are some poeticisms that flaw the toughness of the imagery, but the imagery carries the day as it portrays the peculiar communion between "The sleek little pilot-fish, azure and slim," who has nothing to dread from the shark's "saw-pit of mouth, from his charnel of maw," who does not "partake of the [shark's] treat," but plays "Eyes and brains to the dotard lethargic and dull, / Pale ravener of horrible meat."

MELVILLE'S CIVIL WAR POEMS. Melville's standing as a poet largely rests on his *Battle-Pieces and Aspects of the War*, which, on its publication in 1866, was unsung by critics of the flood of Civil War poems that swept the nation. It now occupies a place beside

Whitman's *Drum-Taps* as one of the two best books of poems occasioned by that woeful war.

That the American Civil War should have elicited poems or volumes of poems from most of the poets then living in the Union and in the Confederacy alike is not surprising. The conflagration was the direst trauma that the new nation, not yet a hundred years old, had yet faced, posing not only onerous moral, political, economic, social, and military problems, but fundamental questions of American identity, of American mythology, from which the country was never fully to recover. How bright was the light to the nations? How could the people who were providing it engage in such massive, brutal fratricide? Had the country always been overadvertised—despite its advertising never really been "the city on the hill"? Combined with such other forces as Darwinism, the rise of science and technology, and accelerating industrialization, such questions were to lead away from romanticism and toward the skepticism, even the naturalism, of the end of the nineteenth century.

What is a little surprising is that during the war, while such questions entered the American consciousness, they were seldom voiced by the poets, almost all of whom dealt with them by ignoring them. Instead, the poets parroted public sentiment by hearkening back to the Puritans. Like the Puritans, the public, North and South, was not bothered by the contradiction of being Christian soldiers and fortifying the New Jerusalem, of serving the Lamb of God by conquest of fellow men. With the Puritans looking over the shoulders of the generations that succeeded them, God has always been on the side of Americans in conflict. During the Civil War He was on both sides. Northerners and Southerners invoked the Deity with equal confidence: "God of the true-hearted, guard them, o'er shadow them. / Strike through each arm, make victorious each blade!"[21] Almost alone among the poets, Melville and Whitman rose above the godliness and romanticizing of warfare and death by dint of their consummate sensitivity to language, their resistance to sentimentality—perhaps even stronger in Melville, who was readier for the sorrow, than in Whitman—and commitment to truth and basic human issues of good and evil and destiny. As a body, Whitman's war poetry looked forward optimistically to America's future; Melville's vision was far darker, focusing on humanity's foolishness—or worse.

Thus in "Donelson" Melville concentrates not on the justice or sanctity of Grant's attack on Fort Donelson, not on the glory of battle or some sentimental view of the suffering, but on the horrid reality of "Some dozen / Hapless wounded men [who] were frozen," some of them "stiffened" as they tried to crawl to safety, and all of them, "Our heedless boys / . . . nipped like blossoms." Melville's mind moves outward to the cosmic question that such anguish engenders, but not to the righteous God who wields the "terrible swift sword" for the Union, but to "The storm, whose black flag showed in heaven, / As if to say no quarter there was given to wounded men in wood, / Or true hearts yearning for the good." The crowd reading the dispatches from the battle can only disperse silently. Melville's quiet, dignified, accurate ending is all that needs to or can be said: "All fatherless seemed the human soul."

Frequently, he meets the complacent suppositions of his fellow war poets head-on. In "The Conflict of Convictions" God, far from taking sides, even in the war that represents "man's latter fall," goes about His business unknowably, and, even more vexingly, in as disinterested a way as fate or nature is implied to be in "The Maldive Shark," "Malvern Hill," and elsewhere in Melville. In that, he anticipates the naturalists, especially Stephen Crane. Ominously, he reminds us that "the Founders dream shall flee"; oppressively, he notes that as always, man's efforts notwithstanding, "death be busy with all who strive— / Death with silent negative." Ecclesiastes reverberates through the poem. "All is vanity," even the Civil War of the last great hope:

> YEA AND NAY—
> EACH HATH HIS SAY;
> BUT GOD HE KEEPS THE MIDDLE WAY
> NONE WAS BY
> WHEN HE SPREAD THE SKY;
> WISDOM IS VAIN, AND PROPHESY.[22]

Over and over in *Battle-Pieces* Melville pries the public's eyelids apart for a look at war with the slogans torn away. The "dying foeman" in "Shiloh" has learned the truth about patriotism: "What like a bullet," Melville demands with rue, "to undeceive!" And in "The March into Virginia: Ending in the First Manassas (July,

1861)" he pictures the lads larking off to war: "All wars are boyish, and are fought by boys, / The champions and enthusiasts of the state"—the same boys who "Shall die experienced ere three days are spent— / Perish, enlightened by the vollied glare."

Two poems in particular demonstrate the distance between Melville's conception of the war and its implications, and that of the other Civil War poets and his countrymen in general. "The House-Top: A Night Piece (July, 1863)" rings with Melville's sense of the baseness of human nature; for him, advocacy of either cause, Union or Confederate, did not equate with nobility. In the poem he castigates the atavism of the participants in the New York City draft law riots of 1863, who, when protesting against the provision of the law that permitted a man to buy his way out of conscription for $300, vented their fury on blacks, burning a black orphanage and church. As in William Faulkner's "Dry September" and Joseph Conrad's *Heart of Darkness*, the setting stirs supposedly reasonable beings to unreasonable, unspeakable acts:

> No sleep. The sultriness pervades the air
> And binds the brain—a dense oppression, such
> As tawny tigers feel in matted shades,
> Vexing their blood and making apt for ravage.[23]

The setting, however, is not to blame, but rather the nature of man, which can be all too easily moved to bestiality—and, incidentally, as Melville discovered, fail to recognize the real contribution of one of the world's greatest writers of fiction. Melville sees the incidents as "The grimy slur on the Republic's faith implied, / Which holds that Man is naturally good, / And—more— is Nature's Roman, never to be scourged." Thus in Melville's cynical view, while it may have been forbidden to scourge citizens of Rome, it seems necessary occasionally to use the whip on American citizens.

The other poem that may most effectively show Melville's perspicacity regarding the Civil War, and his eminence above all the other war poets save Whitman, is "A Utilitarian View of the *Monitor*'s Fight." Here he takes the wind out of the glory-mongers at a stroke. In that war, and especially in the battle between the ironclads, "War . . . laid aside / His Orient pomp," and so " 'twould ill befit / Overmuch to ply / The rhyme's barbaric cymbal." Melville is articulating two penetrating perceptions. The first, which he was among the quickest to understand, is that the American Civil War introduced an extreme change into the very nature of warfare. For the first time industrial might and technological power outstripped human courage in importance, a metamorphosis that was, Melville knew, irrevocable. It was a theme that still preoccupied him two decades later when he lamented the replacement of the heroes of the old sailing navy by the "martial utilitarians" of the new mechanized navy:

> War yet shall be, but warriors
> Are now but hurt operatives; War's made
> Less grand than Peace,
> And a singe runs through lace and feather.[24]

His second exciting insight revealed in the poem is a literary one: the new and baser character of war demands a new kind of verse, a freer one which must be sparing in its use of traditional forms, "rhyme's [now] barbaric cymbal." Emerson and Whitman had long advocated putting the new wine of the times in new poetic bottles, but their reasons were nationalistic and somewhat fuzzily philosophical. Melville tied the imperative of poetic change directly to changes wrought by the Industrial Revolution and specifically to warfare. He realized what most significant twentieth-century poets from the Imagists on would understand and use as an operating principle, that the old forms simply would not ring true in expressing new values. And he used his perception to excellent effect in "A Utilitarian View of the *Monitor*'s Fight." The pounding of the machinery is unmistakable as he marries sound felicitously to sense by roughing up the verse and using appropriate alliteration to convey a remarkable aural impression of the pounding of the pistons:

> . . . plain mechanic power
> Plied cogently in War now placed—
> Where War belongs—
> Among the trades and artisans.
>
> Yet this was battle and intense—
> Beyond the strife of fleets heroic,
> Deadlier, closer, calm 'mid storm;

No passion; all went on by crank,
  Pivot, and screw,
And calculations of caloric.

Needless to dwell; the story's known.
  The ringing of those plates on plates
Still ringeth around the world— . . .[25]

Melville was quite capable of dropping clinkers in his *Battle-Pieces*, as he does in the inverted "fleets heroic," a poeticism, but the faulty spots are noticeable because most of his war poetry is so superb and so superior to that of his contemporaries.

Melville tempered the characteristically optimistic American romanticism. He was certainly always fascinated with the notion of independent and even monomaniacal egos, but the assault on his own sovereign ego by an American public that demanded literature devoid of all complexity and nearly empty of seriousness—the kind of poetry that the public found in that offered by the Fireside Poets—constricted and darkened the romantic content of his poetry.

· FIVE ·

Edgar Allan Poe,
The Hyper-Romantic

> In Heaven a spirit doth dwell
>   "Whose heart-strings are a lute";
> None sing so wildly well
> As the angel Israfel,
> And giddy stars (so legends tell),
> Ceasing their hymns, attend the spell
>   Of his voice, all mute.

> —Edgar Allan Poe, "Israfel"

The work of any serious writer is a strategy to cope with the vicissitudes of life, to re-create the world, to reconstitute its values and relationships to his advantage, to unburden himself by simultaneously confessing (in whatever overt or covert form) his own tensions and projecting the load onto the shoulders of his audience. The writer may not be fully aware of those purposes of his writing among his other motives (making money, calling attention to himself), but those are cardinal exigencies nonetheless. If he spends all of his time in his re-created world, so that he forfeits contact with the world whose features the members of society agree upon, he is adjudged mad, but if he uses his invention intermittently for rest and rehabilitation and returns to society's world to pay the bills and pass the salt and say please and thank you, he ordinarily is not.

Edgar Allan Poe was not, nor was he an opium fiend, despite the calumnies first perpetrated by Reverend Rufus Griswold, the vicious prig whom Poe himself, perversely or naively, appointed as his literary executor and biographer. Given the weird and often antisocial world of Poe's writings; the assortment of deranged, often violent characters and unearthly settings in his poems and tales; and the willingness of many writers stung by Poe's acrid criticism of their work to believe and spread Griswold's lies and half-truths, it was all too easy for the public to credit Griswold's libelous reports that were backed by Griswold's revision of Poe's letters.

Poe has been more of a challenge to biographers and critics than almost any other figure in American literature. But much is now known, and none of it supports the legend that still persists that Poe was mad or a habitual drug abuser, although he did sometimes drink excessively (but no more than literary figures whose sanity has not been a matter of debate), and his drinking sometimes influenced his behavior. Quixotic yes, self-destructive yes, bizarre sometimes, close to the edge often, but insane, no— or perhaps safer to say not quite. He lived very much in the world that was not of his making and with which he had a lot of trouble contending, and he escaped to the alternative world that he constructed. The flights of his ego away from human society to a never-never land of his own concoction, and his delineation of that place, make him, in a sense, the most romantic of all nineteenth-century American poets. The demons that drove him caused him to speak in a voice so hyperromantic that he is on the far edge of American romanticism and without the ap- proval—or understanding—of many of his romantic peers.[1]

Poe's Life as the Psychic Source of His Work

Especially in view of his great sensitivity, the salient facts of his life clearly indicate why Poe lived on the edge. His actor father, David Poe, Jr., was a drunkard who deserted Edgar's mother, Elizabeth Arnold Poe, in Boston when the child was about a year old. Before Poe was three years old, his actress mother died coughing up blood during a consumptive seizure in Richmond, Virginia, where she was performing. The child saw. David Poe dropped from sight after Elizabeth's death, and he may well have died soon afterward. If the Lord taketh away, the Lord also giveth sometimes, now providing Mrs. Frances Allan, wife of John Allan, a Richmond tobacco merchant, to take and raise the baby Edgar. From 1815 to 1820 Poe was with the Allans in England, where he used the Allan name at the good schools to which he was sent. Back in Richmond, the foster parents continued to send him to school, but now, amid the special doubts regarding his origins and circumstances, which could only heighten the usual adolescent identity problems, he took the name of his natural parents. When Poe was about fifteen, perhaps because he defended Mrs. Allan in a disagreement with her husband, John Allan began to display some ill feeling toward Edgar that climaxed in 1824 in Mr. Allan's refusal to pay about $2,000 in gambling debts that Edgar had incurred as a student at the University of Virginia. Allan thought that Poe was profligate; Poe, a good student, although a hard-drinking one, thought that Allan, who had received an enormous inheritance, was parsimonious. Indeed, Poe had wanted to be and been led to believe that he would be Allan's heir, but he had a serious falling-out with Allan in 1827 and left for Baltimore, where he met his father's family, and Boston, where he privately published *Tamerlane and Other Poems*.

The eighteen-year-old's abysmal sense of self at the time of his estrangement from Allan may be inferred from his pseudonymous behavior: when he left for Boston and the army, he was "Henri Le Rennet"; a notation in *Tamerlane* had it that it was "By a Bostonian"; and when he signed into the army, just before the book appeared, he used the alias "Edgar A. Perry." It could not have seemed otherwise to Poe than that a father had rejected him for the second time in his short life. But the deprivation of two fathers was not enough. Now, in 1829, Frances Allan, for whom he cared deeply, died of the same disease, consumption, that had carried off his birth mother. If the Lord giveth, the Lord can also taketh away, and taketh away, and taketh away sometimes. In effect, by the time he was twenty, Edgar Allan Poe had lost four parents in most painful ways.

But not quite. After Mrs. Allan's death, there was an uneasy truce for a time between Poe and John Allan, who helped Poe secure an appointment in the U. S. Military Academy at West Point. The pattern of their relationship had long been stamped, however, and their affiliation doomed. Poe needed an allowance from his foster father to live comfortably at the Academy; Allan, who was siring children out of wedlock and then remarrying, refused. Nor did it help that Allan intercepted a letter from Poe accusing him of being "not very often sober." Edgar's drive for self-destruction was relentless. Now, finally realizing that he must abandon all hope of being Allan's heir, he devised effective tactics to get himself dismissed from the Corps of Cadets. Failing to show up for roll calls and for classes, he was sent down.

The Continuation of Despair

Though his foster father might be, life was far from finished with Poe. In 1831, in his twenty-first year, he returned to Baltimore to live among his Poe relatives, who had fallen on hard times. Death toyed with him again. First his brother died and then, in 1835, his grandmother, whose pension as a war widow from the American Revolution was suddenly denied the family. In considerable torment and penury, Poe secretly married his first cousin, Virginia Clemm, daughter of his aunt, Maria Poe Clemm, members of the Baltimore family circle. There is reason to believe that he utterly etherealized his child bride and never corporeally consummated the marriage. Death watched and played a waiting game now.

Toward the end of 1835 Poe returned to Richmond, with his spirit wife and her mother, to accept an assistant editorship of the newly founded *Southern Literary Messenger*. In Richmond he took his marriage out of the closet and openly remarried Virginia, in his fashion, in 1836. In a town full of ghosts—John Allan was dead now, too, and Poe was cut off from the second Mrs. Allan and the family heirs—and working for hardship wages, Poe drank too much, although he did publish stories in the *Messenger* and attain distinction as an erudite, if acerbic, literary critic. He did help to increase the journal's circulation, but his editor, T. L. White, soon had enough of him and, in 1837, had to dismiss him anyway.

Poe moved on with his aunt and cousin-wife from Richmond to New York in 1837, then on to Philadelphia the following year, in both cities selling some fiction and critical pieces to survive, usually eating poorly if at all, often reduced to doing hackwork. Nothing worked for long. After two years, in the spring of 1839, he was regularly employed again, this time as co-editor of *Burton's Gentleman's Magazine*. He was writing his best tales, but his drinking continued to ensure that his life would be sordid. He lost his job again, going from *Burton's* to *Graham's*, where his challenge to break any cryptograms submitted by readers helped to boost sales. Then another dreadful blow: In January 1842, Virginia, who was a singer, suffered a burst blood vessel in her throat. The effect on Poe, who had seen two mothers succumb to consumption, who had as a baby seen one of them spit up blood in her death throes, can only be imagined. Death was unrelenting, though; it would impose five more years of illness before taking away Virginia. Meanwhile, he resigned his job at *Graham's*, to be replaced, ironically, by his nemesis Griswold. He went to Washington, D.C., to raise money for *The Stylus*, a journal that he meant to start, and to see about a modest post in the administration of President John Tyler, but he ruined his chances on both counts by getting so drunk that he had to be helped onto the train back to Philadelphia.

In the spring of 1844 the forlorn, nomadic little Poe band moved once again, this time back to New York. He enjoyed a measure of success, doing some newspaper work and taking an editorial job at the *Sunday Times*. A number of good things happened to him there, notably in 1845, when James Russell Lowell published a highly favorable article on him in *Graham's* and Poe published "The Raven" in the *New York Evening Mirror* and then in the *Broadway Journal*. Among Poe's many quirky problems was not an inability to recognize an opportunity. Riding the crest of "The Raven" 's instant popularity, he became the primary reviewer for the *Broadway Journal;* hit the lecture circuit, expatiating on American poetry; and saw Evert A. Duyckinck, the writer friend of New York writers, arrange for the publication of a book of Poe's fiction and *The Raven and Other Poems*, both that year. But the wave crashed. Poe managed to assemble the resources to acquire the *Broadway Journal* for himself, but the magazine went under in early 1846, and Poe, attempting now to handle fame as well as sorrow, seemed to go more out of control than ever. His drinking made him more quarrelsome than usual; there is disagreement as to how much he drank, some holding that the quantity was small but that he could not hold liquor. No matter. It is certain that he drank much beyond his capacity, enough to send him out of control at critical times. His involvements with women became even less satisfying. Dire lack of money was still and always would

be a terrible problem for him, but his sense of southern gentle-
manliness seems to have precluded his trying to obtain it other
than with his pen.

In January 1847 Virginia, a semi-invalid by then, went the way
of his four real and surrogate parents. Poe's erratic behavior
temporarily decreased; forgetting when it had begun, he blamed
his alcoholism on Virginia's suffering and credited her death with
its abatement. His own illness that year may have resulted from
a brain lesion. He was nursed by his aunt and a woman who
had charitably attended Virginia and even contributed supplies
during her illness. The next year was frantic; it included a brief
engagement to a widowed Providence poet, Helen Power Whitman,
and an obsessive infatuation with a married Lowell, Massachusetts,
woman, Mrs. Nancy L. Richmond, his "Annie." The extremity in
which he was living reverberates through his letters to them. On
16 November 1848 he wrote to "Annie," whom he had transformed
in his mind into his "own sweet *sister* Annie, my *pure* beautiful
angel—*wife* of my soul—to be mine hereafter & *forever in the
Heavens*—how shall I explain to you the *bitter, bitter* anguish
which has tortured me since I left you?" He even told her, perhaps
truthfully, that in his desperation he attempted suicide by drinking
two ounces of laudanum to force her to keep her sacred vow to
"come to me on my bed of death." That year, in that state of
mind, he gave readings and lectures to raise money for the pet
literary project that preoccupied him during his last years, the
founding of *The Stylus*, which, like the *Broadway Journal*, would
be his own, while unlike its predecessor, it would be successful.

It would never see the light of day. Tormented with a sense of
persecution, Poe left for Richmond in the early summer of 1849
to find money for *The Stylus* but had to get off the train in
Philadelphia with two imagined assassins on his tail. Helped by
friends, he finally did reach Richmond, where he found his last
teasing hope for happiness before his end. He visited his sister
Rosalie, enjoyed old friends, joined a temperance society, even
got engaged again, this time to a sweetheart of his youth, Elmira
Royster Shelton, who had been briefly engaged to Poe in 1825,
then married another man and been widowed. Then came Fate's
last practical joke of his life. He headed north, perhaps to bring
his aunt Mrs. Clemm back to Richmond from New York. He got
only as far as Baltimore, where he gave in to drink and was

picked up in a delirium outside a polling place on Election Day, 3 October 1849. He was in his fortieth year. But the torment chased him beyond the grave: "To vilify a great man is the readiest way in which a little man can himself attain greatness,"[2] he had jotted down among his marginalia in June, not considering how appropriate the observation was to his own designated executor (or did it, with his unerring instinct for self-destruction, cross his mind?). Griswold's calumny, beginning with Poe's obituary notice, was to give him no more respite in death than his woe had granted him in life.

The Effect of His Biography

With Poe as with no other American poet, understanding the biography—the biographical roots of his anguish—is indispensable to understanding his conception of poetry and his poems. It is not difficult to see why he spent his artistic life seeking to change places with the angel Israfel (in the poem of that name, 1831). From "Tamerlane" (1827) on (a poem that encoded his thwarted love for Miss Royster of Richmond, and society's rejection of him), unable to contend with the physical, he cherished the spiritual; unable to fulfill relationships with flesh-and-blood women, he worshipped unearthly or even dead ones; unable to avoid his tormentor Death, he transfigured it, turned it into an object of mysterious attraction. If he tried to love a woman mortally, he could lose her, as indeed he lost them all—mothers, wife, fiancées, flirtations. But if he turned them to ether, he could worship them forever.

And so "To Helen" (1831) idealizes the woman he later called "the first, purely ideal love of my soul!" He was referring to Mrs. Jane Stith Stanard, mother of a Richmond school friend; she died when Poe was fifteen. (Poe claimed to have written the poem when he was fourteen. *Perhaps* he did.) As he conjures her in his poem, the woman does not even begin as woman but as legend, and from there she ascends, as the musicality of the poem magically echoes the ascent, still higher, until she is "Psyche," until she becomes nothing less than pure Soul. Thus, "To Helen" becomes an expression of Poe's sense of ideal beauty as well as an indication of how important and immediate the past was to him.

Women in the Poems

Death repeatedly mediates his relationships with women in his poems. Often, as in "The Sleeper" (1831), "Lenore" (1831), "To One in Paradise" (1845), "Ulalume—A Ballad" (1850), "Annabel Lee" (1850), "For Annie" (1850), and "The Raven" (1845), the female love is dead—not the healthiest, but a safe and enduring arrangement from Poe's point of view in the circumstances of his life. Thus the swain who narrates "The Sleeper," standing in "an opiate vapor" that "Steals drowsily and musically / Into the universal valley," prays "to God that [his deceased love Irene] may lie / Forever with unopened eye, / While the pale sheeted ghosts go by!"—prays that "Soft may the worms about her creep!" In the world that Poe constructs the landscape resembles none ever seen by mortal on this earth; here is precisely where the speaker wants his supernally beautiful lover, and here she is in the optimum condition for him.

In "Lenore" the dead young woman's apparently misguided Guy de Vere rants against those hypocrites who cared only for Lenore's wealth, did her in with their slander, and now would mourn her. Quiet, the pious narrator tells the distraught Guy, in effect: do not disabuse her of the "Hope that flew beside" her but solemnly sing "a Sabbath song." Guy responds with satisfaction that she has escaped the "damnéd Earth!" He wants no conventional bell to ring, will sing no sanctimonious dirge, he announces, but will instead "waft the angel on her flight with a Paean of old days!"—antiquity being one of those baroque places (as in "Tamerlane," "Scenes from Politian," "The Coliseum," and so on) that are part of Poe's paradisaical retreat.

"To One in Paradise" is one of the more thinly veiled poems of psychic autobiography. It is Virginia (who was not yet dead but under a death sentence from the time she had burst the blood vessel), Elizabeth Poe, Frances Allan, Jane Stith Stanard, others, or all of them Poe had in mind when he composed the lines "Thou wast that all to me, love, / . . . a shrine, / All wreathed with fairy fruits and flowers. / And all the flowers were mine." The mood is undeniably of self-pity: "Ah, dream too bright to last! / Ah, starry Hope! that didst arise / But to be overcast!" The future urges the speaker to go on, but his spirit, knowing that life has ceased for him, can only hover "Mute, motionless, aghast!"

No more, he says, "Shall bloom the thunder-blasted tree, / Or the stricken eagle soar!" His final stanza reiterates the dreaminess to which he relegates life again and again ("Dream-Land" [1845], "A Dream Within a Dream" [1827], "Sonnet—To Science" [1829]— in a sense all of his work):

> And all my days are trances,
>   And all my nightly dreams
> Are where thy grey eye glances,
>   And where thy footstep gleams—
> In what ethereal dances,
>   By what eternal streams.

The transmogrification of the physical into some ineffable condition of being is typical Poe and here is Poe at his Svengali, euphonious best, right down to the synecdoche—one of his favorite devices— "footstep gleams."

"Ulalume"

The ballad "Ulalume," another poem in which the ladylove has died, also has great seductive power, making the reader forget for a moment that he has forsaken reality for the poet's dank ideality. What is the dreamscape of "Ulalume" (or "The Valley of Unrest" [1831], or "The Haunted Palace" [1845], or the seascape—if that is the word—of "The City in the Sea," or the scenery of any of Poe's poems)? The descriptions use the language associated with physical nature ("skies," "lake," "woodland," "moon," and so forth), but in the mesmerizing context of the repetitive cadence and diction, with the help of such bizarre rhymes as "Dian"— "dry on"—"Lion," the reader is drawn into a waking sleep.

The dreary dreamland is, in fact, in "Ulalume," a "ghoul-haunted woodland" in the "misty mid region" of a hyperromantic Hudson River school artist (Robert Walter Weir) by a "dank tarn" from a French fairy ballet by Jean François Auber.[3] It is a suitable nowhere for the speaker, an apparently physical entity, or self,[4] to roam with Psyche, his Soul, indulging appropriately "serious and sober" talk that wells up from "palsied and sere thoughts" and "treacherous and sere" memories. The speaker spots Venus ("Astarte's bediamonded crescent," Astarte being the Phoenician goddess of love) in a "liquescent / And nebulous lustre" in the night sky and is attracted to it (her); that is, he is momentarily drawn to physical love, or at least its symbol. Psyche, ever-watchful chaperone of Poe's libido, "uplifting her finger" warns him, "Sadly this star I mistrust, / Her pallor I strangely mistrust." Fair enough; the human women Poe loves acquire a death pallor. "Ah, hasten—ah, let us not linger! / Ah, fly!—let us fly!—for we must," his Psyche urges him "In terror," sobbing and letting her wings trail in the dust. But the speaker is brave enough to trust Venus, which beams "With Hope and in Beauty tonight" and, flickering "up to Heaven through the night," must surely "guide [them] aright." And what does he get for his interest in physical love? He gets a crushing reminder of what such love leads to, as Venus leads them to "the door of a legended tomb," and he asks his "sweet sister" Psyche to read him what is written upon it. "Ulalume—Ulalume!— / 'Tis the vault of thy lost Ulalume!" she replies.

To the psyche of Edgar Allan Poe, who often took walks to Virginia's grave after her lingering death, the message is clear: real amorous entanglements lead to the tomb and sorrow. Better "the spectre of a planet," an antiworld created by the creative imagination. In the last stanza of "Ulalume," the physical self and his Psyche conclude that the "merciful ghouls," knowing that terrible secret, tried "To bar up our way and to ban it," that is, to keep them from the harm of reality, tried to protect them by inventing a spectral world. The "woodlandish ghouls," in other words, are figurations of Poe's own protective imagination.

"Ulalume" is not contrived to work at the rational level. Poe, the man who solves cryptograms, claims to prize ratiocination, and invents the detective story—in Monsieur Dupin of "The Purloined Letter" makes the die in which all rational detectives including Sherlock Holmes are cast—Poe aims his poems not at the brain, but at the viscera (mainly by way of the ears). This is the paradox of Poe, emanating from the two conflicting sides of his personality, the rational, orderly thinker who in fiction and criticism could marshal unimpeachable argument, case-solving scientific logic, and then in his poetry and much of his fiction, too, withdraw to the sanctum of mists and shadows and phantom stars.

That tension is displayed with crystalline clarity in his mellifluous "Sonnet—to Science" (1829). It does not attack science gratuitously; no, Poe honors science as the "true daughter of Old Time." His charge against science is that, with its "peering eyes," it eats away at the other way of perceiving the world, the way of what Coleridge called the "poetic imagination." Science insists on "dull realities." They are the instruments it uses to drive "the Hamadryad from the wood / To seek a shelter in some happier star" and to tear from the poet "The summer dream beneath the tamarind tree."

"Annabel Lee" and "For Annie"

Like Ulalume, as well as Irene, Lenore, and the unnamed lady in paradise, the object of the speaker's love in "Annabel Lee" is dead, resting in a "sepulchre there by the sea" that mirrors Poe's usual sepulchral association of the sea. And why not the sea if his representations of other natural phenomena—lakes, woods, and so on—are also sepulchral? The speaker's retreat here, though, is not really to a vaporous no-place but to a more easily recognizable psychic fortress—the human being's rationalized position of ultimate rectitude and vindication. We were better than the rest and right all the time! He values the love between himself and Annabel Lee, who is usually equated with Virginia Clemm, far above that of mortals, above the power of other mortals even to comprehend. Indeed, "the winged seraphs of Heaven / Coveted her and me" and "The angels, not half so happy in Heaven, / Went envying her and me" because—and this is always the point in Poe's "love" poems—"we loved with a love that was more than love." In "Annabel Lee" he does not shift the relationship in space; he shifts it in kind. So intensely different is it from mere human love that it arouses the jealousy of mortals and immortals alike. Her "highborn kinsmen" bear the child-love away and "shut her up in a sepulchre," and the envy of the angels is "the reason (as all men know, / . . .) That the wind came out of the cloud, chilling / And killing my Annabel Lee." Poe's poems and tales are not wont to let death stand in the way of true unearthly love, however. His soul forever united with his lover's, the speaker lies down with her "all the night-tide . . . / In her sepulchre there by the sea— / In her tomb by the side of the sea."

"For Annie" is a variation on the theme. In it the fundamental love relationship does not change; it is still a necrophilic piece, but here the situations of the male and female lovers are reversed. The live woman is invited to come to the speaker, who is, for practical purposes, a corpse. The "Annie" of the title may be the same "Annie" (Mrs. Nancy L. Richmond) who was, in those embarrassingly desperate letters of 1848, his "own sweet *sister*" and his "*pure* beautiful angel" and "*wife* to [his] soul" to be joined to him "*forever in the heavens*" after his demise, which he claimed to have tried to hasten. Sarah Royster Shelton, Poe's lost fiancée, to whom he became reengaged in his last months, has a counterclaim, though. The "Annie" of the poem may well be a blend of ladies. The speaker, believing that surcease comes only with death (". . . to *sleep*, you must slumber / In just such a [narrow] bed"), sees "Annie" holding him in his deathbed, drowning him in her tresses. The thought of her shuddering "to look at me, / Thinking me dead" so tickles him, that it lightens his heart, which at the end "sparkles with Annie."

"For Annie" is the one that got away from Poe. He could not bring sufficient power to language or music to bear on it—cannot put readers in a deep enough trance—to save it from being merely bathetic. At least one hideous pun does not help, the double entendre of "at length" in the following passage:

> And no muscle I move
> As I lie at full length—
> But no matter!—I feel
> I am better at length.

Poe was capable of deliberate comic and parodic effects, especially in his fiction and criticism, but it is not possible to decide whether the tasteless pun in "For Annie" would be worse if intentional or inadvertent.

"The Raven" and "The Philosophy of Composition"

"The Raven" is much better again than "For Annie." Some, like W. H. Auden in his introduction to *Edgar Allan Poe: Selected Prose and Poetry* (1950), have faulted the poem on grounds that the "thematic interest and the prosodic interest, both of which are considerable, do not combine and are even often at odds";

that is, the sound and sense of the verse live in uneasy wedlock. But the music is so strongly mesmeric, the language so strongly allied to the necessarily dreary, hypnagogic beat, the progression of the speaker's questioning of the bird so suggestive of his increasingly agitated state of mind and logical within the boundaries of the poem that "The Raven," despite its detractors, is one of Poe's most noteworthy successes. It was the poem that finally made him popular as it popped up in a number of magazines and newspapers. Public appreciation of "The Raven" also inspired the clearest statement of his poetic theory, as he attempted to cash in on its popularity.

The source or sources of the idea of the wise bird who can respond to the speaker are uncertain. Similarly prescient birds had, of course, long appeared in literature: in Hamlet's expletive, "Come, the croaking raven doth bellow for revenge," in the biblical account of Elijah's being fed by ravens in the wilderness, in Dickens's raven in *Barnaby Rudge* (a novel that Poe had reviewed in 1841), in the raven that may house the soul of George I in Horace Walpole's *Reminiscences*. More sure it is that Poe took the dominant trochaic octameter cadence from Elizabeth Barrett Browning's "Lady Geraldine's Courtship"; he dedicated *The Raven and Other Poems* (1845) to her.[5]

A discussion of "The Raven" cannot profitably be dissociated from Poe's explanation of his intentions and procedures for writing the poem in his essay "The Philosophy of Composition," which he published in *Graham's* in April 1846, just over a year after the poem had been introduced. The essay is not to be swallowed whole, for it is a self-serving tract designed to foster popular belief in his own genius (he considerably shrinks the length of time it took him to write the poem, for instance). At the same time, however, it offers a sharper insight into his own fragile psyche than he may have been aware that he was revealing, and its contribution to American poetics is important and lasting. Indeed, Poe was among the first American poets (arguably the second, after Emerson) to make such a contribution. The operative words here are "lasting" and "important"; others, Freneau, Barlow, and Bryant, for example, had made attempts.

By southern cultural influence as well as by temperament, Poe was at home in the Gothic branch of romanticism. In poetry and fiction alike, one of Poe's obsessive themes is, naturally, the disintegration of the human mind,[6] more often than not as that process is instigated by some gaping grief and runs its course through otherworldly settings and events. The best of his short stories—"The Fall of the House of Usher" (1845), for example—treat the theme brilliantly, as does his strangely attractive poem "The Haunted Palace," which he published in 1839 and later that year added to the text of "The Fall of the House of Usher" in the form of one of Roderick Usher's "rhymed verbal improvisations." The poem (and, by extension the tale, both together and separately by Poe's own account) explores "a mind haunted by phantoms—a disordered brain." The psychological insight of "The Raven"—well before psychology dreamed of becoming a science—is acute. It is more than a poem in which the sensitive speaker watches madness come on as his grief yields to it. More, it is a poem about the kind of self-destructive impulse that marked Poe's conduct of his own life. In "The Philosophy of Composition" he explains the speaker's questioning of the raven as follows:

I saw that I could make the first query propounded by the lover—the first query to which the Raven should reply "Nevermore"—that I could make this first query a commonplace one—the second less so—the third still less, and so on—until at length the lover, startled from his original *nonchalance* by the melancholy character of the word itself—by its frequent repetition—and by a consideration of the ominous reputation of the fowl that uttered it—is at length excited to superstition, and wildly propounds queries of a far different character—queries whose solution he has passionately at heart—propounds them half in superstition and half in *that species of despair which delights in self-torture* [italics added here]—propounds them not altogether because he believes in the prophetic or demoniac character of the bird (which, reason assures him, is merely repeating a lesson learned by rote) but because *he experiences a frenzied pleasure in so modeling his questions as to receive from the* expected *"Nevermore" the most delicious because the most intolerable of sorrow* [italics added here].

And toward the end of the essay Poe repeats the crucial importance of self-destruction:

The student [speaker-lover] . . . *is impelled . . . by the human thirst for self-torture,* and in part by superstition, to propound such queries to the bird as will bring him, the lover, the most of the luxury of sorrow, through the anticipated answer "Nevermore." With the indulgence, to the extreme, of this self-torture, . . . there has been no overstepping of the limits of the real [italics again added].

Poe did not know its name, but he knew masochism exquisitely. His analysis of it here is at the heart of the poem.[7] As he struggles to get through the night, the lover's resignation over the death of his "rare and radiant" Lenore is at first only pecked at by the odd advent of the raven; the increasingly insistent tapping is unnerving but survivable until the speaker is moved to fling open the shutter to admit the magisterial intruder. From there on, particularly after the speaker asks the dark intruder "what [its] lordly name is on the Night's Plutonian shore," the human is under compulsion to pursue the catechism between himself and the raven inexorably, step by step, to his own bottomless despair, from which he "Shall be lifted—nevermore!" Many a reader who is unwilling to suspend his disbelief of Poe's dark, sonorous blandishments has submitted unwillingly to the spell that he weaves in "The Raven" and the other best poems.

Elements of Poe's Poetic

Of course, much of "The Philosophy of Composition" can be dismissed as Poe's deliberate fabrication to promote himself and his poetry. But the essay both provides clues to the goals and accomplishments of "The Raven" in particular and, with "The Poetic Principle" (published posthumously in 1850 but frequently delivered as a lecture for years before), eloquently states his poetics. The major tenets of his theory are:

1. It is imperative that the poet decide on a specific effect and direct everything in the work to the achievement of that effect (if a plot is involved, this means keeping the denouement in mind from the outset, in a way, working backward).

2. The poet is mandated to keep the poem short, since excessive length must dilute or split the effect (though to excuse from his mandate not only Milton's *Paradise Lost*, but, incidentally, such longer poems of his own as "Al Aaraaf," he allows that a longer poem may be regarded as "a succession of brief ones." Poe suggests that a work should be readable in a single sitting, say a hundred

lines for a poem. Fortuitously, his own exemplary "The Raven" has 108 lines.).

3. "Beauty is the sole legitimate province of the poem." Unlike Emerson and the Transcendentalists, or Shelley, one of his chief models, or most other romantic poets on both sides of the Atlantic, Poe conceives of a tripartite division of art (and experience), instead of working through the imagination toward an ultimate appreciation of cosmic oneness. To Poe, the members of the triumvirate are "Truth, or the satisfaction of the intellect"; "Passion, or the excitement of the heart"; and Beauty . . ., the excitement, or pleasurable elevation of the soul" (in "The Poetic Principle" the three elements of "the world of mind" are labeled Pure Intellect, Taste, and Moral Sense, but these are essentially equivalents of Truth, Passion, and Beauty).

Poe decided while ratiocinating (ex post facto?) about "The Raven," "the death . . . of a beautiful woman is, unquestionably the most poetical topic in the world." Poetry is indeed, to Poe, as he defines it in "The Poetic Principle," "The Rhythmical Creation of Beauty," although ". . . the incitements of Passion, or the precepts of Duty, or even the lessons of Truth, may . . . be introduced into a poem," but only toned down to best "subserve . . . that Beauty which is the atmosphere and real essence of the poem." Beauty, to Poe, is a matter of harmony, largely a function of sound, to be attained through the exercise of creative imagination.

4. Language must be suited to the material in the poem. Poe's insistence on this is implied, rather than stated, in his discussion of his choice of the word "nevermore" as perfectly expressive of the tone of sorrow that he had decided upon for "The Raven."

5. Just as the language must be natural to the material, so must the rhythm, Poe implies in recounting the thinking that went into his choice of meters for "The Raven."

The Effects of Poe's Poetic Theories

Poe's equation of poetry with a nonverbal art form, music, in the achievement of what he took to be poetry's sublime task, the representation of supernal beauty, caused him much trouble with critics in his own time and with posterity. By his reckoning, literature can deal with passion and truth—a function of intellect— through prose, with beauty primarily through the music of poetry. There is the implication that passion-truth-prose is somehow a matter of precision, beauty-poetry of—what, ambiguity, even obscurantism? Ah, but poetry *is* a verbal art: it uses words; words mean things. Poe's paradoxically well-reasoned conception of the essential nebulosity of poetry was alluring to the late-nineteenth-century French Symbolist poets Baudelaire, Mallarmé, Verlaine, and their followers, to Charles Swinburne, and to some extent William Butler Yeats because it permitted him, and them, to build and rationalize their antiworlds. But in the main, American poets, while intrigued by the vast scope that Poe gave the imagination (Whitman, for example, defended him; and Wallace Stevens felt the pull but decided that death was not beauty, only beauty's parent or intensifier), have much preferred the tangible world tangibly represented. In that respect, the mainstream flowed around Poe, through Emerson, Whitman, Dickinson, the Imagists, even T. S. Eliot, who was drawn to Poe but helped channel the mainstream away from him. American poets might be fascinated by a musical travelogue to neverland, but they hardly would wish to go where earthly objects and linguistic sense are contraband. Poe was interested in finding ways to express *essence* directly; "No ideas, but in things," William Carlos Williams would say, speaking for the majority.

What American poets would like about Poe's ideas would be the urging of the use of language and rhythms organic to the material. Emerson had begun to get at that in "The Poet" (and overlooked Poe's contribution when he dismissed Poe as a jingle-man); Whitman would live by the precept; the Imagists would hammer the idea home in their manifestos; it is arguable that every significant American poet since Poe got the message, from Poe or others, and applied it. That much they have had in common with Poe.

Beyond that, however, Poe's voice has remained eerily disembodied from the preponderance of American poetry, as that voice was disembodied from the physical America of his day and its issues—democracy, reform, industrialization, slavery. Even in a rare poem that touched on American matter—"El Dorado" (1850), a phenomenally disguised poem of the gold rush—the event is severed from the present and moved well to the rear, to the time of "a gallant knight," detached not just from America, but safely from all the earth (Poe could not be too careful), to that place in his imagination free of consumption and blood and betrayal, "Over the Mountains / Of the Moon / Down the Valley of the Shadow."

The critical ambivalence toward Edgar Allan Poe has not really changed since his lifetime. His necromancer ways are transparent, yet his readers are hoodwinked while they watch themselves being hoodwinked. His magnetic power is scarcely deniable and often irresistible. The verdict that James Russell Lowell handed down in *A Fable for Critics* still stands: "There comes Poe, with his raven, like Barnaby Rudge, / Three fifths of him genius and two fifths sheer fudge." Oh, that powerful genius! And oh, that cloying fudge!

· SIX ·

Ralph Waldo Emerson and the Transcendental Poets

> The kingly bard
> Must smite the chords rudely and hard,
> As with hammer or with mace;
> That they may render back
> Artful thunder, which conveys
> Secrets of the solar track,
> Sparks of the supersolar blaze.
>
> —Ralph Waldo Emerson, "Merlin I"

No other theoretician or practitioner of American poetry in the nineteenth century influenced American poetry in the long term—the mainstream of American poetry—nearly to the extent that Ralph Waldo Emerson did. Yes, Bryant helped to foster the dominant romantic mode; and Poe, by his popular example (popular, at least from "The Raven" of 1845 on) and strictures on rhythm and appropriateness of language, made a significant contribution; and Lowell, Longfellow, and others by word and by model would affect the direction of poetry in the United States. Emerson, though, was close to being its polestar. The two greatest American poets of the century, Walt Whitman and Emily Dickinson, would admire his work exceedingly. Dickinson's would be affected mainly by Emerson's worldview, Whitman by that and by Emerson's pronouncements on technique as well. In fact, Whitman would appropriate the whole package of ideas concerning poetry and its relation to life that Emerson wrapped appealingly in his essay

"The Poet" (1844) and proffered in large or small parts in myriad other essays and poems (of which "Merlin" (1847) is but one). Through Whitman, who chose to remake himself in Emerson's image of the ideal, complete American poet (but not in the mold of Emerson himself, a very different shape indeed), and from Whitman through such seminal twentieth-century poets as Ezra Pound (sometimes grudgingly), William Carlos Williams, Theodore Roethke, and Allen Ginsberg, Emerson has continued to light the way beyond any byways that American poets have taken.

Emerson and Poe

Because Emerson and Poe were such close contemporaries (Emerson, born in 1803 was some half a dozen years Poe's senior, though, dying in 1882, he outlived Poe), because they published much of their influential poetry and critical pronouncements in the 1840s, and because they were so artistically similar and yet unlike, it is fascinating and instructive to consider the two poets together for a moment. Emerson's father died when the boy was eight and he grew up in an impoverished family; Poe lost both of his parents at an earlier age, and though he was taken in by the well-to-do Allans for the first unhappy half of his life, poverty would stalk him later, throughout the second, even more somber, half. But then, Emerson was not immune from death. Like Poe, he fell in love with and married a teenager (Ellen Tucker was seventeen and Emerson twenty-four when they met, although they were not married for another two years). She died about a year and a half after their marriage. Death would visit Emerson often, taking his brothers in 1834 and 1836, and his beloved five-year-old son Waldo by his second wife Lidian in 1842. Transcendentalism was his survival mechanism as much as supernal beauty was Poe's.

Both men sought something beyond the materiality of everyday life and were concerned in their work with, in a sense, spirit worlds. The realms for which they yearned were terribly different, however. Poe hankered for a supernal beauty to be attained by escape from earthly pain to a kind of phantom necropolis or fairy wasteland resort where one can bask by scoriac rivers or fetid, vaporous lakes. To Poe, escaping into the shadows of imagination, even an effulgent unreality, was preferable to life as he perceived

it. Emerson quested, too, but his search was for a nondenomi-
national religious ideality, an *external* beauty, inexorably associated
with philosophical truth, rather than Poe's gossamer *supernal* beauty.
His spirit world was an Eastern one of higher reality,[1] which, far
from ignoring the here and now, relishes it as emblem of some
pervasive and benevolent spiritual force and the means to apprehend it.

Nature and Transcendentalism in Emerson vs. Nature in Poe

That difference in the objects that they pursued helps to explain
the difference in their treatments of nature. To Emerson, as to
Edward Taylor and the Puritan forebears whom he revered, the
things and the processes of nature were of primary importance
for their symbolic value; they were messages to be read and
interpreted, the means for the sensitive and open observer to
derive truths about God and His intentions. That much the Reverend Emerson took from the Reverend Taylor and the others
even when Emerson left the pulpit of the Unitarians' Second
Congregational Church in Boston in 1832, left the clergy for good
over a crisis of conscience to become a poet and sage. Taylor had
used nature as evidence of an all-too-stern Old Testament God
for Emerson to accept, and so he more or less abandoned formal
Christianity, but in a basic way Emerson used nature in the same
way as Taylor. Emerson simply redirected the Puritans' querulous
emphasis on a deity who demanded strict ritualistic observance,
an angry God, to an immanent God or Will or Over-Soul. That
is, instead of acquiescing to the Puritan God, Who was, to Emerson,
objectionably antiquated and remote, like Blake and Wordsworth
a little earlier, he elected to search in nature for an immediate
and present God, still very much alive and active in the cosmos
and the affairs of human beings, in short, *immanent.* Since He
moved through nature, nature was the book in which to read His
presence—or *intuit*, really. "Intuit" would be a better word than
"read" because the truths of the universal spirit (which Emerson
variously referred to as the "Over-Soul," the "One," "Unity," the
"Law," and so forth) cannot precisely be read the way one reads,
say, documentary prose or even Scripture (for all its sanctimonious

malleability). They *transcend* cognitive thought—hence the term *Transcendentalism* applied to Emerson and his philosophical associates (including Henry David Thoreau, Bronson Alcott, Jones Very, Margaret Fuller, W. H. Channing, and others).[2] Moral (and religious) truths can only be arrived at by the application of an intuitive understanding of nature and human behavior in it. No intermediary, no church or ritualism is necessary. Every person should be his or her own priest, perhaps his or her own god, through application of sensitive, poetic divination which the Transcendentalists presumed to be present, or at least latent and developable, in everyone. The true poet, among all categories of people, was exemplary in having that capacity innately and best developed. The keys were, as Emerson declared them, nature, where the answers lay, and the courage of self-trust or self-reliance to search out the answers there and not be afraid to know the answers when God conveys them through intuition and conscience. Transcendentalism, in its egocentricity, is an intensely devout, religiously unorthodox romanticism. Poe's romantic conception of nature was poles away from all of that—as far away as "Mount Yaanek / In the realms of the Boreal Pole," in fact. That is partly why Emerson, as perspicacious as he usually was, missed what he did have in common with Poe and dismissed him as a mere "jingle-man." Poe was not troubled by a crisis of conscience as Emerson was, but rather by the familial and material personal crises of a gloomy soap opera. Poe simply transported nature to the domain of imagination. He kept the names of nature because no other language would have been recognizable, and transformed its essence into the dream or nightmare sanctuary removed from the ordeal of his life.

It is important to understand, however, that for all of the differences between Emerson's and Poe's use of nature and the autobiographical forces that motivated them, both had a compulsion to withdraw behind the lines of their own egos—Emerson to what one critic has termed "the imperial self."[3] In filling the need of his audience to find a substitute for received faith that many in America were finding it hard to accept in the 1830s and 1840s, Emerson provided many with

. . . [a] guarantee of their connection with the universe . . . their existential uniqueness. No doubt many found in Emerson simply a fresh and rather titillating way to be good, to announce their ties to right feeling despite their having discarded a creed [i.e., like Emerson himself, revealed, ritualistic Christianity]. But we have reason to believe that many of Emerson's hearers understood and welcomed the tie between themselves and the nature of things because it answered the same emotional need in them that it fulfilled in Emerson himself: *the road to transcendence lay through self-absorption, one had to take possession of the imperium of one's own consciousness* [my italics].[4]

Substitute "retention of sanity" for "transcendence" in the last sentence and the insight readily shifts from Emerson to Poe.

Both Emerson and Poe were faced with the task of constructing an aesthetic that would harness their poetry to their goals—that would account for the formulation of language and structures that could convey their listeners into their special worlds. Poe treated himself to the luxury of advocating a poetic theory that was, in large measure, a description of poems that he had made, so if there is a tight consistency between his theory and practice, that should scarcely come as a shock; hindsight tends to be clear. Emerson's theory of poetry—inextricably entwined with his transcendental worldview and its aim of fusing Self and Other, spirit and nature—evolved later in life and more slowly (one must remember that Emerson was, as artist and thinker, a considerably later starter than Poe). There is not infrequently a disparity between his theory and practice, but then, there was also a good deal of internal conflict between the visionary and practical sides of his character.

Emerson's Poetics

In his most direct commentary on poetics, his 1844 essay "The Poet" (first published in *Essays*, Second Series), which summarized his cogitations on the subject over his highly productive years, especially during the late 1830s, Emerson called for a poet who would not only use the material of new times, and especially of the United States, as the stuff of his poetry (by now a familiar theme in American criticism), but would use, would invent, new bottles to hold that heady new wine. He had learned well from Wordsworth and Coleridge, and sang beyond the voices of the masters. The major thrust of his argument, as far as the development of American poetry is concerned, was this imperative: that the relationship between matter and form should be absolutely organic, with matter necessarily dictating form: "it is not metres, but a metre-making argument that makes a poem," he proclaimed, "—a thought so passionate and alive that like the spirit of a plant or an animal *it has an architecture of its own*" (my italics here emphasize both the importance of the idea and the aptness of its phrasing). The argument, or "content," of a poem is to be so new and spirit-waking that the architectural blueprint for its expression—its form—inheres within it. Arguably, ever after in American poetry, form would subserve matter. It is not that form is of no consequence. Poetry, to Emerson, was obviously not chaos. "The thought and the form are equal in the order of time, but in the order of genesis the thought is prior to the form."

Emerson's conception of the poet is nothing less than visionary. The true poet is "representative"—like other people in kind but different in magnitude in that he or she has fulfilled the potential that is present in everyone for union with the All. "The people fancy they hate poetry, and they are all poets and mystics!" That is why the poet's function is prophetic; the others need to have their intuitive faculty awakened and learn to be self-reliant and trust their insights into the meaning of experience and its relation to the Over-Soul. The "imagination [that] intoxicates the poet [is] not inactive in other men." But more intensely imaginative at the outset, the poet uses symbols, which have "a certain power of emancipation and exhilaration for all men." The poet can make others "dance and run about happily, like children." With their "tropes, fables, oracles and all poetic forms," that is to say, "poets are thus liberating gods." A reader of British Platonists, Emerson sees poets leading the rest of humanity "out of a cave or cellar into the open air." In some ways a spiritual son of Edward Taylor, Emerson is advocating what he would have been banished to the wilderness for in Taylor's time. Worse than an antinomian, the Sage of Concord teaches that the true poet will make a priest of everyone. And to do that, the poet must be what prophets are, "the sayer, the namer," as the best American poets from Emerson and Whitman on have been. How burstingly optimistic Emerson was compared to Poe—compared to almost anyone! "The poet . . . represents beauty [not Poe's airy-fairy beauty but real earthly beauty through which one can attain cosmic understanding and fuse with God]. He is a sovereign, and stands on the centre. For the world is not painted or adorned, but is from the beginning beautiful." Beauty is indeed the informing principle of the world; it is indistinguishable from God:

. . . God has not [merely] made some beautiful things, but Beauty is the creator of the universe. Therefore the poet is not any permissive potentate, but is emperor in his own right. Criticism is infested with a cant of materialism, which assumes that manual skill and activity is the first merit of all men, and disparages such as say and do not, overlooking the fact that some men, namely poets, are natural sayers, sent into the world to the end of expression, and confounds them with those whose province is action but who quit it to imitate the sayers.[5]

Emerson knew perfectly well that a prophet-poet needs language equal to his vision and that the arguments entailed by that vision would determine the shapes of his poems. Science is one means of understanding nature, but understanding in and of itself is certainly not the end of prophecy. The poet as "Namer or Language-maker" must be able to put "eyes and tongue into every dumb and inanimate object," and to do that he or she must use fresh and appropriate language, defining things, identifying their essences, "thereby rejoicing the intellect, which delights in detachment or boundary." It has always been thus. "The poets made all the words," and "though the origin of most of our words is forgotten, each word was at first a stroke of genius, and obtained currency because for the moment it symbolized the world to the first speaker and to the hearer." In other words, there is no variance between Emerson's transcendental epistemology and his poetics.

Emerson was quite right in his plaint toward the end of "The Poet" that "I look in vain for the poet whom I describe"; he could not even find him in his own mirror, and he knew it, although he did, overall, at least approximate his ideal as a poet. *The poet* of Emerson's desires did not yet exist; Walt Whitman was incarnated, but would have to reincarnate himself as a poet. With too little affinity himself for the cross, Emerson had to play John the Baptist, but to his credit, when Whitman showed himself in 1855, Emerson would recognize the stupendous advent that he had annunciated. But meanwhile, in the artistic timidity of the 1840s, Emerson regretted that artifice passed for real art, that there was no poet who could mediate between spirit and substance, even in America, with its boundless potential:

We do not with sufficient plainness or sufficient profoundness address ourselves to life, nor dare we chaunt our own times and social circumstance. . . . Dante's praise is that he dared to write his autobiography in colossal cipher, or into universality. We have yet had no genius in America, with tyrannous eye, which knew the value of our incomparable materials, and saw, in the barbarism and materialism of the times, another carnival of the same gods whose picture he so much admires in Homer; then in the Middle Age; then in Calvinism.

"The Poet," p. 246

The English poets, Emerson's distress continues, have tended to be "wits more than poets, though there have been poets among them." There are "difficulties" even with Milton and Homer, however; "Milton is too literary, and Homer too literal and historical." But Emerson does not despair; as a young and youngish man he seems almost never to have done that. Beginning with the penultimate paragraph of "The Poet," with the direct exhortation to the as-yet-unknown true poet, "Doubt not, O poet, but persist. Say 'It is in me and shall out,' " Emerson's prose becomes rhapsody in one of the most moving passages of musical, poetic prose in all of his frequently musical, poetic prose works. How passionate the irritatingly dispassionate Emerson could wax at important times—almost to galvanize himself to action beyond "saying."

The Function of the Poet

From his essay "The Poet," from other essays and journal entries and such poems as "Saadi" (1847), "Merlin" (1847), "Bacchus" (1847), "Uriel" (1847), and others, a dual task emerges for the poet. The two functions fit perfectly into the broader spectrum of Emerson's thought.[6] Both flow from the poet's position as representative—yet really model—man. In brief, first, he is to show the fusion between substance and spirit, the world of physical experience and the Over-Soul, that was central to Emerson's quest (see, for example "Brahma" [1867] and "Mithridates" [1847]). The job here is not to reconcile differences as much as to show that what appear to be differences are parts of the same All, arcs of the same circle.[7] "The rhyme of the poet," he writes in "Merlin II," must reflect how "Balance-loving Nature / Made all things in pairs," how "Flavor gladly blends with flavor," how "two married sides / in every mortal meet," and "Thoughts come also hand in hand." No things are separate or excluded, the poet must reveal. "Justice is the rhyme of things; Trade and counting use / The self-same tuneful muse." There are no real opposites, he must reflect:

> And Nemesis,
> Who with even matches odd,
> Who athwart space redresses
> The partial wrong,
> Fills the just period,
> And finishes the song.

Part of the poet's mandate to break down what Emerson takes to be a fallacious duality between experience and spirit is to be a "liberating god," as he terms it in the essay "The Poet." The poet is to remove the fetters and untie the blindfold so that everyone can let his spirit soar, not around experience, but through it. Merlin and Saadi (the latter a Persian poet whom Emerson read and admired) are both free, natural men whose energy is natural inspiration. They can free others because they are free. Merlin "mount[s] to paradise / By the stairway of surprise" (Merlin I), while Saadi, in whose speech "Suns rise and set," is he who can "Open innumerable doors . . . [and] Those doors are men."

The second part of the poet's task is to be a national poet, to be at one with the people, taking the material of the nation from them and making of it a great and heroic national poetry for them. Paradoxically, Emerson's purpose here is not at all chauvinistic, but rather the achievement of an intensely spiritual, universal corpus of poetry, rooted in national lore, as he knew that the greatest world poetry, Homer's, say, and Shakespeare's, had always been, but moving outward beyond borders to the timelessness and spacelessness of truth. Shakespeare was his touchstone for the movement from the national to the universal:

The poet needs a ground in popular tradition on which he may work, and which again, may restrain his art within the due temperance. It holds him to the people, supplies a foundation for his edifice, . . . leaves him at leisure and in full strength for the audacities of his imagination.[8]

Thus in "Merlin" Emerson incites the poet to be unfettered by timidity of both form and of substance, to be free, natural, to reflect in his song the bold rhythms of nature, yes, but also "the voice of orators; . . . [and] the din of city arts." He often equaled in practice this plank in his poetic platform. In "Hamatreya" (1847), for instance, he anchors a universal observation concerning mortality and pride of possession in the history of Concord, in its landowners and builders, "Bulkeley, Hunt, Willard, Hosmer, Meriam, Flint," the earth's "boastful boys," who could not "steer their feet / Clear of the grave." The "Ode Inscribed to W. H. Channing" (1847) works from references to American geographical names (Contoocook, Agiochook, New Hampshire, Boston Bay, Bunker Hill) and political offenses ("Harrying Mexico / With rifle and with knife," and "The jackals of the negro-holder") outward to the universality of man's misdeeds ("The Cossack eats Poland, like stolen fruit"), the repetitive nature of evil and stupidity, and the need for individuals to "Live for friendship, live for love," the rottenness of states notwithstanding. The title of "Musketaquid" (1847) is the name that the local native Americans gave to the Concord River; Emerson manages to unite history, place, and fusion with the Transcendental Over-Soul in this poem, too, as the speaker finds along the river the "true liberty / In the glad home plain-dealing Nature gave." Here the speaker becomes the passive receptor of the wood-gods, can hear them murmuring: "Canst thou shine now, then darkle, / And being latent, feel thyself no less?"

And "Concord Hymn" (1847), sung at the completion of the Revolutionary War Battle Monument, 4 July 1837 (the ceremony had been scheduled for the previous July Fourth but had been delayed a year), commemorates the opening battle of that conflict, when "the embattled farmers stood / And fired the shot heard round the world." Yet, fixed though it is in specific human history, the poem is more importantly a dignified hymn to the universal human spirit that urges men to sacrifice to "leave their children free," though in the long run death plays the inescapable equalizer: "The foe long since in silence slept; / Alike the conqueror silent sleeps." Examples of Emerson's adherence to his belief in the poet's need to start with the national and expand to the universal are numerous. In this, as in other respects, Emerson's practice was closer to his theory than criticism has sometimes given him credit for.

Three's a Crowd: Merlin, Saadi, and Israfel

On both sides of the Atlantic the figure of the lyre or Aeolian harp, an instrument that could resonate with the impulses of nature, was a great favorite to romantic poets.[9] In "Israfel" Poe hung one in the breast of that angel, "Whose heart-strings are a lute." There, ensconced as he is in heaven, blessed beyond the tribulations of such mortals as Edgar Allan Poe, no wonder the angel has "the sweetest voice / of all God's creatures." There "Where deep thoughts are a duty" and "Love's a grown-up God" and "the Houri glances are / Imbued with all the beauty / Which we worship in a star," no wonder Israfel casts his gorgeous spell and despises the "unimpassioned song" of a mere mortal poet. In perfectly controlled hypnotic lines, which, presumably, mimic the perfection of Israfel's heart-strumming, Poe yearns (as all his poems yearn for his dream world) to trade places with him. No trick to produce what Israfel creates when one's lyre is in the sky, but if the angel were earthbound, where "flowers are merely— flowers," he might not do "so wildly well" as Poe at singing "A mortal melody." Vastly different are the instruments of Merlin and Saadi, Emerson's embodiments of the ideal poet in two poems in which Emerson's theory and execution of poetry may be prof- itably examined. If Poe's lute of Israfel and technique for playing are distinctly Apollonian, not so Emerson's harp of Merlin or lyre of Saadi. No, these are strictly Dionysian; the secret of their lovely music is their being attuned to undisciplined, natural inspiration. Emerson, after all, is the poet who in "Bacchus" craves the wine of inspirational abandon so that, intoxicated by it, he "May float at pleasure through all natures; / The bird-language rightly spell, / And that which roses say so well." Emerson, after all, is the poet who wrote in his copy of his *Poems* this telling thought from the *Phaedrus:* "The man who is his own master knocks in vain at the door of poetry." Emerson, after all, is the poet who knew very well that he was, at times, awfully decorous for his own liking, a man who could stay at home when many of his Transcendentalist friends tried to live their beliefs at Brook Farm and, when Thoreau experimented with matching deed to word at Walden Pond, a man who deplored slavery but did little enough to act on his condemnation of it, a man who spoke against the Mexican War but chided his friend Thoreau for making even a minimal gesture against the war by refusing to pay a tax and spending a night in the lockup. Aware of that conventional side of his personality, Emerson opted for the unconventional, bold-spirited Merlin as his poetic alter ego. No "jingling serenader's art" (presumably Emerson had his "jingle-man" Poe quite specifically in mind when he imagined Merlin's antithesis here), "Nor tinkle of piano strings" for Merlin in Emerson's poem of that name.[10] Like any truly "kingly bard," he "Must smite the chords rudely and hard, / As with hammer or with mace" to produce the "Artful thunder" of his music, which conveys "Secrets of the solar track / Sparks of the supersolar blaze"—insights into the constitution of creation. Merlin does not strum; he does not pluck the strings; he strikes them with "blows of fate" that resound with nature, with "the forest tone" of "boughs buffet[ing] boughs in the wood" and the "gasp and moan / Of the ice-imprisoned flood"—yes, and because Emerson is the breaker down of barriers, with the "pulse," "voice," "din," "cannonade," "marches," and "prayers" of the human drama. Far from wanting to escape human experience like Poe, Emerson insists upon an intense cognizance of nature and life as the only way to arrive at the All. Saadi, whose words to his own accompaniment "like a storm-wind can bring / Terror and beauty on their wing," owes his success to two traits: he is solitary ("Ever when twain together play, / Shall the harp be dumb"), and he is not tempted by forces external to his own humble self—not by approbation, not by material things. On the latter count, "Saadi" is closely related to such poems as "Hamatreya."

Poe, fleeing the earth, plays his lute with the otherwordly harmony of an Israfel, while Emerson's Merlin, inspired by the cadences of nature and the human drama, "can make the wild blood start / In its mystic springs" with his unrepressed playing; utterly free himself, he sets others free with his uninhibited rhythms. Emerson takes Poe to task in this accolade for Merlin: "He shall not seek to weave, / In weak, unhappy times, / Efficacious rhymes," yet the two poets have in common the conviction that form must subserve and be appropriate to content, and both influence American poetry with that belief.

"Merlin II" certainly complements the first section of the poem, but it is more indirect. Now Merlin is not mentioned directly, and much of the poem turns to upholding Emerson's doctrine of compensation, which holds that "An inevitable dualism bisects nature, so that each thing is a half, and suggests another thing to make it whole; as spirit, matter; . . . yea, nay."[11] This notion, involving the reconciliation of polarities—Emerson takes them to be necessary halves of the same whole and parts of the greater Whole—is absolutely central to his epistemology and explains what sometimes seems to be his trying habit of blithely accepting misadventure or evil as part of the cosmic scheme of things. Compensation is a kind of law of the conservation of everything through interrelatedness (in "The Sphinx" [1847] the merry Sphinx declares, "Who telleth one of my meanings / Is master of all I am."). Here, in "Merlin II," the rhyme of the poet is seen to act as mediator between the items of the pairs of nature, "grooms and brides," "health and age," and so forth. Poetry is the glue that somehow makes the compensatory force work: "The animals are sick with love, / Lovesick with rhyme," and in the working out of the events of the world, "The rhyme of the poet / Modulates the king's affairs." At the end of the poem Emerson suggests that the poet produces something akin to the "Subtle rhymes . . . / Sung by the Sisters as they spin"; the free and naturally inspired poet actually produces a result something like Fate.

Emerson's Prosody: The Poetry as Extension of His Prose

In a letter to his wife-to-be Lydia Jackson (he dubbed her "Lidian" after their marriage, fearing that New England pronunciation would make her "Lidiar Emerson," and, perhaps even worse, would make him "Mr. Remerson")[12] on 1 February 1835, Emerson wrote,

I am a born poet, of a low class without doubt, yet a poet. That is my nature and vocation. My singing, to be sure, is very "husky," and is for the most in prose. Still I am a poet in the sense of a perceiver and dear lover of harmonies that are in the soul and in matter, and especially of the correspondences between these and those. A sunset, a forest, a snowstorm, a certain river-view, are more to me than many friends and do ordinarily divide my day with my books. Wherever I go therefore I guard and study my rambling propensities with a care that is ridiculous to people, but to me is the care of my high calling.

In calling his singing "husky," he led with his chin, giving detractors an opening much as Whitman was to do when he referred to the "barbaric yawp" of his own singing in "Song of Myself." But the word cannot be taken out of the full context of Emerson's self-assessment. He saw himself as representative of his conceptualized poet, who was representative man, or at least he would conform to the ideal as closely as his personality would allow. That meant, specifically, not practicing "the jingling serenader's art" and not being a poet by occupation, but by writing in such a way that substance ("meter making argument") would determine form and by being a "poet"—in the broadest sense of the term—in every facet of his life.

Perhaps more than anyone else Ralph Waldo Emerson is responsible for deemphasizing sound in favor of sense in American poetry—for making poetry, in that respect, less artificial. He would be a poet, one who intuited the correspondences between the physical and the spiritual, on walks in sunsets and forests and snowstorms; he would be a poet when he sat down to compose an essay, a journal entry, or a letter no less than when he sat down to compose a poem. His essay "The Poet" and his poem "The Poet" would be of the same essence, his essay "Compensation" and his poem "Compensation" likewise. And so on through the body of his work, which runs to fourteen volumes (in the edition of 1867 and 1876). There, close to the center, are his poems in Volume 9, comprising the two fairly thin separate volumes that he had published in his lifetime, *Poems* (1847) and *May-Day and Other Pieces* (1867), along with other pieces. That the poems should be among his other works, his prose works, but near the middle, seems fitting. But then again, his poems are not really limited to the space between those two covers. Many of the essays in the other volumes are prefaced by verses, and, in the sense that he meant by "poetry," all the volumes comprise his poetic output. That, surely, is what he had in mind when he confessed to singing in a "husky" voice. All of his writing is rhythmical, gnomic, spirit-expanding, underpinned at its best by images and pithy anecdotes. That is not a proposition that needs to be defended, really, for *random* selections from his work reveal the truth of it. Speaking in a letter to Caroline Sturgis (4 February 1842) of the loss of young Waldo, and mourning, too, his own aloofness, Emerson wrote, "Alas! I chiefly grieve that I cannot grieve; that this fact [his son's death a week earlier] takes no more deep hold than other facts, is as dream-like as they; a lambent flame that will not burn playing on the surface of my river." Finding miracles in nature to replace the biblical ones to which he could no longer subscribe, he wrote in his *Journal* in November 1837 (recorded by Bliss Perry, ed., *The Heart of Emerson's Journals* [Boston and New York: Houghton Mifflin Co., 1926], p. 118):

Who sees a pine-cone, or the turpentine exuding from the tree, or a leaf, the unit of vegetation, fall from its bough, as if it said, "the year is finished," or hears in the quiet, piny glen the chickadee chirping his cheerful note, or walks along the lofty promontory-like ridges, which, like natural causeways, traverse the morass, or gazes upward at the rushing clouds, or downward at a moss or a stone and says to himself, "Miracles have ceased"?

In the essay "Self-Reliance" (1841), he reflects, "Society is a wave. The wave moves onward, but the water of which it is composed does not. The same particle does not rise from the valley to the ridge." There is scarcely any of his prose that cannot be chanted— or practically chanted—with its carefully orchestrated repetitions, balanced phrases, and homey, evocative tropes.

The poems differ from the other writing mainly in their frequent conservatism of form. He was constitutionally unable to be quite the bold tradition-breaker that he called for. There is no denying that. That role would have to wait for the free-verse measures of Whitman, for whom Emerson's admiration would, after a while, be circumscribed by moral, maybe social considerations. *Leaves of Grass* "is a wonderful book," he would say; "I had great hopes for Whitman until he became Bohemian."[13] But Emerson did influence American poetry by example as well as by proclamation; his poems are somewhere between the rigid prosody that was still the rule in the American poetry of his day and the freedom of form that, given the impetus of his blessing, would become dominant in the United States.

In general, his earliest poems are the most metrically regular, with blank verse and heroic couplets two of the common English meters he often used (blank verse, for example, in such poems as "The Summons," "The River," and "Self-Reliance," heroic couplets in "To-day" and "The Rhodora"). It must be said, however, that virtually from the outset, he seldom permitted himself to be a slave to a traditional form. He was capable of varying syllable counts and moving accents about and missing rhymes to rough up established patterns for effect—particularly, as opposed to Poe, to prevent the listener from falling under the spell of the music and failing to focus on the "argument" of the poem. The "Channing Ode" is remarkably loose in form. The blank verse of "Hamatreya" is so irregular that one commentator correctly remarks that its "lines deserve to be called blank verse only because they have an average of ten syllables and do not rhyme."[14] The instances of roughing verse are many, either in whole poems or key passages. The four-stress, loosely octosyllabic lines of "Each and All" (1847) (an important poem to understand Emerson's Transcendental egocentrism as its consciousness moves from the periphery of a bucolic scene at the beginning to the spiritual center at the end, when the speaker "yielded [himself] to the perfect whole") and the alternating four-beat, three-beat hymnal rhythm of "The Humble-Bee" (1847) offer further examples of Emerson's ability to loosen the metrical screws to let his "arguments" move more freely.

How to Locate a Ralph Waldo Emerson

Emerson's readers almost inevitably feel a kinship with the "Frenchies" who hunted the Scarlet Pimpernel: they seek him here, they seek him there, they seek Ralph Waldo everywhere.[15] Is he in Christianity?—not quite. "I like a church; I like a cowl; / I love a prophet of the soul," he admits in "The Problem" (1847), but unable to heft "The burdens of the Bible old," he concludes that "not for all his faith can see / Would I that cowled churchman be." Yet he was the most religious American poet since the Puritans, and his worldview was strongly influenced by the eighteenth-century Swedish Christian mystic Emanuel Swedenborg. Is he in nature?—yes, but not quite. His nature is certainly "more real" than that of Poe; at least it does not smell of the graveyard or beyond. But is somehow less real, more curiously theoretical than that of Thoreau or Melville. It is real all right, but not something in which to get one's hands dirty or feet soaked,[16] any more than evil (which, in such forms as slavery, he most certainly recognized) was something to get involved in. After all, like death—for which he grieved he could not grieve—it was part of God, and so the necessary (and so ultimately benevolent) other half of something good. He embarrasses the nay-sayers, but one is haunted by the thought that in order for his approach to life to work, all the world would have to subscribe to it wholeheartedly, and everyone, like Emerson, would have to look down from so high that distinctions between good and evil lose their outlines and consequence. Only from outer—or inner—space can the difference between the slayer and the slain be eradicated, as he suggests in "Brahma" that it can be.

Is he in his definition of a poet? Ah, there he is, only partially hidden. Unlike Poe, he based his definition less on what he was than on what he longed to be. It is surprising not that there is inconsistency between his theory and practice of poetry, but that there is so little. He is to a large extent the sayer and namer that he said and named; with the soul of a mystical seeing eye, he could scarcely have been otherwise. And if his vision is not in totally new skins, they are far from the old skins, too. Matthew Arnold sensed that Emerson was creating something different, but, because he could not classify it, he could only condemn it as being "not legitimate," by which he meant new and not British.[17] Emerson read the British poets, all the standard ones, past and contemporary; he enjoyed the metaphysicals greatly, particularly Herbert. But his model was more an internal affair than a literary one. Yes, that is where he is. If Emerson is hard to find in the sum total of his thought, which is so liberating that it is kaleidoscopic, he can be found there in his conception of the American poet and in the work of Whitman, whom he called forth as an idea called "The Poet." Emerson said and named American poetry; it sprang from the seed of his words, and so he is in the organic form and prophetic-naming quality of the best American poetry ever after. And finally, no less he is in the powerful grace of his own writing.

Other Transcendentalist Poets

Predictably, since the Transcendentalists' doctrine held that every human being is a poet, all of them wrote poetry (a notion and a habit that scarcely endeared them to the materialistic business and industrial mainstream in the United States, against which they were swimming). And since they had their own journal, *The Dial*, at their disposal, much of their verse, often edited by Emerson, found its way into print there. Some of the group were quite atrocious poets, with not a lot of equipment for composing poems other than conviction—little ear for musicality, little eye for figurative language, little nose for linguistic concentration. Emerson's poems were part of the body of thought that subsumed prose writing as well, but he had ample talent to make poems that stood on their metrical and imaginative feet as poems, many of them fine ones. But the poems of Bronson Alcott (1799–1888), for instance, were, fundamentally, essays in rhyme (he spent his poetic instinct in rapturous prose), and William Ellery Channing (1818–1901), the friend who accompanied Emerson on long, ruminating walks, churned out such awful verse that Thoreau judiciously called it "sublimo-slipshod."[18] He typically turned out such vapid stanzas as the following:

> I rest forever on my way,
> Rolling around the happy sun,
> My children love the sunny day,
> But noon and night to me are one
> ("The Earth," *The Dial*, 4, 64)

> He talks to himself
> Of what he remembers,
> Rakes over spent embers,
> Recoineth past pelf, . . .
> ("An Old Man," *The Dial*, 4, 103)

There was only one Emerson in the crowd, but some of the others could at least outdo Channing; it was not hard. Margaret Fuller (1810–50), a bundle of energy that helped to power the movement, wrote some ebullient lyrics celebrating life and nature that are of mild interest. "A Dialogue" reflects the veiled sexuality that was sometimes a feature of the Transcendentalists' poems, either out of an Adamic innocence or a deliberate intention to sexually liberalize American verse.[19] If they proposed to spice up American literature (the more likely choice, since their naiveté stopped short of blindness), they were in for a disappointment. With the odd mild exception (e.g., Walt Whitman, a shocker in his time), American literature wore white into the twentieth century. In "A Dialogue," though, the bride puts on a shade of red; Dalia entices the Sun (who refuses her, though he loves her, pleading work commitments):

> My cup already doth with light o'errun.
> Descend fair sun;
> I am crimsoned for the bridal hour,
> Come to thy flower.
> ("A Dialogue," *The Dial*, 1, 134)

Ellen Sturgis Hooper (1815–41) and Caroline Sturgis Tappan (1818–88), an Emerson confidante, wrote a variety of lyrics, some of them appreciations of Emerson, a number of others antimaterialistic pieces that were sure to raise the hackles on people increasingly busy running American society's maze for material rewards. "I slept, and dreamed that life was Beauty, / I woke, and found that life was Duty," Hooper lamented. But do not give up on the dream: "Toil on, sad heart, courageously," she incited, "And thou shalt find thy dream to be / A noonday light and truth to thee" (*The Dial*, 1, 123). And the other subversive sister Caroline wanted to know in "Life" (*The Dial*, 1, 195) "Why for work art thou striving / Why seek'st thou for aught?" To the Transcendental mind, the alternative to material endeavor was clear: "To the soul that is living / All things shall be brought." Puritans would have approved of her trust in something beyond herself, but that would not have prevented them from sending her, her sister, Emerson, and all their Transcendentalist cohorts into the desert or the forests for their individualistic spirituality and their aestheticism, which amounted to seeming sloth. Yet the religiosity, the individualism, the conviction-driven aesthetic, and the materialism were all fruits of the seeds that the ideologically complex Puritans had planted in the soil of New England.

For all of their paltry versification, the Transcendentalists had three poets among them, apart from Emerson, who command some attention: Jones Very (1813–80), Christopher Pearse Cranch (1813–92), and Henry David Thoreau (1817–62).

Jones Very

Jones Very is, in the extremity of his self-involvement and isolation, so utterly a romantic poet that he is, paradoxically, on the fringes of American romanticism, yet so burning in his religious ardor that his poems ring of, say the "Meditations" of Edward Taylor, though with an overlay of egocentricity. Emerson approved of Very and his poetry early on; indeed, Emerson volunteered to edit Very's poems (by which, to a great extent, he meant to punctuate them). He recognized in the younger man—Emerson was born in 1803, Very ten years later—one who was in harmony with his Transcendentalist exhortations to abandon oneself to nature in order to intuit Truth and God and their harmony with the world of matter and experience. That is, Very was more fundamentally Christian and receptively Quaker-like than Emerson, more intuitive, and therefore able to practice what Emerson preached somewhat better than Emerson could practice it. When Very's driving force, his religious obsession, cooled in about 1840, so did Emerson and the world at large cool toward him. Very's name was pretty much lost until his resurrection in the mid-twentieth century by Ivor Winters and others. Too romantic for romantics, Victorians, naturalists, and realists alike, a spectral figure among the Transcendentalists, his revival had to await a time when mystical eccentricity was comprehensible, when it was thoroughly acceptable for a man to measure not himself by the world, but the world by himself; and if the man happened to suppose that the resulting measurement was the revelation of God, that was all right, perhaps even arresting to a modern audience so utterly absorbed in materialism that it could tolerate spiritual eccentricity.

It was as a student that Very lapsed into religious ecstasy and had to leave the Harvard Divinity School in 1838. After a month in an asylum, he was released, but ever after he felt himself to be God's amanuensis, not even *interpreting* but *hearing* the words of God and *reporting* them in his poems and in lay sermons that he delivered in Unitarian churches.

His self-defined role as recorder of God's impulses rather than as artist causes Very's poetry to be extremely uneven in quality. In the plainness of his style and his use of nature, as well as in his fervor, he is reminiscent of the seventeenth-century Puritan poets, especially Edward Taylor, though he avoids Taylor's tendency to make a religious connection explicit after the imagery has already done the job. Very works close to the border of the pathetic fallacy, but he often manages to keep shy of it. Both qualities may be found in his 1830 sonnet "The Dead," for example, in which the godless are represented as zombie-like trees which "crowd on crowd . . . walk the earth" but can "mimic life" and must "borrow words for thoughts they cannot feel." But Very's artlessness shows at the end of this poem as it does elsewhere in his poetry, as in the sonnet "Love" (1839), in unnecessarily awkward syntax that does not quite smooth down and leaves the poem with splinters. In the light of God's truth he is blissfully unconcerned with literal truth, and so he often leaves furrows on a reader's brow. Very's approach is rather like that of the primitives in American painting; its naive forms and colorations are attractive, but wanted effects are sometimes unachieved, and there is lapsing into boredom and repetition.

The tediousness about much of Very's work must be admitted, though James Russell Lowell was probably right in asserting in about 1840 that some of Very's sonnets were the best poetry yet published in the United States.[20] His greatest and most charming strength is his frequent capacity to go beyond merely presenting objects in nature as useful and well-drawn images. He actually fuses his being mystically with that of a nonhuman creature (say, a canary or a columbine) in a way that perhaps Emily Dickinson (and Walt Whitman, though Whitman in his very different maximalist manner) could project later in the nineteenth century and that no one could do again as well until Robert Bly, James Wright, and other poets of the mid-twentieth century (e.g., Wright's identification with the bird crying in the elder trees in his poem "The Cold House").

Christopher Pearse Cranch

Christopher Pearse Cranch was as forgettable as any bromidic nineteenth-century American poet until Transcendentalism twanged a chord in him and he became, after Emerson, the outstanding and most direct versifier of Transcendentalist epistemology. "Correspondence" is the most interesting piece among the five that he published in *The Dial* in 1840–41. The form of the poem is so prosy, with its long unrhymed and unrhythmic syllabic lines, and so short on fresh imagery, that only its dominant six-accent pattern and unjustified lines argue for its classification as a poem at all. The piece does, however, contain a series of aphoristic statements of the notion of correspondence that Emerson seems to have gotten from Swedenborg through the nineteenth-century American Swedenborgian Sampson Reed.[21] Here are a few of them: "All things in Nature are beautiful types to the soul that would read them"; "Every object that speaks to the senses was meant for the spirit: / Nature is but a scroll,—God's handwriting thereon"; "When we perceive the light which breaks through the physical symbol, / What exultation is ours! *we* the discovery have made!"; ". . . the lordly sun shine[s] out a type of the Godhead; / Wisdom and Love the beams that stream on a darkened world." Thus does Cranch summarize in his quasi-poem the Transcendentalists' essential bridge between nature, mind, and spirit, for which nature is symbolic.

Considerably better as poems are the pieces that Cranch published decades later in *The Bird and the Bell with Other Poems* (1875), when he had purged much Transcendentalism from his system but retained the wayward instinct to push aestheticism against the no-nonsense current of materialism—that, it should be pointed out, had grown much stronger since the *Dial* poems with the rise of robber barony and industrialism that had been hastened by the Civil War. The poems now were more attractive melodic artifacts, much more traditional in form, but still freshened somewhat with the Transcendentalists' intellectual freedom. In "The Garden," for example, the speaker leans on the "balmy breast" of summer and heeds the gospel of "Repose and Beauty" rather than "how the moralist toils or talks." He doubts the part that the "Pale priest of a thorn-girded church" plays "in this wide breathing universe," and he rejects the soul-inhibiting "Thin prayers and moralisms" of the priest and his kind, concluding: "Better thy cowl befits thy cloister's gloom: / Its shadow blots the garden and its bloom." Thus Cranch easily resolves for himself the conflict between freedom of spirit and inspiration versus ideological rigidity and moralism that Emerson had temporarily settled in "The Problem" ("I like a church; I like a cowl; . . . Yet not for all his faith can see / Would I that cowled churchman be") and then wrestled with for the remainder of his life.

Henry David Thoreau

Henry David Thoreau probably became Emerson's protégé in 1837, the year of his graduation from Harvard, when he tied his poem "Sic Vita" to a bunch of violets and threw them into the window of Lucy Jackson Brown, Emerson's sister-in-law, who was a boarder in the house where Thoreau lived; she called the poem to Emerson's attention. Emerson, as he did from time to time, proved himself to be a better Transcendentalist thinker than a literary critic when he declared that young Thoreau "writes genuine poetry that rarest product of New England wit." His admiration for Thoreau's poetry was, indeed, a factor in Emerson's establishing *The Dial* as the Transcendentalists' voice. "My Henry Thoreau will be a great poet for such a company, and one of these days for all companies." Editor Margaret Fuller was not convinced, but Emerson was not to be denied, and so a number of Thoreau's efforts were published. Thoreau seems to have had a better sense than his mentor about where his own strength lay, for by no later than the middle 1840s, he was himself rightly convinced that as a poet, he was a fine writer of prose.[22]

Like most of the other contributors to *The Dial*, notably Cranch, Thoreau wrote poems that are restatements of Transcendentalist doctrine, though his are sometimes also personal, romantic lyrics. Thus, the central metaphor of "Sic Vita" (later published as "I Am a Parcel of Vain Strivings Tied") is of a bunch of violets (presumably the one that Thoreau loosely tied with straw and shyly conveyed to Emerson's sister-in-law with this poem appended) which sees itself as useless until it intuits that there is a purpose in its existence. Its flowers were plucked and "by a kind hand brought / Alive / To a strange place" so that the "stock thus thinned" can, "by another year," bear "More fruits and fairer flowers" while the narrator-nosegay "droop[s] here"—now aware of nature's scheme and so glad of its destiny.

Thoreau rarely achieves the tightness of imagery of "Sic Vita," but he does often manage a sprightly epigrammatic manner in his poetry that is reminiscent of his prose style. He reprinted some of his *Dial* poems in *A Week on the Concord and Merrimac Rivers* (1849), where they blend nicely with the prose. "Sic Vita," for example, appeared in that prose work some eight years after the poem had been published in *The Dial*, 3, 224–225 (July 1841). Another such poem is "My Books I'd Fain Cast Off, I Cannot Read," first published in *The Dial*, 2, 81–82 (October 1842). Here he echoes the Transcendentalist insistence on limiting the importance of books; one should gain his own insights and write of them. Thoreau muses

> Here while I lie beneath this walnut bough,
> What care I for Greeks or for Troy town,
> If juster battles are enacted now
> Between the ants upon this hummock's crown?
>
> Tell Shakespeare to attend some leisure hour,
> For now I've business with this drop of dew,
> And see you not, the clouds prepare a shower,—
> I'll meet him shortly when the sky is blue.

There are too few passages so delectable in his poetry, however; he chose to channel his poetic instinct into *Walden* and his other magnificent prose works. Probably no one after Emerson ever regretted the choice.

Meanwhile, at about the time Thoreau was coming to realize that his metier was prose, Walt Whitman, the only important American Transcendentalist outside of New England and the only one posterity would honor as a poet, was in Brooklyn beginning to reinvent himself as America's archetypal poet.

· SEVEN ·

Walt Whitman

I teach straying from me, yet who can stray from me?
I follow you whoever you are from the present hour,
My words itch at your ears till you understand them.

I do not say these things for a dollar or to fill up time
while I wait for a boat,
(It is you talking just as much as myself, I act as the
tongue of you,
Tied in your mouth, in mine it begins to be loosen'd.)

If you would understand me go to the heights or water-
shore,
The nearest gnat is an explanation, and a drop or motion
of waves a key,
The maul, the oar, the hand-saw, second my words.

— Walt Whitman, "Song of Myself"
(Sec. 47)

When Emerson dolefully commented in 1844 in "The Poet," "I look in vain for the poet whom I describe," he had reason to lament. Poe may have been undeserving of much of the abuse aimed at him from Frogpondia, but he was the last poet in the world to fit into the mantle of vatic poetry that Emerson tailored. Emerson himself tried it on and realized that he could fill out the general outline reasonably well, but the garment was, overall, too big for him. It dwarfed the members of the Boston and New York poetic establishments. Emily Dickinson was but fourteen years old, and though she would become, with Whitman and Emerson (if one counts him) and Poe (if one counts *him*) one of the two (or three or four) great American poets of the nineteenth century, when she grew into a poetic style, she would not accept Emerson's off the rack, but would borrow some of it to cut her own singularly independent pattern. And while Walter Whitman was twenty-five years old in 1844, Walt Whitman, who would personify Emerson's ideal American poet, was not yet born. Walt Whitman would be a magnificent dybbuk that Walter would create, like an inerrant Dr. Frankenstein, out of the blueprint that Emerson drew. To become Emerson's poet, Whitman would perform a feat of self-reconstruction that may well have no equal in the annals of sanity.[1]

Whitman was born in 1819 near Huntington, Long Island, the second of nine Whitman children (including one who died at birth).[2] He was to know personal tragedy as Poe and Emerson had, and evolve his own psychic strategy for coping with it. Times were seldom good with the family. The baby, Ed, would prove to be retarded; Jesse, the eldest, would be committed to an asylum as violent and die there; Andrew, the third son, would die of tuberculosis and his wife would resort to prostitution; Hannah would make a bad marriage and become an inveterate hypochondriac. George and Mary would be closest to normal, though Walt would be closest to younger brother Jeff, who was cursed with a nervous, depressive personality. These were the brood of Louisa Whitman and Walter Whitman, a farmer who turned to carpentry for a living as economic circumstances dictated. When the boy Walter Whitman was five, in 1824, those circumstances dictated that the family move to Brooklyn, where the senior Whitman could ply his trade in a building boom. The family roved from house to house as the father would build one, move the family into it, and then attempt, with little success, to make a profit on its sale. Young Walter ended his formal schooling at eleven, becoming an office boy for a lawyer and for a physician. At twelve he got a job in a newspaper printing office where he even saw an occasional piece of his own in print, an important event for him, for like many another American poet and fiction writer, from Bryant to Hemingway and beyond, he would spend much of his life (for him, the next two decades) as a newspaperman.

In his mid-teens, when the Whitmans returned to Long Island he stayed behind and continued to contribute (probably conventional little poems) to newspapers, now to the respected *New York*

Mirror in Manhattan. He was employed for a time as a journeyman printer, then in 1835 went back to the family on Long Island, where amid conflicts with his father, whose temper was not calmed by his large son's balking at farm labor, young Whitman taught at a number of schools, worked for an Island newspaper, even broke off his teaching to attempt his own paper. There are three significant trends to be distilled from the biographical outline of his early years: a restless independence; an affinity for language and a resultant determination to write; and a relentless curiosity that led him to devour books from a very early age. His independence manifested itself in clashes with his father, frequent changing of jobs, and a liking for quiet, solitary reflection, often on long solo walks (many older people ascribed his unusual behavior to plain indolence).

In the beginning he read romantic novels, especially those of Scott (his semiliterate mother could see to it that he absorbed the rhythms and substance of the Bible from the outset); later, he took advantage of press passes to cultural events, including the theater, in Brooklyn and Manhattan. He even attended and participated in debating societies. Much used to be made of Whitman's lack of education. He was uneducated the way gathering rain clouds lack moisture. He was sufficiently educated to work on various newspapers in the 1840s and become the twenty-two-year-old editor of a daily in Manhattan, the *Aurora* (a post from which he was dismissed for that old charge of laziness), and then, briefly, of the *Evening Tatler*. Between editorships of the *Aurora* and the *Brooklyn Eagle*, a good newspaper until it folded in modern times, he covered New York's theater and music scene for the *Long Island Star*, and once on the job at the *Eagle*, he kept the literary beat for himself, reviewing books by Goethe, Thomas Carlyle, Emerson and the other Transcendentalists. He was a great afficionado of opera, later claiming that he could not have written *Leaves of Grass* without opera.

When he was fired from the *Eagle* in 1848, it was for political reasons, certainly not for want of sufficient education. Long a participant in the Democratic party (for example, as a speaker at rallies) and something of a jingoist in his advocacy of American expansionism (the expansion of American territory would spread the light of American democracy, he supposed), he was now let go because of his stand on the crucial Free Soil issue. He vehemently opposed the addition of more land to slave territory. While Poe was yearning for his dark nebula and Emerson was finding ways to merge with the Over-Soul, Whitman, in his twenties, was not above getting sullied in the political trenches and bars of New York.

The word *hack* is the first adjective that leaps to mind to describe Whitman's writing before *Leaves of Grass*. He published a temperance novel, *Franklin Evans, or the Inebriate*, in a special number of the *New World*; it is a poor specimen of a wretched genre, a portrait of sordid Southern life found in magazines, replete with sexually corrupt slave owners and sexually corrupt slave women, which he painted half a dozen years before he actually visited the South for a newspaper job in 1848, after he had lost his job with the *Eagle*.

His short fiction, for which he was better known in the 1840s than he was for his unremarkable, conventional poems, was generally no better, though he could turn a good epigrammatic phrase and seems to have had compassion for his characters. He generally wrote sentimental and highly derivative stories of home life, although they are distinctive in one particular that is fascinating in view of Whitman's home life and especially his stormy relationship with his father. His stories often involve the homecoming—in one way or another—of a son who has been missing; there may be warmth in the return, but, through some grotesque twist, the parents are made to suffer.[3] As good an example as any is "Wild Frank's Return," printed in the *Democratic Review* in 1841, in which Frank has run away from a home where "Oh, it had been a sad mistake of the farmer [i.e., Frank's overbearing father] that he did not teach his children to love one another." After seeing something of the world, the son decides to return to hearth, home, and daddy—even anticipates the reunion with pleasure, but alas, the best-laid plans of mice and prodigals. . . . On the way home a storm frightens Frank's horse, which drags him to death and deposits him at the door before the waiting parents. In the temperance tale "Reuben's Last Wish," published in the *Washingtonian* of 21 May 1842, a drunken father is the cause of one son's leaving home forever and of the son Reuben's becoming an invalid. Reuben's slow death tears the father's heart out (as the innocent mother must watch), and with his last breath, the boy thrusts a temperance pledge at him.

Strangely, in a way, while Whitman's father may have been somewhat severe, was sometimes quick to temper, bibulous, and surely inept as a businessman, there is no evidence to show that, apart from not especially unusual flare-ups of temper between them, relations between father and son were worse than many. Yet the father in "There Was a Child Went Forth," would be described as "strong, self-sufficient, manly, mean, anger'd, unjust, / The blow, the quick loud word." Whatever troubled Whitman about his father was deep seated, just as the perfect mother figure of his work bears minimal resemblance to his mother Louisa Whitman, who apparently could be a nagger. More and more from the late 1840s to the death of Walter Whitman, Sr. in 1855 after years of illness, Whitman became head of the household; when the father died, the event seems not to have caused much of a ripple on the surface of the family.

While Whitman's fiction and early poetry was primarily hackwork, his editorial writing was often much better than that. For the most part, he espoused Jacksonian democracy and the Democratic party line. He sometimes expressed them in the standard bombastic terms of American journalism in the forties, but his flair for language and his bold honesty frequently made for powerful journalism. Like Horace Greeley,[4] Whitman was a progressive and a reformer who believed that newspapers were instruments of pedagogy, and as much as any editor, he took himself to be not only the teacher of the public, but its voice. That view of himself would square nicely with his self-concept as Emerson's representative poet who was representative man.

Moreover, Whitman's editorials reflected two traits that would be important to his poetry that were beyond Emerson's practice, if not his theory: an urban consciousness, even bravado (Whitman was urban man much more than country lad, Emerson very much the Sage of village Concord, not of Boston), and a true and thorough embracing of democracy (Jeffersonian in its emphasis on individual potential and minimal government) even in its most unseemly behavior by the most unsavory elements of the populace. Whitman had a streak of compassion that even showed up in his attitude toward the characters in his turgid temperance novel. His people were the folk, the bus drivers he met on his lonely wanderings through the city and the firemen to whom he would later introduce a discomfited Emerson on one of the New Englander's trips to New York, as much as they were fellow writers and the cultured people he met at the theater. And politics could be— should be—turbulent, even violent, at times: "all the excitement and strife, even—are *good* to behold. They evince that the *people act;* they are the discipline of the young giant, getting his maturer strength," he declared in an *Eagle* editorial, calling the person who is alarmed by political turmoil a "popinjay priest of the mummery of the past." He allowed, "We know well enough that the working of Democracy is not always justifiable in every trivial point," but to him democracy had to have "great winds that purify the air," and could those winds "be condemned because a tree is prostrated here and there in their course?"

Whitman's Early Poetry

Only with acute hindsight can themes or traits be found in the early prose that hint at the phenomenon *Leaves of Grass;* even less is there the faintest clue in Whitman's poems through the early 1840s that the sensibility that wrote them could be transmuted into the intellect that was to begin publishing in 1855 the great work of his life. Random samples from *The Early Poems and the Fiction* volume[5] of his *Collected Writings* clearly illustrate the point. "The Inca's Daughter," for example, from the *Long Island Democrat,* 5 May 1840, is an utterly conventional piece, in galloping quatrains, about a nobly savage young Inca woman who, brought before her captors, "the dark-brow'd sons of Spain," produces a poisoned arrow from her robe and shows the white men how to die well, saying:

> "Now, paleface see! the Indian girl
> Can teach thee how to bravely die:
> Hail spirits of my kindred slain,
> A sister ghost is nigh!"

Two weeks later, the same newspaper printed his "The Love That Is Hereafter," a plaint, standard in form and content, of a lonely twenty-one-year-old. The last stanza reads as follows:

> For vainly through this world below
> We seek affection. Nought but wo [sic]

> Is with our earthly journey wove;
> And so the heart must look above,
>   Or die in dull despair.

He was to be allowed his wish for a "second life," not in the sense he intended in the poem, but with his rebirth as a fine poet and, eventually, mountainous fame and affection. Later that year, on 27 October, the *Long Island Democrat* published one of Whitman's chauvinistic verses, "The Columbian's Song," similar to the flag-waving poems that were epidemic in American newspapers and magazines. "O, My soul is drunk with joy, / And my inmost heart is glad, / To think my country's star will not / Through endless ages fade," Whitman banged out on the drum. The poem bears Whitman's personal stamp only in its celebration of the country's brawling brand of democracy; all will come together in strength when danger threatens, "Though parties sometimes rage, / And faction rears its form."[6]

Through those early years he used numerous traditional verse forms in his political, philosophical, parodic, and other poems, in a competent but surely undistinguished way. About as close as he came to prosodic freedom, and that was not close at all, was in the modestly irregular blank verse of the introduction and conclusion of a routine expression of thwarted youthful ambition, in the piece called "Ambition," published in *Brother Jonathan*, 19 January 1842.

The Birth of the Poet

On 5 March 1842 something of extreme consequence happened to the journalist born Walter Whitman, Jr. Ralph Waldo Emerson, the popular lecturer, whose first group of published essays was well known, came to New York to deliver a series of lectures, and young Whitman, then editor of the *Aurora*, went to hear him at the Society Library. The talk was "Nature and the Powers of the Poet" (which Emerson was to revise as "The Poet" for publication in his next collection of essays in 1844). Emerson's aesthetic views need not be repeated here; suffice it to say that that must have been the occasion when Emerson brought the simmering Whitman to the boil, or at least tossed a lot of wood on his fire. Whitman, in the afterglow of the event, said two days later in the *Aurora* that Emerson's lecture had been "one of the richest and most beautiful compositions, both for its matter and style, we have heard anywhere, at any time."[7] Why would Whitman not have been impressed, galvanized? He must have recognized himself in Emerson's description of the poet as "Yankee born," in touch not with nature alone but with humanity at all levels: "He is in the forest walks, . . . He visits without fear the factory, the railroad, and the wharf." Furthermore Emerson's notion of the poet as prophet and teacher squared beautifully with the didactic role Whitman had written for himself as editorialist, Democratic speechifier, temperance fiction writer, and poet of the paltry early poems. He heard the great man say, "When he lifts his great voice, men gather to him and forget all that is past, and then his words are to the hearers, pictures of all history; and immediately the tools of their bench, and the riches of their useful arts, and the laws they live under, seem to them weapons of romance."[8] One can almost feel Whitman stirring in the audience, thinking "That's me. When do I begin?"

Emerson did not re-create Whitman; Whitman did. After the publication of *Leaves of Grass* in 1855, Whitman would call the older man his "master," but then Whitman was big enough to acknowledge the older man's great influence (later on in his life he would back away from the concession, as Emerson's enthusiasm for his accomplishment waned), and, anyway, he was not above being either hyperbolic or self-serving. Emerson tapped strains in Whitman that had been largely dormant; Whitman responded to harmonies and tonalities in Emerson that were very close to his own[9]—some of which Whitman had never quite realized. And resonating to them, Walt Whitman emerged from the cocoon of Walter Whitman. He began to fill his journalist's notebooks—for artistic purposes, close equivalents of Emerson's journals—with sympathetic observations of human behavior, many of which would form the bases of the things that he would "name" and "say" as the embodiment of Emerson's prophetic yet representative man-poet. The earliest extant notebook from 1847[10] (or, more exactly, from between 1847 and 1854), shows that in the years following his attendance at Emerson's lecture on "Nature and the Powers of the Poet," Whitman, who had long kept notebooks as an observant journalist, began to rehearse, mainly in private, largely in prose, the wholly new kind of American poetic utterance that would be sprung on the public in 1855 in *Leaves of Grass*.

Generally speaking, the crucial thing that Emerson seems to have shown him is the critical, transcendental importance of the Self and how to discover and express it. A few poems that Whitman published during the years of transition, such as "The House of Friends" (*New York Tribune*, 14 June 1850), clearly anticipate the pulsing free verse of the gestating book. There are even some lists in them, prototypes of one of his frequent devices in the volume, but the central, universal "I" into which his experiment with Self would develop is not quite present in them, even when he uses the first person singular. "Look well to your own eye, Massachusetts— / " he enumerates in the political protest poem "The House of Friends," "Yours, New-York and Pennsylvania; / —I would say yours, too, Michigan"; he tells Virginia not to blush for being a "mother of slaves" because she "might have borne deeper slaves— / Doughfaces, Crawlers, Lice of Humanity— / Terrific, screamers of Freedom." The poem "Blood-Money," first printed in the *New York Tribune* Supplement of 22 March 1850 (wrongly dated 1843), almost certainly as a fusillade aimed at Daniel Webster for a speech promoting the Fugitive Slave Law, is a way station between Whitman's earlier traditional verse and the "thought rhythm"[11] that characterizes *Leaves of Grass*. His fine biblical parallelism was developing, and the free verse lines of the piece do run on, but Whitman was trying out "phrasal or clausal units"; he had not yet felicitously subjugated sound to sense.

Ideas, of course, and sometimes passages, lines, phrases found their way from the notebooks into the poems of *Leaves of Grass*, though usually after much astute revision, for Whitman was a careful, indefatigable reviser with an acute instinct for what was needed for improvement. Alone among the poems composed by 1850, "Resurgemus" from the *New York Tribune* of 21 June 1850 was included in the original *Leaves of Grass* as the eighth of its twelve poems (its substantial revision, including a new title, "Europe and the 72ᵈ and 73ᵈ Years of These States," came between the 1855 and 1860 editions). Even more than "The House of Friends" and "Blood-Money," "Resurgemus" demonstrates what came to be known as Whitman's mature poetic style. Here is "the emphatic parallelism and contrast, and the freedom of the rhythmic line, characteristic of his great poems of 1855 and later," as one editor summarizes; here is "his unconcern for the syllabic formalism and metrical regularity of traditional verse"; now he depends "on the rhythm of the accented syllables in a loosely iambic-anapestic line. . . ."[12]

And so Whitman remade himself as a poet and into a poet in his search for and assertion of his universal Self, his cosmic eye. Nothing was lost to him in the Emersonian Transcendentalist merging of external world with the soul that he determined to make representative—family, friends, and acquaintances (the notebooks list many names of tantalizingly unidentifiable people among those who have been identified), American folks he met and places he saw on his travels wherever he went (he was fascinated with Boston, though toward the end of his life, it would ban his book), literature, numbers, philosophy, theater, music (especially opera), science. He was enthralled by phrenology and fixated on matters of health but led the cheer for biology, geology, virtually all the science and technology he could soak up. The phenomena of America's culture and speech and the events of her history, all of creation were his materials. Conceivably as religious a figure as ever picked up a pen in the New World, he would often be accused of unreligion by the narrow-minded who could not begin to fathom the depth of his vision; that is one of the great paradoxes of his life.

The "Twoness" of Whitman

Emerson is not the only half of the mentor-disciple pair of Emerson and Whitman who is hard to pin down. So is Whitman, though in a different way. Where the difficulty in tracing the "real" Emerson basically stems from the sometime discrepancy between his theory and practice, the problem with Whitman is caused by the "twoness"[13] of his personality. "Here is the baffling, often irritating source of Whitman's temperament: that he was a hack and yet was also America's most original poet. Time and again, in his journalism, in his attempts at fiction, even in *Leaves of Grass* (especially the plodding programmatic poems he filled his books out with)," notes a recent incisive Whitman critic, "he sank to the lowest level of popular taste with a homey directness that is not without charm. . . . His 'twoness' was apparently integral and fertile." There is an irony here: In the problem is

Whitman's strength. Emerson had one part of the "twoness," the structured literary genius. The other, the spirit that could commune with and rouse the common man, that could make the representative man-poet, Emerson called for but could not be, though he liked to think he could. Whitman had both parts of the "twoness" in plenty. He was an infinitely more careful, cultured craftsman than his free-verse, apparently free-swinging great bear hugs of poems reveal—a deception that is at the core of his genius. The two halves nourished each other; the self conscious artist (and he gave new meaning to that term "*Self*-conscious") created him as "Walt Whitman, an American, one of the roughs, a Kosmos, / Disorderly fleshy and sensual. . . . eating, drinking and breeding" ("Song of Myself," Sec. 24) and gave him meticulously articulated expression. And the artist believed what he wrote about that great companion of the open road, that tireless procreator in thought, and became him—at least did the things, or most of them, that that omnipresent democratic "I" would have done. He hobnobbed with the common folk and named them and said democracy until the two parts of the "twoness," which in almost all other poets, including Emerson, were finally incompatible, were integrated with astonishing completeness in a single human being—two personae fused in one person.

The Emerson Legacy: Preface to *Leaves of Grass*

By 1855, Whitman had long since absorbed the elements of Emerson's conception of the ideal poet, had used them in the remaking of his own image (down to his mode of casual workingman's dress) and had become that image, had put himself through a long, almost unprecedented introverted apprenticeship, and was ready to publicize his new matter and means of utterance. Unable to find a publisher who would acquiesce in his literary-philosophical coup, on (or close to) July Fourth of that year, to underscore the Americanness of the book and his own independence, he published the twelve poems of the first *Leaves of Grass* himself.

The prose preface to the 1855 edition is married to the poems both thematically and rhythmically, presenting a microcosm of the world of the poems. No one familiar with Emerson's ideal or prose style can be much surprised by the preface; but for its euphoric expansiveness, it is wholly Emersonian. "America" is Whitman's first word in the essay, and it points toward a culmination of all that crowing in the American poetry of the eighteenth and early nineteenth century about "the future glory of America." For Whitman, the glory, the future are here and now—or at least within immediate grasp—in America. "America does not repel the past," he begins, but America does recognize that its "opinions and manners and literature" best served the past and must now give way to a new artistic, political, social order. And that order, exemplary for the rest of the world, is to be established in the United States because "The Americans of all nations at any time upon the earth have probably the fullest poetical nature. The United States themselves," he indeed proclaims, "are essentially the greatest poem." The nation's genius is not expressed through its leaders, "but always most in the common people," in the characteristics of the common folk—in "their manners, speech, dress, friendships," in "their deathless attachment to freedom," even in "the fierceness of their roused resentment" (an echo of his past approval of the turbulence of American politics).

There is no distinction for Whitman, any more than theoretically for Emerson, between life and art. The lives and traits of the people "too are unrhymed poetry." America needs only the right representative man-poet to transform it into "unrhymed poetry. It awaits the gigantic and generous treatment worthy of it," he declares, and, of course, that is exactly the work that he is about in the poems and here in the Preface, where he names a litany of American geographical places and features, flora, fauna, groups of people, industry, science, and the bad as well as the good ("slavery and the tremulous spreading of hands to protect it, and the stern opposition to it which shall never cease till it ceases or the speaking of tongues and the moving of lips cease").

To express all of that, the poet will sing in a way that is "transcendant and new . . . indirect and not direct or descriptive or epic." He is to be somewhat like Shelley's "unacknowledged legislator," but Whitman's will, presumably, be acknowledged; the great democrat is to be "the arbiter of the diverse . . . the equalizer of his age and land." Whitman's prose in describing the ideal poet—that is, in describing his own intentions and method—has no less cryptic, aphoristic power than Emerson's. "He is no arguer . . . he is judgment," Whitman elegantly expounds: "He sees eternity less like a play with a prologue and denouement. . . . he sees eternity in men and women . . . he does not see men and women as dreams or dots." Whitman's "poet hardly knows pettiness or triviality." Like Emerson's poet, he fuses everything with the All. "If he breathes into any thing that was before thought small it dilates with the grandeur and life of the universe. He is a seer . . . he is individual . . . he is complete in himself." As representative man, he is no better than anyone else, "only he sees it and they do not." But he teaches the people until they are prophets like him. When they learn to see, no priests will be needed; "prophets en masse shall take their place." A supremely self-reliant soul, "he does not stop for any regulation . . . he is the president of regulation."

Whitman took more political action than Emerson. He helped runaway slaves, publicly fought the Free Soil issue, and so on, while Emerson's action was generally confined to the pages of his works. But like Emerson, he may seem, at times, to be infuriatingly blind to evil in any form. Yet both men were keenly aware of maleficence, tyranny, of corruption of body and soul in all of its forms, and, far from ignoring it, believed that by folding it into a Transcendentalist view, it could be seen as part of a beneficent whole in which badness is compensated for by goodness. The understanding of that (through the auspices of the vatic poet) would so improve the human spirit that wickedness would diminish and disappear. Men and women are equal; science and poetry love each other; "The spirit receives from the body just as much as it gives to the body." In the Preface he delivers his own shining sermon on the mount: "This is what you shall do: Love the earth and sun and the animals, despise riches, give alms to everyone that asks, stand up for the stupid and crazy, . . . hate tyrants, argue not concerning God." He goes on at length, urging his people to "dismiss whatever insults your own soul"; "to reexamine all you have been told at school or church or in any book"; to realize that "your very flesh shall be a great poem"— in words, yes, but in the body itself and its every motion. We are tempted to shout to Whitman's audience, to ourselves: Listen to him, but remember to keep your hands on your wallet in a crowd, lock your car doors, and go to the poll to keep the most porcine of the swine out of office next Election Day. But the intensity of Whitman's vision and language may be overwhelming; he shames us into sharing it.

His poetics, like Emerson's, are inseparable from the revelation. The poet "shall go directly to the creation. His trust shall master the trust of everything he touches . . . and shall master all attachment. The known universe has one complete lover and that is the greatest poet." Some of the essentials of the ideal poet's craft are a bit less abstruse, however. His attitude toward the necessity of "not metres," but a "metre-making argument" is that of Emerson; "The poetic quality," as Whitman puts it in the Preface, "is not marshalled in rhyme or uniformity of abstract addresses to things nor in melancholy complaints or good precepts, but is the life of these and much else and is in the soul. . . . Who troubles himself about his ornaments or fluency is lost." In a famous passage Whitman asserts, "The art of art, the glory of expression and the sunshine of the light of letters is simplicity. Nothing is better than simplicity . . . to speak in literature with the perfect rectitude and insouciance of the movements of animals and the unimpeachableness of the sentiment of trees in the woods and grass by the roadside is the flawless triumph of art." Later in the work he insists, "The great poets are also to be known by the absence in them of tricks and by the justification of perfect personal candor. . . . How beautiful is candor!" The candor is, naturally, to be couched in English, for that "language befriends the grand American expression"; "it is," he says, "brawny enough and limber and full enough," this English that "is the powerful language of resistance . . . the dialect of common sense. It is the speech of the proud and melancholy races and of all who aspire." He knows the job that English will have to do to attach all things in the world to each other and to the All, and he considers it worthy of the task: "It is the medium that shall well nigh express the nigh inexpressible."

The preface to the 1855 *Leaves of Grass* is a fundamentally American document with a promise of the universality that Emerson wanted the ideal poet to attain eventually. In another preface, that to the 1876 edition, Whitman would write that he wanted to produce after *Leaves of Grass*, with its "songs of the body and existence," another "equally needed volume, based on the convictions of perpetuity and conservation which, enveloping all precedents, make the unseen soul govern absolutely at last." He never got to do that because he made *Leaves of Grass* the occupation of his life, constantly revising and augmenting it. But perhaps Emerson, who may have distanced himself from Whitman out of disappointment that Whitman did not produce such a second book,[14] and even Whitman himself missed the point; *Leaves of Grass* becomes as symbolic of the universal human condition as any second book could have, just as the character he created as the representative "I" of the book comes to signify every man and woman.

The Emerson Legacy: "Song of Myself"

Emerson's ideas, adapted to Whitman's purpose and genius, informed all of Whitman's poems as well as his theory of poetry. A point-by-point enumeration of those ideas[15] (any list of them must be somewhat arbitrary because they are fluid and flow into each other) as they were reflected in Whitman's most representative poem "Song of Myself" is paradigmatic.

1. Emerson's notion of the ideal poet as representative man: Whitman loses no time in establishing the idea. His opening chant of the long poem, "I celebrate myself, and sing myself, And what I assume you shall assume," is calculated to merge or equate the reader's consciousness with that of the visionary singer. He failed to get many readers, who took the pronouncement to be merely lunatic braggadocio, to concede his representativeness (closely associated with the principle of identification with all people and matter in creation), but the motif repeats through much of "Song of Myself." From the carefully posed photograph of the casual workingman's companion, through the poem and beyond, Whitman presents his common-folk credentials. He loafs in the grass (sec. 1 and 33); walks among all, sees all, loves all spiritually and sometimes physically, even *is* all (e.g., "the hounded slave" and "mash'd fireman," sec. 33); feels degraded by the degradation of any person (sec. 24); takes part in all the activities of American life (sec. 33); is the father and companion of travelers ("Shoulder your duds dear son, and I will mine," sec. 46).

Moreover, to deepen the sense of equality with the reader, Whitman has a trick (he has tricks despite his injunction against them in the Preface), unprecedented and unequaled in poetry, of forging an intimacy with the reader by verbally nudging him in the ribs and speaking as if to him alone. Thus, for example, he closes section 19 on this note of extraordinary personal revelation: "This hour I tell things in confidence, / I might not tell everybody, but I will tell you." In section 51 he actually looks up from the page at the reader and exchanges innermost confidences with him: "Listener up there! What have you to confide to me? / Look in my face while I snuff the sidle of evening, / (Talk honestly, for no one else hears you, and I stay only a minute longer)." The most striking example of the illusion of intimacy that the representative poet achieves with his coequal reader appears in "Crossing Brooklyn Ferry," the splendid symbolic voyage through time and space that Whitman added to *Leaves of Grass* in the 1856 edition as "Sun-Down Poem" (he gave the poem its present title in the 1860 edition): "Just as you stand and lean on the rail, yet hurry with the swift current, I stood yet was hurried," he reminds his reader, drawing him close. In the ways that matter, they are as one; referring to sailors and boats and buildings visible from the ferry he confides (in sec. 4) that "These and all else were to me the same as they are to you. . . ." And in section 7 he comes even nearer: "Closer yet I approach you, / What thought you have of me now, I had as much of you— / . . . Who knows, for all the distance, but I am as good as looking at you now, for all you cannot see me?"

2.   Emerson's notion of man's divinity: Whitman asks in section 20 of the 1855 version of "Song of Myself," "Shall I pray? Shall I venerate and be ceremonious" when he "find[s] no sweeter fat than sticks to my own bones. / . . . To me the converging objects of the universe perpetually flow"; "I know I am deathless," he declares. There are many such passages aimed at asserting human divinity. As powerful as any is this one from section 24: "Divine am I inside and out, and I make holy whatever I touch or am touch'd from; / The scent of these arm-pits is aroma finer than prayer. / This head is more than churches or bibles, or creeds." Regarding himself as representative of a divine species in an intricately interconnected and benign universe makes Whitman

radiantly optimistic in nearly every line of "Song of Myself." He is impatient only with the "trippers and askers" who surround him, those who are recalcitrant in their acceptance of his epiphany.

3. Emerson's notion of the vatic function of the ideal poet: the idea is pervasive in "Song of Myself" (as well as through much of Whitman's work). He is the prophet of the personal religion that has at its heart a recognition of the divinity of humankind and the interrelationship of everything, and of everything to the All. Though he sees himself as the wild Old Testament prophet speaking a new tongue (e.g., in sec. 52 he is like the spotted hawk: "I too am not a bit tamed, I too am untranslatable"; he is also like a comet: "I depart as air, I shake my white locks at the runaway sun, / I effuse my flesh in eddies and drift it in lacy jags."), he rejects the Judeo-Christian religious tradition, among all others. "Magnifying and applying" he comes in section 41, "Outbidding at the start the old cautious hucksters," that is, the prophets of other religions who failed to perceive the divine nature of man and even of the lowest creatures. At times religions may have come close, but "The bull and the beetle [Egyptian deities, among others, were] never worshipped half enough." In section 42 Whitman even has the vocal equipment of a prophet: "A call in the midst of the crowd, / My own voice, orotund sweeping and final."

4. Emerson's notion of the ideal poet as a kind of filter for the divine processes of the great Brahman force: Whitman uses this idea most obviously in section 24 of "Song of Myself," stating specifically, "Through me the afflatus surging and surging, through me the current and index." Through him are filtered not the divine spirit in the abstract, but such earthy manifestations of it as "many long dumb voices, / Voices of the interminable generations of slaves, / . . . of thieves and dwarfs," and even the rights of "Fog in the air and beetles rolling balls of dung."

5. Emerson's notion of the ideal poet as the great democrat: Whitman's commonplace family and working-class friends and his training as a journalist and Democratic party operative were excellent preparation for his self-assertion as the poet of egalitarianism. Even more, his open temperament drove him to like and trust people of all classes and categories and to undermine values

of status—economic, political, intellectual—and property. At the same time, he promulgated alternative, humanistic values—love, including sexuality, and the inestimable value of all persons and things equally in the oneness of the universe. "Have you reckon'd a thousand acres much? Have you reckon'd the earth much?" he demands to know (sec. 2); "Have you felt so proud to get at the meaning of poems?" All one need do to avoid perishing in meaningless materiality is to heed this prophet: "Stop this day and night with me," he says, to possess "the origin of all poems . . . the good of the earth and sun." And finally, seeing first through him, everyone will be able to filter the cosmic essence through and for himself. Thus Whitman also echoes Emerson's notion of ultimate self-reliance.

He often aims to break down the oppositions upon which the English language is made to turn—body and soul, man and woman, birth and death ("it is just as lucky to die [as to be born], and I know it," he says in sec. 7), all contrarieties. His very word, "a word of the modern," is "the word En-Masse" (sec. 23 of the deathbed edition).

Closely allied to his role as poet of democracy is his posture as "The Great Camerado" (sec. 45), the comrade and companion, with a bedfellow sleeping at his side, replacing the bridegroom in the bridal bed. He is the father, too, the brother, and the teacher of athletes, at one with all he loves and teaches.

In part at least, the basis of his commitment to democracy is his belief that ultimate fusion with the All is the only kind of distinction that means anything. "Have you outstript the rest?" he demands in section 21; "Are you the President? / It is a trifle, they will more than arrive there every one, and still pass on."

6. Emerson's notion of the ideal poet as a "scientist": Whitman extols science as useful to, though different from, his art of prophetic poetry. Not in the least incompatible with art, science is to be cheered: "Hurrah for positive science! long live exact demonstration! / . . . this the . . . chemist, . . . / This is the geologist, . . . and this is a mathematician. / Gentlemen, to you the first honors always!" Whitman too humbly concedes. Then through a tidy metaphor he hints at how he uses science as an entryway: "Your facts are useful, and yet they are not my dwelling. / I but enter by them to an area of my dwelling" (sec. 23). In fact, science,

about which he was endlessly curious, subtly helps to form a good deal of his vision; for instance, four years before the publication of Darwin's *Origin of Species* (1859), Whitman, sensitive to the breeze of evolution already blowing through Western thought, pictured himself as the end product of trillions of years of evolution guided by the magnificent pantheistic force that is at the center of his and Emerson's thought. "I waited unseen and always," he recounts, / "And slept . . . through the lethargic mist, / And took my time . . . and took no hurt from the fetid carbon." Before his mother bore him "Monstrous sauroids transported . . . [his embryo] in their mouths and deposited it with care" (sec. 44).

7. Emerson's caution against the domination of the past: Whitman shares Emerson's attitude—due respect for the past but not a veneration of it. Past and present is one of the sets of opposites that he shatters, for in the measureless size and possibility of cosmic oneness the distinction evaporates. "Creeds and schools in abeyance, / " he says in section 1, "Retiring back a while sufficed at what they are, but never forgotton. / I harbor for good or bad, I permit to speak at every hazard, / Nature without check with original energy." It is not that there is anything a priori wrong with the past. It is that every man and woman coming to apprehend transcendental trust must, as self-priest, reassess the world and its taught values and formulate a new, personal set of values. The approach is very brash, very pragmatic, very New World, very American. Values of the past may be admissible, but if they are, it is because they are reconsidered and found to be right, not because they have been historically acceptable. "You shall no longer take things at second or third hand, nor look through the eyes of the dead, nor feed on the spectres in books, / " Whitman cries (sec. 2); "You shall not look through my eyes either, nor take things from me, / You shall listen to all sides and filter them from yourself." He aims to spread not a system but an intuitive religion—a way of knowing and so of living, based on love, decency, and common sense. Those forces are timeless: "These are the thoughts of all men in all ages and lands, they are not original with me" (sec. 17). The very symbolism of his title, *Leaves of Grass*, suggests commonality of time and place and feeling as well as the obvious growth and vitality. "This," he says, referring to "the thoughts of all men in all ages and lands, "is grass that

grows wherever the land is and the water is; / This is the common air that bathes the globe."

Another of Whitman's tricks, the substitution of an archaic Indian name like "Paumanok" for the contemporary English one, "Long Island," or of the Greek letter *k* for the English *c* (especially in "Kosmos"), is designed to eradicate the past-present opposition in a way that does not arouse undue reverence for the past.

8.   Emerson's idea of organic form (which Emerson really appropriated from Coleridge): As Melville and Thoreau groped toward organic form in prose, Whitman reinvented poetic form, deriving it from what he had to say. He developed his characteristic free-verse long lines, with their strongly rhythmic repetitions and parallelisms, precisely because that is the pattern that inhered in his vision. He would have insisted on the reverse of Marshall McLuhan's popular observation on the medium and the message; for Whitman, the message was the medium. To him, to see was to prophesy—to prophesy in the only language and form that were possible. "Speech is the twin of my vision, it is unequal to measure itself, / " he explains in section 25; "It provokes me forever, / It says sarcastically, / *Walt you contain enough, why don't you let it out then?*" Even further, to prophesy, to utter, was to see: "My voice goes after what my eyes cannot reach, / With the twirl of my tongue I encompass worlds and volumes of worlds." Whitman gave his detractors a useful weapon in section 52 when he boasted, "I sound my barbaric yawp over the roofs of the world," but those who turned the phrase against him tended to be unready to recognize as poetry anything that violated their hidebound conceptions of poetic form, poetic language, and poetic worldview. By "barbaric yawp" Whitman meant nothing less than the *natural, innate* language and form that he chanted as the most exactly appropriate expression of his transcendental perception.

9.   Emerson's notion that there should be no restrictions on subject matter: Whitman, of course, with his swaggering unconstraint, carried this idea, among others, considerably further than Emerson did in his own work. And sex, essentially absent in Emerson, is the subject to which Whitman most obviously applied Emerson's license. Whitman said in the 1855 Preface that the greatest poet takes his audience "with firm sure grasp into live regions previously unattained." He meant it. Never before in

American literature had there been such openly sensual treatment of sexuality, and not until well into the twentieth century would such overt sexuality reappear. He used it to seduce the reader into acquiescence to his spiritual program. Approaching the reader closer and closer in "Crossing Brooklyn Ferry," he finally "fuses into" "the woman or man that looks in my face"; he "pours [his] meaning into you" (sec. 8). But as much as his innovative form—probably more—Whitman's sensuality created a barrier between him and contemporary critics and between him and the American public he wanted desperately to gather into his embrace. In his day as in ours, the natural habitat of prurience is in the small mind of its hunter.

He was sensitive to the value of shock—his hyperbole was principally designed for it—but he did not use sex primarily to titillate. Among the distinctions that he dissolved was that between spiritual and physical love; they were not morally equal as much as they were the same. That included all of the practices of physical love, for he intuited that sex is a natural, motivating human force and a means of human expression. It is not dirty. The dirt is apart from sexuality. "Clean and vigorous children are jetted and conceived," he says in the Preface, "only in those communities where the models of natural forms are public every day." "Song of Myself" is full of clean and vigorous jettings. In section 3 he sings, "Urge and urge and urge, / Always the procreant urge of the world. / Out of the dimness opposite equals advance, always substance and increase, always sex. . . ." Every human organ, he insists, is "hearty and clean, / Not an inch nor a particle of an inch is vile," and he rejoices that a "hugging and loving bedfellow sleeps at . . . [his] side."

Section 5 contains one of the poem's most sensual celebrations of physical love, as Whitman causes the beauty of sex to resonate in the beauty of language. He recalls "How you settled your head athwart my hips and gently turn'd over upon me, / And parted my shirt from my bosom-bone, and plunged your tongue to my bare-stript heart, / And reach'd till you felt my beard, and reach'd till you felt my feet." Section 11, too, transforms an ecstasy of universal love, into physical love, here in the gorgeously delicate physical fantasy of a woman spying on twenty-eight young men bathing nude. She moves among them unseen, passing her hand over them as they float. "their white bellies bulge to the sun, they do not know who seizes fast to them, / They do not know who puffs and declines with pendant and bending arch." One might naively think that the sheer beauty and power of the expression and the reflection of cosmic love would have over-whelmed objection. It did not. For many, it still does not.

Whitman's use of sex comprises more than such direct descriptions of human sexual encounters. When the portrayals are direct, the sex acts are both sex acts and metaphors of the divine love that is the glue of cosmic oneness. Additionally, though, he often uses sex in a figurative way to convey the orgasmic intensity of his union with the universe. So in Section 21, one of the passages of "Song of Myself" that soars into exquisite lyricism, he expresses the intensity of his communion with night in sexual terms: "Press close bare-bosom'd night—press close magnetic nourishing night! / Night of south winds—night of the large few stars! / Still nodding night—mad naked summer night!" And the sea, too, in Section 22 becomes a metaphorical sexual partner, as he gives himself to the sea, undresses, and urges, ". . . hurry me out of sight of the land, / Cushion me soft, rock me in billowy drowse, / Dash me with amorous wet, I can repay you."

10. Emerson's notion that America is the stuff of poetry: Whitman's adaptation of the idea is everywhere evident in "Song of Myself" and throughout *Leaves of Grass*. He not only uses the people, places, history (e.g., the Battle of Coleto in the Texas Revolution and the massacre of the Texas prisoners at Goliad, magnificently in sec. 34), and current events (e.g., the Civil War and death of Lincoln) like no poet before him, he articulates them in a language and cadence that is exclusively American. No one but an American could have written *Leaves of Grass*. In his catalogues, for example, of American occupational and regional types (sec. 16), he accommodates another Emersonian idea to his own use, that unadorned words may be poetry and that as "namer" the poet is entitled to use them as such.

The Poetry after 1855

All told, Walt Whitman published ten versions of his magnum opus *Leaves of Grass* at the following irregular intervals: 1855, 1856, 1860, 1867, 1871, 1876, 1881 (the second Boston edition dated 1881–82), 1882 (published in Philadelphia after the second Boston edition had been declared immoral by the Society for the Suppression of Vice), 1888, 1892 (the "deathbed" or "authorized" edition that Whitman gave to the care of his friends and executors, Horace Traubel, R. M. Bucke, and Thomas B. Harned). He would add individual poems and whole clusters of poems (e.g., he added the "Drum Taps" section after it and *Sequel to Drum Taps* had been separately released); he would revise poems, often several times and radically over the book's printing history, and change the order of the poems. From the slim dozen poems of the 1855 edition the work grew vastly to the 384 poems of the deathbed edition. Not only is the change in size obviously perceptible over time, but so, more subtly, are changes in feeling. The Civil War poems, for example, introduce a somber note to his song that is not present in the unfettered ebullience of the first edition. In general, over the years, while generally retaining his optimism, the poems tended to move in the direction of greater control.

Among the nearly four hundred poems and passages of poems that Whitman made by the end, are "a thousand of brick" to use Thoreau's metaphor,[16]—scattered ones, chipped and fractured ones, half-baked ones—that mar the view of wonders that he prepared his audience to see from "upon a hill or in the midst of a plain." But the wonders are wonderful. *Leaves of Grass* is surely without serious competition as the most influential volume of poetry ever published by an American, and is arguably among the most important expressions of a quintessentially American spirit (or of the way Americans like to conceive of that spirit when they are feeling psychically free). The pulsating, primal sexuality of the "Enfans d'Adam" and "Calamus" sections (added in 1860) is an artistic as well as a cultural and moral coup. "Crossing Brooklyn Ferry" (added as "Sun-Down Poem" in 1856) uses water and the blaze of sunset to destroy the conception of space and time as obstacles to universal brotherhood and oneness. "Out of the Cradle Endlessly Rocking" (added as "A Word Out of the Sea" in 1860) may be the most beautiful and remarkable poem of artistic birth ever composed; do even Proust or Joyce approach it in prose? The *Drum-Taps* pieces, with their sharp vignettes and fatherly sympathy, are among the most sensitive war poems of not merely the Civil War, but of any war.

They, like some of the sexual passages in "Song of Myself," "Enfans d'Adam," "Calamus," and other poems and clusters, gave Whitman an outlet for his androgynous impulses. There is evidence that he may have acted out his homosexual tendencies with Peter Doyle and other male friends and acquaintances. He certainly did, for instance, lovingly preserve a lock of Doyle's hair among his effects. What is clear from poems and letters is that he had such proclivities and that the poems enabled him to give vent to the pressures sanely in a culture in which they were strictly taboo.

"When Lilacs Last in the Dooryard Bloom'd" (first printed as an appendix to the *Drum-Taps* volume) is simply among the best half dozen or so elegies in the English language, as Whitman uses the death and funeral of Lincoln to attune his feelings concerning death to an understanding of the cosmos. Like a master composer of symphonic music, he weaves the symbolic motifs of lilacs, warbling bird, star, pines, and funeral train through the poem until he pulls them together in a brilliant life-affirming coda in the sixteenth and final section.

The "Lilacs" poem brings up a facet of Whitman's art that is sometimes overlooked. The poet did not so totally divorce himself from the traditions of English-language poetry[17] as he chose to lead people to believe. Mainly well camouflaged, the poem contains virtually all of the elements of the classical elegy, from invocation to reconciliation. Further, a number of his poems, not just the other (and unjustly more popular) elegiac poem on Lincoln's death, "O Captain! My Captain!" (also first printed in *Drum-Taps*), use more or less regular rhyme: when he felt that the creative occasion called for rhyme, he could use it well and unobtrusively. "Song of the Broad Axe" (probably written in 1856), the first part of "By Blue Ontario's Shore" (the rhymed opening was added to the 1856 poem in 1867), "The Singer in Prison" (written in 1869), and "Ethiopia Saluting the Colors" (1871), for example, all have regular rhyme patterns—some, like "Song of the Broad Axe," contain quite intricate internal rhyme. A number of poems, too, including "Pioneers! O Pioneers!" (1856), "Old War Dreams" (1865–66), "Gods" (1870), and "Eidolons" (1876) contain more-or-less regular traditional metrical lines and stanzaic divisions. Like Picasso, Whitman understood the value of being able to draw horses that looked like horses before he made them look like dominoes.

Prose Work

Walt Whitman published two important books of prose after he was fifty years of age, *Democratic Vistas* in 1870 (though dated 1871) and *Specimen Days and Collect* in 1882–83. The first is an American cultural study of some consequence, comprising three essays, "Democracy" and "Personalism," both published earlier in *Galaxy* magazine, and "Literature," which that journal rejected. If close reading of the poems is not enough to do it, *Democratic Vistas* gives the lie to any sense that Whitman was a Pollyanna. It is, of course, in the long run optimistic, but it upbraids America for having so far violated—for example, because of the corruption of her ward-heeling politics—its opportunity to fulfill its boundless democratic promise.

The second, *Specimen Days*, by Whitman's own account (in a letter of 8 October 1882 to a member of the *Boston Daily Herald* staff), "is a great jumble . . . an autobiography after its sort . . . the gathering up, and formulation, and putting in identity of the wayward itemizings, memoranda, and personal notes of fifty years, under modern and American conditions." It was, he said correctly, "a good deal helter-skelter but I am sure a certain sort of orbic compaction and oneness" (in *Walt Whitman: The Correspondence, Vol. III: 1876–1885*, ed. Edwin Haviland Miller [New York: New York University Press, 1964], 308). The diary entries concerning the war and Abraham Lincoln are among the most sensitive and vivid of the period.

Of great interest, too, naturally, are Whitman's judgments of contemporary American poets in *Specimen Days*. His perspicacity and generosity of spirit, even in assessing poets as different from him as his favorite Bohemian watering hole, Pfaff's Bar, was from a Boston gentlemen's club, is evident. He regards Poe with the kind of ambivalence many have felt. Poe, he says, "probably belongs among the electric lights of imaginative literature, brilliant and dazzling, but with no heat." Whitman quotes from a piece that he placed in the *Washington Star* of 16 November 1875, on the occasion of Poe's reburial in Baltimore: " 'For a long while, . . . I had a distaste for Poe's writings. I wanted, and still want for poetry, the clear sun shining, . . . not delirium . . . with always the background of the eternal moralities.' " But Poe's magic got to him, he confesses: "Poe's genius has yet conquer'd a special recognition for itself, and I . . . have come to fully admit it, and appreciate it and him."

In *Specimen Days* Whitman pays homage to four other contemporaries as well, three of them surprisingly. "I can't imagine any better luck befalling these States for a poetical beginning and initiation than has come from Emerson, Longfellow, Bryant, and Whittier." To him, of course, Emerson "stands unmistakably at the head . . . for his sweet, vital-tasting melody, rhym'd philosophy, and poems as amber-clear as the honey of the wild bees he loves to sing." One would expect the conventionality of form and morality of the other three to have irked Whitman, but he is eclectic in his taste and openhanded in his praise. After putting Emerson first, he has trouble ranking the others, but they have all contributed. Longfellow, with "rich color, graceful forms and incidents—all that makes life beautiful and love refined"—has competed with "the singers of Europe on their own ground, and, with one exception [probably Tennyson, a favorite of Whitman], [has produced] better and finer work than that of any of them." Bryant's nature poems succeeded in "pulsing the first interior verse-throbs of a mighty world" and through "poems, or passages of poems, touching the highest universal truths, enthusiasms, duties— morals as grim and eternal, if not as stormy and fateful, as anything in Aeschylus." That from Whitman! As for Whittier, in him "lives the zeal, the moral energy, that founded New England—the splendid rectitude and ardor of Luther, Milton, George Fox—I must not, dare not, say the willfulness and narrowness—though doubtless the world needs now, and always will need, almost above all, just such narrowness and willfulness." This tribute, too, from Whitman, who was undeniably as willful as they come, but broad enough to contain multitudes! Could he have written it a quarter of a century earlier, before the Civil War, the assassination of his beloved Lincoln, the gilding of America, the death of his mother, almost two decades of poor health (including his paralytic illness of 1873)? Did he need a measure of external constriction to counterbalance his own internal infinite breadth?

Whitman's Reputation and Influence

The intrusion of Whitman's voice into the serenity of nineteenth-century American culture was so jarring that the controversy over

Leaves of Grass began immediately and continued until well into the twentieth century. From one side came cascades of rotting fruit and dollops of vitriol. Typical of that critical genre was an anonymous review in the *Cincinnati Daily Commercial* of 1 January 1860,[18] occasioned by the printing of "Out of the Cradle Endlessly Rocking" in the *Saturday Press*, a respected literary weekly; to the reviewer, the *Press* is "a gentle garden . . . [into which] that unclean cub of the wilderness, Walt Whitman has been suffered to intrude, trampling with his vulgar and profane hoofs among the delicate flowers . . . and soiling . . . [it] with lines of stupid and meaningless twaddle." That is the kind part of the review; it goes on: "He has undertaken to be an artist without learning the first principle of art, and has presumed to put forth 'poems' without possessing a spark of the poetic faculty." Whitman "affects swagger" and represents his "vulgar impertinence" as "originality." In *Leaves of Grass*, as in the new poem, "All that is beautiful and sacred in love was dragged down to the brutal plane of animal passion" by the awful creature who "revel[s] in language fit only for the lips of the Priapus." The reviewer claims to have searched the book for redeeming value, but he has found only "drivel," a work "destitute of all the elements which are commonly desiderated in poetical composition; it has neither rhythm nor melody, rhyme nor reason, metre nor sense." And so forth. The review is interesting not because it is particularly rabid, but because it is unexceptional. It articulates the grounds for the general run of attacks—no civilized sexual restraint, no reign on Whitman's bragging, no traditional poetic patterning, no sense. The reviewer was in good company. Matthew Arnold said in a letter dated 16 September 1866 to W. D. O'Connor: "while you think it is . . . [Whitman's] highest merit that he is so unlike anyone else, to me this seems to be his demerit." A review in the London *Critic* of 1 April 1856[19] also captured the sense of outrage on both sides of the Atlantic very nicely: "Walt Whitman is as unacquainted with art, as a hog is with mathematics. His poems—we must call them so for convenience—. . . resemble nothing so much as the war-cry of the Red Indians." The offended Briton raised the most pertinent question of the moment: "Is it possible that the most prudish nation in the world will adopt a poet whose indecencies stink in the nostrils?"

There were those who hoped so. The defenders were fewer and less vehement than the crucifiers, but they rallied to the new call, led by a voluble reviewer who placed three unsigned reviews of *Leaves of Grass* in various outlets. In the *Brooklyn Daily Times* of 29 September 1855,[20] he affirmed Whitman's genius as that of "A rude child of the people!—no imitation—no foreigner—but a growth and idiom of America." He proclaimed that Whitman was "the begetter of a new offspring out of literature, taking with easy nonchalance the chances of its present reception, and, through all misunderstandings and distrusts, the chances of its future reputation." He seemed to understand the nature and purpose of Whitman's controversial egotism very well: "Other poets celebrate great victories, personages, romances, wars, loves, passions," and so on, but "This poet celebrates natural propensities in himself; and that is the way he celebrates all. He comes to no conclusions," but to taste his work is like tasting the fruit of the tree in the Garden; the taste is "never to be erased again." The anonymous reviewer should have crystal-clear insight into what Whitman was about, for he was Walt Whitman exercising his penchant for self-advertising.

To Emerson's surprise—though not entirely to his pleasure—he also used Emerson's delight in the volume to serve his own interest. Whitman had sent Emerson a review copy of the 1855 *Leaves of Grass*, and Emerson immediately recognized in it the work of the unknown great American transcendental poet he had heralded a decade and more earlier. It was a recognition that Emerson shared with other Transcendentalists, Bronson Alcott, for example, who became Whitman's friend, and Thoreau, who exclaimed in his 7 December 1856 letter to Harrison Blake,[21] "Though rude and sometimes ineffectual, it is a great primitive poem—an alarm or trumpet note ringing through the American camp. Wonderfully like the Orientals, too, considering that when I asked him if he had read them, he answered, 'No: tell me about them.'" On 21 July 1855, soon after receiving the book, Emerson wrote a private letter to Whitman saying "I find it the most extraordinary piece of wit and wisdom that America has yet contributed. . . . I find incomparable things said incomparably well, as they must be. . . . I greet you at the beginning of a great career, which yet must have had a long foreground somewhere for such a start." On reading *Leaves of Grass*, the Sage of Concord must have felt somewhat the way Dr. Frankenstein felt on first seeing the humanoid move his limbs and stand. "I rubbed my eyes a little," Emerson wrote, "to see if this sunbeam were no illusion." He must have rubbed his eyes again a year later when the 1856 edition came out and he discovered that Whitman, without Emerson's permission or knowledge, had appropriated his name and the encomium "I greet you at the beginning of a great career" and stamped them on the spine of the book.

One of the paradoxes of Whitman's life is that his wish to become the poet of the American people has never really come true; he has been too avant-garde for the democratic En-Masse in the twentieth century, as he was in the nineteenth. But to finish the answer to the anonymous reviewer's question in the London *Critic*, by early in the twentieth century Walt Whitman had become the poet of at least the poets and intellectuals of what that reviewer had called "the most prudish nation in the world"—at times grudgingly. With all of his display of Old World erudition, Pound eventually came to him "as a grown child / Who has had a pighead father," and he invited "commerce between us," admitting that "Mentally, I am a Walt Whitman who has learned to wear a collar and a dress shirt (although at times inimical to both)."[22] Pound and Amy Lowell and the Imagists knew what they owed Whitman (and, through him, Emerson) for their rejection of metronomic prosody and insistence on the right to any subject matter. Through Whitman directly, or from the Imagists, or from other poets who derive from him, all important American poetry of the twentieth century owes much to him, almost everything: all of the "naming" and "saying," William Carlos Williams's understanding of the relationship between poetry and the American language, Williams's variable foot and the Black Mountain poet's breath group as they develop from Whitman's long line, the freedom of confessional poets to confess, of experimental poets to experiment. A list of poets affected by Whitman in America would be virtually endless: Carl Sandburg and Edgar Lee Masters and Hart Crane and William Carlos Williams and Allen Ginsberg and Charles Olson and Robert Creeley and Lawrence Ferlinghetti, and all those with obvious lineage; Ezra Pound and T. S. Eliot and Denise Levertov and Sylvia Plath and Wallace Stevens and John Berryman, and the host less obviously indebted to him. The compilation is, in fact, nearly identical to a total list of American poets and groups of poets. And not just Americans. Poets everywhere have absorbed Whitman—Russian poets, like Mayakovski and Soviet ones through the translations of Chukovski, for example; Lorca and European poets; Jorge Luis Borges and the Latin Americans. The influential Borges said, "For a time, I thought of Whitman not only as a great poet, but as the *only* poet. In fact, I thought that all poets the world over had been merely leading up to Whitman until 1855, and that not to imitate him was a proof of ignorance."[23]

In the beginning were the Puritans and in Whitman's time were still the Puritans, or their heirs unto the eighth generation. Whitman came along, and goaded by what Emerson stirred in his temperament, he got different answers for a new time to the old Puritan questions—cosmic questions of the nature of the universe and humanity's place in it, and human questions of responsibility to what is external and internal to the individual human consciousness. The frame of reference of his contemporary audience tended to be too Puritan-controlled for him to bend it, but he would not stop chanting his vision with a music that was indistinguishable from it. And in the end Whitman had much of what he wanted; in reshaping himself and his poetry he reshaped American poetry and perhaps even the culture a little, insofar as the poetry expresses it.

Whitman understood that man did not have to be idealized; a person has only to be self-reliant, to live up to his potential, to achieve harmony with the benignant universe. Like his friend the painter Thomas Eakins, he used the real people and things of his nation, very much of this world, to show how little distance there was between reality and ideality. That light reflected in his vision accounts for the inevitable, if slow, growth of his recognition. Like Eakins, he revealed the romantic nobility that he knew was present in the reality of the nineteenth century. The naming was no casual naming; it was seeing the real heroically. Walt Whitman was a romantic realist, and romantic realism was to become the dominant mode of American poetry.

• *Notes and References* •

Chapter One

1. Perry Miller, *The American Puritans: Their Prose and Poetry* (Garden City, N.Y.: Doubleday & Co., 1956), 171.

2. For a full and excellent discussion of Ramist logic in Puritan New England, see Perry Miller, *The New England Mind from Colony to Province* (Cambridge, Mass.: Harvard University Press, 1939). Walter J. Ong, S. J., *Ramus: Method, and the Decay of Dialogue* (Cambridge, Mass.: Harvard University Press, 1958), presents a full explanation and critical appraisal of Ramism. Both are cited by Roy Harvey Pearce, *The Continuity of American Poetry* (Princeton, N.J.: Princeton University Press, 1961), 31–35, in his examination of the effect of Ramist logic on Puritan poetry.

3. Samuel Sewall, *Diary of Samuel Sewall 1674–1729, Vol. I* (New York: Arno Press, 1972), 460.

4. In Miller, *American Puritans*, 277. The ninth meditation, which follows immediately, is quoted from the same source.

5. Quoted by Jane Donahue Eberwein, ed., *Early American Poetry: Selections from Bradstreet, Taylor, Dwight, Freneau, and Bryant* (Madison and London: University of Wisconsin Press, 1978), 91. Subsequent quotations from Eberwein's edition will be cited in the text by the page numbers in parentheses.

6. Quoted by Harrison T. Meserole, ed., *Seventeenth-Century American Poetry* (New York: W. W. Norton & Co., 1968), xxvii. Meserole's introduction to his fine sampling of seventeenth-century American poetry is commendable. Subsequent quotations from this edition will be cited in the text by the page numbers in parentheses.

7. The discussion here of literary influences on Puritan poets owes much to Meserole's discussion of the subject in his introduction to *Seventeenth-Century American Poetry*.

8. In Eberwein, *Early American Poetry*, 14. A footnote remarks that Nathaniel Ward, a New England author who was an older contemporary of Anne Bradstreet, "saluted" her as " 'a right Du Bartas girl.' "

9. Meserole speaks of this in *Seventeenth-Century American Poetry*, xxix. He also points out that all extant records of Puritan library holdings,

Notes and References

including those of Harvard, list copies of Quarles's work, and that poems as different as those of Bradstreet, Taylor, and Wigglesworth reflect the influence of Quarles.

10. Ola E. Winslow's *American Broadside Verse* (New Haven, Conn.: Yale University Press, 1930) shows something of the range and often the doggerel quality of the broadsides.

11. It is certainly not lost to the view of Sacvan Bercovitch. Taking off, in a sense, from the place where the important work of Perry Miller ended, his *The American Jeremiad* (Madison and London: University of Wisconsin Press, 1978), persuasively follows the spoor of the jeremiad through American culture.

12. Quoted by Ellman Crasnow and Philip Haffenden, "New Founde Land," in *Introduction to American Studies*, eds. Malcolm Bradbury and Howard Temperley (London and New York: Longman, 1981), 32.

13. John Berryman, *Homage to Mistress Bradstreet* (New York: Farrar, Straus & Giroux, 1956), stanza 2.

14. Berryman, *Homage*, stanza 2 of the opening exordium.

15. Eberwein, *Early American Poetry*, 46–54. The citations of Anne Bradstreet's poems in this section are all from Eberwein.

16. Figures attesting to the extraordinary popularity of *The Day of Doom* are cited by Meserole, *Seventeenth-Century American Poetry*, 37, and by Pearce, *Continuity of American Poetry*, 21. The latter offers a figure of one copy for every twenty people. Meserole, incidentally, observes that a hundred years after the appearance of the poem's first edition, "New England grandmothers and grandfathers were able still to recite *The Day of Doom* from memory."

17. In *The Poetical Works of Edward Taylor, Edited with an Introduction and Notes by Thomas H. Johnson* (Princeton, N.J.: Princeton University Press, 1966), 146–47.

18. Cotton Mather, *Manuductio ad Ministerium*, in *American Poetry and Poetics: Poems and Critical Documents from the Puritans to Robert Frost*, ed. Daniel G. Hoffman (Garden City, N.Y.: Doubleday & Co., 1962), 253.

19. Ibid., 254–55.

20. Ibid., 256.

21. In *Colonial American Poetry*, ed. Kenneth Silverman (New York and London: Hafner Publishing Co., 1968), 354. Silverman cites Frederick B. Tolles, *Quakers and the Atlantic Culture* (New York: Macmillan, 1960), 80.

Chapter Two

1. Alexander Pope, "Essay on Man," *Alexander Pope: Selected Poetry & Prose*, edited with an introduction by William K. Wimsatt, Jr. (New

York, Chicago, San Francisco, Toronto, London: Holt, Rinehart and Winston, 1964), 137.

2. Memorandum from the *Letter-Book* of Samuel Sewall, in Silverman, *Colonial American Poetry,* 201. Further excerpts from Silverman will be cited in the text with page numbers in parentheses.

3. Noted by Silverman in "Later New England Verse," *Colonial American Poetry,* 207.

4. Winslow, *American Broadside Verse,* 65.

5. Quoted by Pearce, *Continuity of American Poetry,* 55.

6. Ibid., 55–56, quoted from Constance Rourke, *The Roots of American Culture* (New York: Harcourt, Brace & World, 1942), 3; Pearce notes that he has not been able to track down the original in Franklin.

7. Both observations are cited by Silverman, *Colonial American Poetry,* 130. The first is from *New-England Courant,* 5 November 1772, n.p., the second from *New-England Courant,* 5 August 1723, n.p.

8. Benjamin Franklin, *The Papers of Benjamin Franklin,* ed. Leonard W. Labaree (New Haven, 1959), 1:259, quoted by Silverman, *Colonial American Poetry,* 356.

9. Smith's interesting biography has been told by Albert F. Gegenheimer, *William Smith: Educator and Churchman (1727–1803)* (Philadelphia: University of Pennsylvania Press, 1943).

10. Horace Wemyss Smith, *Life and Correspondence of the Reverend William Smith, D.D.* (Philadelphia: S. A. George, 1879), 341, quoted by Silverman, *Colonial American Poetry,* 359.

11. William Smith, "The College of Mirania," *The Works of William Smith, D.D.* (Philadelphia: Hugh Maxwell and William Frye, 1803), 1:192–93, cited by Silverman, *Colonial American Poetry,* 358.

12. Ibid., 187–88, cited by Silverman, ibid.

13. William Smith, "Copy of Verses, Addressed to *The Gentlemen of the House of Representatives,*" *Some Thoughts on Education* (New York: J. Parker, 1752), 19–36, in Silverman, *Colonial American Poetry,* 380–86.

14. Noted by Silverman, *Colonial American Poetry,* 359–60.

15. The ensuing discussion of Southern colonial verse is heavily based on Kenneth Silverman's excellent "Southern Verse," in *Colonial American Poetry,* 257–67.

16. Arthur M. Schlesinger, "A Note on Songs as Patriotic Propaganda 1765–1776," *William and Mary Quarterly,* 3d ser., 11 (1954): 80–81. Quoted by Silverman, *Colonial American Poetry,* 265.

17. Silverman, *Colonial American Poetry,* 260–61, derived from Thomas Jefferson Wertenbaker, *The Shaping of Colonial Virginia* (reprint, New York: Russell & Russell, Inc., 1958), 2:136.

18. Pattie Cowell, *Women Poets in Pre-Revolutionary America, 1650–1775, An Anthology* (Troy, N.Y.: Whitston Publishing Co., 1981). The discussion

of colonial women poets owes much to Cowell's introduction and head-notes to the poets. References to women's poems in this section of the text are from Cowell's anthology and are cited in the text.

19. John Woodbridge, "Epistle to the Reader," *The Works of Anne Bradstreet in Prose and Verse*, ed. John H. Ellis (New York: Peter Smith, 1932), 84. Quoted by Cowell, *Women Poets*, 11.

20. John Winthrop, *The History of New England from 1630–1649*, ed. James Savage (Boston: Little, Brown & Co., 1853), 2:265–266. Quoted by Cowell, *Women Poets*, 8.

21. Thomas Parker, *The Copy of a Letter Written by Mr. Thomas Parker . . . to His Sister, Mrs. Elizabeth Avery . . . Touching Sundry Opinions by Her Professed and Maintained, November 22, 1649* (London: John Field, 1650), 13. Quoted by Cowell, *Women Poets*, 8.

22. Sarah Wentworth Morton, *Ouâbi: Or the Virtues of Nature. An Indian Tale* (Boston: Thomas & Andrews, 1790), viii. Quoted by Cowell, *Women Poets*, 11.

23. Quoted by Cowell, 11.

24. "The Lady's Complaint," *Virginia Gazette*, 2 October 1736, p. 3. Quoted by Cowell, *Women Poets*, 21.

25. Judith Sargent Murray, "On the Equality of the Sexes," *Massachusetts Magazine* 2 (March, 1790):132. Quoted by Cowell, *Women Poets*, 21. The male attitude against which Murray and the others cited here remonstrate has lingered in the air of, not only American, but world culture generally. In the British satirical novelist Barbara Pym's 1961 novel *No Fond Return of Love*, a woman warns Dulcie Mainwaring, the central character, "You read too much. They [i.e., men] don't like it."

26. Quoted by Silverman, *Colonial American Poetry*, 355.

27. Even from such an excellent one as Silverman's *Colonial American Poetry* (except for Silverman's inclusion of Anne Bradstreet and his passing mention of such facts as "The ladies [of pre-Revolutionary Philadelphia society] wrote, too," p. 355).

28. Winslow, *American Broadside Verse*, xvii. The discussion of broadside poetry in this section owes much to Winslow's pioneer work on the subject; hereafter cited in the text and followed by page numbers in parentheses.

Chapter Three

1. Silverman, *Colonial American Poetry*, 419–20. The discussion of the nationalistic pastoral that follows is mainly based on Silverman's, 419–21.

2. Pearce, *Continuity of American Poetry*, 65–66.

3. Donald Barlow Stauffer, *A Short History of American Poetry* (New York: E. P. Dutton & Co., 1974), 52. Stauffer points out that between 1782 and 1820 there were over twenty editions of the poem.

4. Ibid.

5. Quoted and discussed by Pearce, *Continuity of American Poetry*, 67–68.

6. Ibid., 68.

7. Philip Freneau, *The Poems of Philip Freneau, Poet of the American Revolution*, vol. 1, ed. Fred Lewis Pattee (New York: Russell & Russell, Inc., 1963), 141.

8. Ibid., vol. 2, 281.

9. Ibid., vol. 3, 91.

10. Ibid., vol. 2, 370.

11. M. A. Richmond, *Bid the Vassal Soar: Interpretive Essays on the Life and Poetry of Phillis Wheatley and George Moses Horton* (Washington, D.C.: Howard University Press, 1974), 14. Richmond is quoting from Wheatley's early biographer Margaretta Matilda Odell, *Memoir and Poems of Phillis Wheatley* (Boston: George W. Light, 1834), 9–10.

12. Richmond, *Vassal*, 20–21.

13. Phillis Wheatley, *The Poems of Phillis Wheatley*, ed. Julian D. Mason, Jr. (Chapel Hill: University of North Carolina Press, 1966), 7.

14. Ibid.

15. Ibid., 34.

16. William H. Robinson, Jr., *Early Black American Poets: Selections with Biographical and Critical Introductions* (Dubuque, Iowa: William C. Brown, 1969), 19.

Chapter Four

1. Discussed briefly by Pearce, *Continuity of American Poetry*, 206.

2. Quoted by Pearce, ibid., 210.

3. Ibid.

4. Quoted by George Perkins, ed., *American Poetic Theory* (New York: Holt, Rinehart & Winston, 1972), 14–19.

5. Though not by Stauffer, *Short History*, 83–84.

6. Gay Wilson Allen, *American Prosody* (New York: American Book Company, 1935), 86. Stauffer also notes and concurs with Allen's assessment, 70.

7. Noted by Stauffer, *Short History*, 74.

8. According to Robert E. Spiller, Willard Thorp, Thomas H. Johnson, and Henry Seidel Canby, eds.; Howard Mumford Jones, Dixon Wector, and Stanley T. Williams, associate eds., *Literary History of the United States* (New York: Macmillan Co., 1959, 289.

9. Perkins, *Poetic Theory*, 71–81.

10. Quoted by Hyatt H. Waggoner, *American Poets from the Puritans to the Present* (Boston: Houghton Mifflin Co., 1968), 56. Waggoner has a valuable short discussion of Holmes's aversion to Calvinism, 55–59.

11. Waggoner, ibid., 258, says correctly that "Tuckerman was a doubting, despairing, grief-stricken Episcopalian," although he accommodates that judgment within a full and fair treatment of the poet.

12. Ibid., 259.

13. Frederick Goddard Tuckerman, *The Complete Poems of Frederick Goddard Tuckerman*, ed. N. Scott Momaday (New York: Oxford University Press, 1965), 69–70.

14. As noted by Waggoner, ibid., 236–40.

15. Ibid., 192.

16. Simms and Hayne are discussed briefly by Stauffer, *Short History*, 189–90.

17. Nathaniel Hawthorne, *The English Notebooks*, ed. Randall Stewart (New York: Modern Language Association of America, 1941), 432–33.

18. Walter Bezanson, "Melville's 'Clarel': The Complex Passion," *ELH* 21 (1954):146–49.

19. Quoted by Waggoner, *American Poets*, 229.

20. Herman Melville, *Clarel: A Poem and Pilgrimage in the Holy Land*, part 2, vol. 14 of *The Works of Herman Melville, Standard Edition* (New York: Russell & Russell, Inc., 1963), 255.

21. From an untitled poem in Clara H. von Moschzisker, *Poems* (Philadelphia, 1868), quoted by Lee Steinmetz, *The Poetry of the American Civil War* (n.p.: Michigan State University Press, 1960), 52.

22. Melville, vol. 16, 10.

23. Ibid., 64.

24. Ibid., 45.

25. Ibid., 44.

Chapter Five

1. For any virtues, though not for any defects, the discussion of Poe here owes much to Daniel Hoffman's exciting interpretive book *Poe Poe Poe Poe Poe Poe Poe* (New York: Vintage Books, 1985). Any disquisition on Poe and his work by anyone who has read the Hoffman study is bound to be at least partially shaped by it.

2. Edgar Allan Poe, *Essays and Reviews*, ed. G. R. Thompson (New York: Library of America, 1984), 1467.

3. Probably Auber's "Lac des Fées." Lewis Leary treats the references to Auber and Weir in *Explicator* 6 (1948):25. Hoffman refers to Leary and also identifies "Mount Yaanek" as Mount Erebus, a volcanic mountain in Antarctica discovered in Poe's time. Hoffman also sheds light on the name "Ulalume" as perhaps meaning "light of the dead." He points out

that *Ule* is turkish for "dead" and that in a note to "Al Aaraaf" Poe
incorrectly took "Ule Deguisi" as Turkish for "Dead Sea." Hoffman
succinctly concludes: "With these exotic names—Auber, Weir, Yaanek,
Ulalume—Poe is being at once exact and diaphanous, imputing the
meaning in the music, such as it is."

4. As Hoffman calls him, *Poe*, 71–72.

5. All four possibilities for sources mentioned here are suggested
in *Selected Writings of Edgar Allan Poe*, ed. Edward H. Davidson (Cambridge, Mass.: Riverside Press, 1956), 495, in Davidson's extremely helpful
note on "The Raven." As for the meter, which is reasonably referred to
in the present discussion as trochaic octameter, Poe has a long-winded
and technically more precise description in "The Philosophy of Composition." In it he acknowledges that he borrowed the line configurations
from unnamed poets, but he congratulates himself on his originality in
grouping them into his stanza form.

6. Poe's fixation with madness is fascinating, so profound and repetitive that it suggests a dread of the affliction. At times, his identification
with other writers to reassure himself is touching. Witness his attribution
to Shakespeare of his own fusion with mad characters in his title essay
on the nature of Shakespeare's greatness, "The Characters of Shakespeare." Speaking of the character of Hamlet, Poe says:

> It must have been well known to Shakespeare, that a
> leading feature in certain more intense classes of intoxi-
> cation, (from whatever cause,) is an almost irresistible im-
> pulse to counterfeit a farther degree of excitement than
> actually exists. [How well must Poe have known.] Analogy
> would lead any thoughtful person to suspect the same
> impulse in madness—where beyond doubt it is manifest.
> This, Shakespeare *felt*, not thought. He felt it through his
> marvellous power of *identification* with humanity at large—
> the ultimate source of his magical influence upon mankind.
> He wrote of Hamlet as if Hamlet he were; and having in
> the first instance, imagined his hero excited to partial in-
> sanity by the disclosures of the ghost—he (the poet) *felt*
> that it was natural he should be impelled to exaggerate
> the insanity.

How much is Poe saying about himself here? A great deal, one suspects.

7. Another of Poe's treatments of self-destruction is his story "The
Imp of the Perverse" (1845), almost as absorbing as the poem "The
Raven." In "The Imp of the Perverse" Poe insinuates that human beings
are psychogenically driven, against their wills and self-interests, to act in
ways that make them unhappy and bring evil to the world. In *Poe Poe
Poe Poe Poe Poe Poe* Hoffman often appropriately chalks up Poe's perverse

behavior to the imp of that name. That busy little imp is at work in Poe's 422-line poem of 1829, "Al Aaraaf." On the mystical, distant nowhere of that star, Ianthe resolves to become mortal to experience mere mortal pleasures, while Michael Angelo, a mortal, chooses to die in order to be with Ianthe, of whom he has had a vision, in pleasure. Giving up the unearthly in favor of the earthly can lead to no good in Poe. In a clear analogy to the Judeo-Christian fall the two lovers unintentionally bring disharmony to Al Aaraaf and, even worse, in so doing, destroy the plan of its leading spirit, Nesace, to bring harmony to all the universe by spreading the power of creative imagination.

Chapter Six

1. A good short article on Emerson's Eastern thought is Andrew M. McLean's "Emerson's *Brahma* as an Expression of Brahman," *New England Quarterly* 42, no. 1 (March 1969):115–22.

2. Emerson, who had a strong measure of dispassion in his personality and was often more comfortable as a spectator and commentator than as a doer, was beautifully suited to an epistemological approach (Transcendentalism is too unsystematic to be legitimately called a philosophical system) that called for calm surveillance and reflection upon the meaning of experiences observed. He actually got his Transcendentalist concepts from such European philosophers as Emanuel Kant by way of British and Continental writers, notably Coleridge, Carlyle, and Goethe, tailoring the ideas as a result of discussions with the New England Transcendentalist cohort at meetings of the Transcendental Club (formerly the Symposium Club and Hedge Club) in Concord. The group was in the forefront of such reform movement in the 1840s intuiting the need for such libertarian political causes as political rights for women, though Emerson himself, the most articulate—and detached—spokesman of Transcendentalism, generally abstained from activity other than stating theory. He did help edit the Transcendentalist journal, *The Dial*, an important outlet for his work, however. An absorbing treatment of Emerson's own view of the association between nature and the human observer is Carl M. Lindner's "Newtonianism in Emerson's *Nature*," *Emerson Society Quarterly* 20, no. 4 (1974):260–69. And Hyatt Waggoner, whose book *Emerson as Poet* (Princeton, N.J.: Princeton University Press, 1974) is a must for any serious Emerson scholar, treats the matter of Emerson's Transcendentalism in his excellent essay on Emerson in *American Poets from the Puritans to the Present*, 90–114.

3. Quentin Anderson, *The Imperial Self: An Essay in American Literary and Cultural History* (New York: Alfred A. Knopf, 1971).

4. Ibid., 46–47. Quoted by Waggoner, *Emerson as Poet*, 59.

Notes and References

5. Ralph Waldo Emerson, "The Poet," *The Best of Ralph Waldo Emerson: Essays, Poems, Addresses* (Roslyn, N.Y.: Walter J. Black, Inc., 1941), 228. There is a hint of self-justification in this passage. Emerson, who realized that he was "such as say and do not," that is, a man far more of words than of action, erases the difference by making *saying* an action.

6. John Q. Anderson, *The Liberating Gods: Emerson on Poets and Poetry* (Coral Gables, Fla.: University of Miami Press, 1971), 31–41, sees the poet's function as tripartite, since Anderson chooses to divide in two what is here described as demonstrating the union between the physical and spiritual worlds. Thus, Anderson discusses (1) cosmic unity and (2) the poet's job of freeing "men from the prison of their everyday thoughts by bringing them glimpses of the higher realm of spirit" as distinct, though related issues. His scheme is perfectly defensible. The chapter "The Function of the Poet" is an excellent one in a first-rate study of Emerson's aesthetic.

7. A favorite metaphor of Emerson; see, for example, his soaring, mystical essay "Circles."

8. Quoted by Anderson, *Liberating Gods*, 33–34, from *Emerson*, 4:194.

9. And to those who liked to prick the skin of romanticism—Melville, for example, who in his "The Aeolian Harp" nicely contrasts Ariel's false rendering of the Real in *The Tempest* (1.2), when the storm he reports on to Prospero is quite harmless, with the dumb fatality of a real tempest, which is much different and more deadly.

10. The poem "Bacchus" helps to introduce abandon as a motif in American poetry. Emily Dickinson's "I Taste a Liquor Never Brewed," Wallace Stevens's "A High-Toned Old Christian Woman," Archibald MacLeish's "Theory of Poetry," e. e. cummings's "My Father Moved Through Dooms of Love," Hart Crane's "The Wine Menagerie," not to mention almost all of Whitman, are just a few examples among literally innumerable American poems that play variations on the theme.

11. See Emerson's "Compensation"; the essay contains a full exposition of the idea.

12. Noted also by Waggoner, *Emerson as Poet*, 78–79. The letter appears in *The Letters of Ralph Waldo Emerson*, Vol. 1, ed. Ralph L. Rusk (New York and London: Columbia University Press, 1939), 435.

13. Reported by Charles J. Woodbury, *Talks with Emerson* (New York: Horizon Press, 1970), 62–63. Quoted by Anderson, *Liberating Gods*, 119.

14. Allen, *American Prosody*, 99. Hyatt Waggoner points out the debt that Edgar Lee Masters and Marianne Moore owe to the technique of "Hamatreya," observing that "each, along with many other American poets since Whitman, owe part of their inspiration to the Concord bard. He is in the blood of every American original."

15. A penetrating essay on the difficulty of locating Emerson the man is Joel Porte's "The Problem of Emerson," in *Romanticism: Critical Essays in American Literature*, ed. James Barbour and Thomas Quirk (New York and London: Garland Publishing, 1986), 59–81. Porte mentions that some, such as Charles J. Woodbury, wanted to elevate him to sainthood ("He is a shining figure on some mount of Transfiguration").

16. For Emerson's safety, that was just as well. Woodbury, in *Talks with Emerson*, 76–77, recounts this anecdote: "Mr. Emerson was a man of meditation for whom action was too severe; and his success at garden tending is suggested by the expostulation of his son, who alarmed at certain gestures with the spade, cautioned as follows: "Look out, papa! you'll dig your leg."

17. Noted also by Waggoner, *American Poets*, 90–94.

18. Stauffer, *Short History*, 94.

19. The two possibilities are posed by Perry Miller in his handy book *The Transcendentalists: An Anthology* (Cambridge, Mass.: Harvard University Press, 1950), 402. The lines quoted in this section from Channing, Fuller, the Sturgis sisters, and Cranch are all from Miller's anthology.

20. Cited by Waggoner, *American Poets*, 126.

21. Gay Wilson Allen, in Miller, *The Transcendentalists: An Anthology*, 49–50, 385.

22. The brief essential facts of Thoreau's poetic career are in *Collected Poems of Henry David Thoreau*, enlarged edition, ed. Carl Bode (Baltimore: Johns Hopkins Press, 1964).

Chapter Seven

1. Paul Zweig's account of this process of transformation, *Walt Whitman: The Making of the Poet* (New York: Basic Books, 1984), is the best source on the subject and one of the best studies of Whitman of any kind. Inevitably, it colors much of the present discussion; it must affect anyone's perception of Whitman who reads it.

2. An excellent, and perhaps the best written, general critical biography of Whitman is Justin Kaplan's *Walt Whitman: A Life* (New York: Simon & Schuster, 1980), although many critics still regard Gay Wilson Allen's *The Solitary Singer: A Critical Biography of Walt Whitman* (New York: Macmillan Co., 1955) to be the best for its detail. There is really no competition; both are excellent.

3. Zweig, *Walt Whitman*, 34, calls this plot pattern "Whitman's signature as a fiction writer." The following quotation from "Wild Frank's Return" is also used by Zweig, ibid.

4. Ibid., 28–29.

5. Walt Whitman, *The Early Poems and the Fiction*, ed. Thomas L. Brasher (New York: New York University Press, 1963).

6. Jerome Loving, *Emerson, Whitman, and the American Muse* (Chapel Hill and London: University of North Carolina Press, 1982), 19–20, finds another crack in Whitman's conventionality in his poem "Time to Come," from the *Aurora* of 9 April 1842. A revision of "Our Future Lot," published on 31 October 1838, which anticipated a Christian afterlife, "Time to Come" confesses to an inability to accept the Christian belief; "this struggling brain is powerless . . . / To rend the mighty mystery." All the human can do is await death "In dark, uncertain awe." The ideological change does signal an opening of Whitman's mind, although he expresses it in prosody as conformist as ever.

7. Joseph Jay Rubin and Charles H. Brown, eds., *Walt Whitman of the New York "Aurora"* (State College, Pa.: Bald Eagle Press, 1950; reprint, Westport, Conn.: Greenwood Press, 1972), 105. Quoted also by Loving, ibid., 10.

8. *The Early Lectures of Ralph Waldo Emerson,* ed. Stephen E. Whicher, Robert E. Spiller, and Wallace E. Williams, 3 vols. (Cambridge, Mass.: Harvard University Press, 1959–1972), 3:362. Quoted also by Loving, ibid.

9. The spiritual distance between the two men has been exaggerated, often by Emerson worshippers or Whitman deprecators (not infrequently the same persons), on grounds, for instance, that Whitman's sexuality, including his extolling of masturbation, both heterosexual and homosexual love, and prostitutes, was distasteful to the far more reserved Emerson. Few would argue that Emerson was not more conservative, but much prudery seems to have been projected upon him by others. He did not complain of the sensuality of the original *Leaves of Grass* when he wrote his famous congratulatory letter to Whitman in 1855, and when he walked with Whitman on Boston Common in 1860 and tried to talk him out of adding the "Enfans d'Adam" cluster to the collection, his reasons, according to Whitman, were pragmatic, not moralistic. Emerson "wanted the book to sell" and urged Whitman to excise "bits here and there that offended the censors so that the book "might . . . go through editions—perhaps many editions" (Horace Traubel, *With Walt Whitman in Camden,* 5 vols. (Boston, 1906), 1:439. Emerson, admitting that without the "Enfans d'Adam" poems the book would be good but not as good, had to acquiesce to Whitman's argument that the sexuality was the "root" of the book and so could not be omitted. Indeed, Whitman appears to have antedated Freudian psychology in his perception of sex as a wellspring of human behavior.

10. Dated by Edward F. Grier, "Walt Whitman's Earliest Known Notebook," *PMLA* 83 (October 1968):1453–56. Grier is the editor of *Notebooks and Unpublished Manuscripts, Vol. I: Family Notes and Autobiography, Brooklyn and New York* in *The Collected Writings of Walt Whitman*

Notes and References

(New York: New York University Press, 1984); quotations are taken from Grier's volume. Floyd Stovall, "Dating Whitman's Notebooks," *Studies in Bibliography* 24 (1971):197, disputes the 1847 date, suggesting 1854 instead, but Grier's argument is convincing.

11. Gay Wilson Allen, *Walt Whitman Handbook* (New York: Hendricks House, 1962), 394.

12. Grier, *Notebooks* 1:38–39.

13. A term used by Zweig, *Walt Whitman*, 115–16, in his enlightening discussion of the two sides of the poet. The quote that follows is from the same source.

14. A supposition suggested by Anderson, *Liberating Gods*, 90.

15. The listing here is based on the handy one provided by Anderson, ibid., 116. n. 62.

16. In a letter to Harrison Blake dated 7 December 1856.

17. See Allen, *Walt Whitman Handbook*, 422–28.

18. Reprinted in James Woodress, ed., *Critical Essays on Walt Whitman* (Boston: G. K. Hall & Co., 1983), 44–46.

19. Ibid., 41–43.

20. Ibid., 23–25.

21. Ibid., 40–41.

22. Quoted from the poem "A Pact" and the prose note "What I feel About Walt Whitman" in *Walt Whitman and the Measure of His Song*, ed. Jim Perlman et al. (Minneapolis: Holy Cow! Press, 1981), 29–31.

23. Jorge Luis Borges, *The Aleph and Other Stories, 1933–1969* (New York: E. P. Dutton & Co., 1970), 217.

• *Selected Bibliography* •

PRIMARY SOURCES

Bradstreet, Anne. *Works of Anne Bradstreet.* Edited by Jeannine Hensley. Cambridge, Mass.: Harvard University Press, 1967.

Bryant, William Cullen. *The Poetical Works of William Cullen Bryant.* Edited by H. C. Sturges. New York: D. Appleton & Co., 1903.

Emerson, Ralph Waldo. *The Collected Works.* Edited by R. E. Spiller, A. R. Ferguson, et al. Cambridge, Mass.: The Belknap Press of Harvard University Press, 1971– .

———. *The Complete Works of Ralph Waldo Emerson,* Centenary Edition, 12 vols. Edited by E. W. Emerson. Boston: Houghton Mifflin & Co., 1903–4.

Freneau, Philip. *The Last Poems of Philip Freneau.* Edited by Lewis Leary. New Brunswick, N.J.: Rutgers University Press, 1945.

———. *The Poems of Freneau.* Edited by Harry Hayden Clark. New York: Harcourt Brace, 1929.

Holmes, Oliver Wendell. *Oliver Wendell Holmes: Representative Selections.* Edited by S. I. Hayakawa and H. M. Jones. New York: American Book Co., 1939.

Longfellow, Henry Wadsworth. *The Complete Poetical Works of Henry Wadsworth Longfellow.* Boston: Houghton Mifflin & Co., 1893.

Lowell, James Russell. *James Russell Lowell: Representative Selections.* New York: American Book Co., 1947.

Melville, Herman. *The Works of Herman Melville.* Standard edition, 16 vols. London: Constable & Co., 1922–24. Reissued, New York: Russell & Russell, 1963.

Poe, Edgar Allan. *The Complete Works of Edgar Allan Poe,* Virginia edition, 17 vols. Editied by J. A. Harrison. New York: Crowell, 1902.

Taylor, Edward. *The Poems of Edward Taylor.* Edited by D. E. Stanford. New Haven: Yale University Press, 1960.

———. *The Poetical Works of Edward Taylor.* Edited by Thomas H. Johnson. Princeton, N.J.: Princeton University Press, 1939. Reissued, Princeton University Press, 1943.

Selected Bibliography

Thoreau, Henry David. *Collected Poems of Henry David Thoreau.* Enlarged edition. Edited by Carl Bode. Baltimore: Johns Hopkins Press, 1964.

Timrod, Henry. *The Poems of Henry Timrod.* Edited by Paul H. Hayne. New York: Hale & Sons, 1873.

Tuckerman, Frederick Goddard. *The Complete Poems of Frederick Goddard Tuckerman.* With a Critical Foreword by Yvor Winters. Edited by M. Scott Momaday. New York: Oxford University Press, 1965.

Very, Jones. *Poems and Essays.* Complete and revised edition. Edited by James Freeman Clarke and C. A. Bartol. Boston and New York: Houghton Mifflin & Co., 1886.

Wheatley, Phillis. *The Poems of Phillis Wheatley.* Edited by Julian D. Mason, Jr. Chapel Hill: University of North Carolina Press, 1966.

Whitman, Walt. *The Collected Writings of Walt Whitman,* 22 vols. Edited by Gay Wilson Allen and Sculley Bradley. New York: New York University Press, 1961—84.

———. *Leaves of Grass: A Textual Variorum of the Printed Poems.* Edited by Scully Bradley, Harold W. Blodgett, et al. New York: New York University Press, 1980.

Whittier, John Greenleaf. *The Complete Poetical Works of John Greenleaf Whittier.* Edited by Horace E. Scudder. Boston and New York: Houghton Mifflin & Co., 1894.

SECONDARY SOURCES

Adkins, Nelson F. *Fitz-Green Halleck: An Early Knickerbocker Wit and Poet.* New Haven, Conn.: Yale University Press, 1930. Adkins's book is helpful on both Halleck and the Knickerbocker milieu.

Allen, Gay Wilson. *American Prosody.* New York: American Book Co., 1935. This is a standard, often technical examination of the development of American prosody through specific contributions made to it by important American poets.

———. *The Solitary Singer: A Critical Biography of Walt Whitman.* New York: Macmillan Co., 1955. This is a standard and exhaustive study of Whitman and his work.

———. *Waldo Emerson.* New York: Viking Press, 1981. Allen did his characteristically thorough scholarship in producing this readable critical biography.

———. *Walt Whitman as Man, Poet, and Legend.* Carbondale: Southern Illinois University Press, 1961. Allen updated and expanded upon his earlier fine work on Whitman.

Selected Bibliography

————. *Walt Whitman Handbook.* New York: Hendricks House, 1962. The *Handbook* is a valuable and usable guide to Whitman by one of the great Whitman scholars.

Anderson, John Q. *The Liberating Gods: Emerson on Poets and Poetry.* Coral Gables, Fla.: University of Miami Press, 1971. The volume is an excellent, well-documented study of Emerson's aesthetic.

Anderson, Quentin. *The Imperial Self: An Essay in American Literary and Cultural History.* New York: Alfred A. Knopf, 1971. Anderson's discussion is both far-ranging and incisive; it is a must for students of American Literature.

Arvin, Newton. *Herman Melville.* New York: William Sloane Associates, 1950. Arvin's study is basic and useful.

Asselineau, Roger. *The Evolution of Walt Whitman.* Cambridge, Mass.: Harvard University Press, 1960–62. This two-volume translation of Asselineau's work in French is a distinguished critical biography.

Barbour, James, and Thomas Quirk, eds. *Romanticism: Critical Essays in American Literature.* New York and London: Garland Publishing, 1986. Though necessarily limited in its coverage of poets, the volume includes excellent essays on Emerson, Poe, and Whitman.

Bartlett, William I. *Jones Very: Emerson's "Brave Saint."* Durham, N.C.: Duke University Press, 1942. Not only is the biography good, but Bartlett printed many poems omitted from Clarke and Bartol's supposedly "complete" edition of 1886.

Bercovitch, Sacvan. *The American Jeremiad.* Madison and London: University of Wisconsin Press, 1978. Bercovitch traces the jeremiad through American culture. The work sheds important light on Puritan thought and its underpinning of American culture.

Berryman, John. *Homage to Mistress Bradstreet.* New York: Farrar, Straus & Giroux, 1956. The volume consists of a poem that expresses Berryman's highly personal humanizing sense of Bradstreet.

Bezanson, Walter. "Melville's 'Clarel': The Complex Passion." *Journal of English Literary History* 21 (1954):146–59. Some of Bezanson's interpretation is arguable, but his reading of Melville's long and difficult poem is strongly reasoned.

Campbell, Killis. *The Mind of Poe and Other Studies.* Cambridge, Mass.: Harvard University Press, 1933. Campbell's work is worth reading, particularly on Poe.

Chase, Richard. *Herman Melville: A Critical Study.* New York: Macmillan Co., 1949. Chase's is still a handy, reliable biography of Melville.

Cowell, Pattie. *Women Poets in Pre-Revolutionary America, 1650–1775, An Anthology.* Troy, N.Y.: Whitston Publishing Co., 1981. This is an invaluable collection of poems with good little introductions to their women poets. Cowell brings light to a subject about which there was only darkness for too long.

Crasnow, Ellman, and Philip Haffenden. "New Founde Land." In Malcolm Bradbury and Howard Temperley, eds., *Introduction to American Studies.* London and New York: Longman, 1981, 23–44. The essay perceptively examines the Puritan culture and its contribution to the mythology of America.

Daly, Robert. *God's Altar: The World and the Flesh in Puritan Poetry.* Berkeley, Los Angeles, and London: University of California Press, 1978. Daly's discussion of Ramism in Puritan poetry is especially helpful in what is, overall, a good survey.

Davidson, Edward H., ed. *Selected Writings of Edgar Allan Poe.* Cambridge, Mass.: Riverside Press, 1956. Davidson's notes are invaluable.

Eberwein, Jane Donahue, ed. *Early American Poetry: Selections from Bradstreet, Taylor, Dwight, Freneau, and Bryant.* Madison and London: University of Wisconsin Press, 1978. The title is too modest, for the volume also contains selections from Wigglesworth, Cooke, and Barlow. The editorial choices are intelligent and the introductions to the book and the poets valuable.

Fogle, Richard Harter. "Melville's *Clarel:* Doubt and Belief." *Tulane Studies in English* 10 (1960):101–16. This is a helpful interpretation of the complex poem by an excellent student of Melville's work.

———. "The Themes of Melville's Later Poetry." *Tulane Studies in English* 11 (1961):65–86. The essay contains a full and intelligent treatment of the subject.

Foster, Charles Howell. *Emerson's Theory of Poetry.* Iowa City: Midland House, 1939. Foster's is a useful, well-documented treatment of the subject.

Gross, Seymour L. "Emerson and Poetry." *South Atlantic Quarterly* 54 (1955):82–94. This essay is an outstanding one on Emerson's theory and practice of poetry.

Halbert, Cecelia L. "Tree of Life Imagery in the Poetry of Edward Taylor." *American Literature* 38 (1966):22–34. This is a useful article relating Taylor's imagery to Puritan thought.

Hoffman, Daniel G., ed. *American Poetry and Poetics: Poems and Critical Documents from the Puritans to Robert Frost.* Garden City: Doubleday & Co., 1962. This is a handy anthology with well-chosen selections.

———. *Poe Poe Poe Poe Poe Poe Poe.* New York: Vintage Books, 1985. Hoffman's is simply the best interpretive study of Poe written to date.

Hopkins, Vivian C. *Spires of Form: A Study of Emerson's Aesthetic Theory.* Cambridge, Mass.: Harvard University Press, 1951. Hopkins's study is admirable and essential to understanding the subject.

Selected Bibliography

Howard, Leon. *The Connecticut Wits.* Chicago: University of Chicago Press, 1943. This is a rare and valuable examination of Trumbull, Dwight, and Barlow.

Johnson, Thomas H., ed. *The Poetical Works of Edward Taylor.* Princeton: Princeton University Press, 1939. Johnson, one of the best scholars and editors of American poetry and the man who produced the crucial variorum edition of Emily Dickinson, discovered the work of Edward Taylor in 1937 and edited this volume. It has a helpful introduction and notes.

Kaplan, Justin. *Walt Whitman: A Life.* New York: Simon & Schuster, 1980. Along with Gay Wilson Allen's *The Solitary Singer,* Kaplan's book is essential to a thorough knowledge of Whitman.

Kummings, Donald D. "A Note on the Americanness of Walt Whitman." *Calamus: Walt Whitman Quarterly: International* (Tokyo) 10 (April 1975):18–27. Kummings explores a number of Whitman's key poems to show the centrality of Americans' preoccupation with process to *Leaves of Grass.*

———. *Walt Whitman, 1940–1975: A Reference Guide.* Boston: G. K. Hall & Co., 1982. The work is an exhaustive, well-annotated compilation of Whitman criticism during the period covered.

Lindner, Carl M. "Newtonianism in Emerson's *Nature.*" *Emerson Society Quarterly* 20, no. 4 (1974):260–69. The article helps to clarify Emerson's conception of the relationship between nature and the individual observer.

Loving, Jerome. *Emerson, Whitman, and the American Muse.* Chapel Hill and London: University of North Carolina Press, 1982. The book is useful for an understanding of the development of the two poets and the relationship between them.

Matthiessen, F. O. *American Renaissance: Art and Expression in the Age of Emerson and Whitman.* New York: Oxford University Press, 1941. Matthiessen's work is a standard one that should not be missed.

McLean, Andrew M. "Emerson's *Brahma* as an Expression of Brahman." *New England Quarterly* 42, no. 1 (March 1969):115–22. This is a helpful article on the relationship between Emerson's thought and Eastern religion.

Meserole, Harrison T. *Seventeenth-Century American Poetry.* New York: W. W. Norton & Co., 1968. This is a fine anthology with a good introductory essay and helpful notes and comments.

Metzger, Charles R. *Thoreau and Whitman: A Study of Their Esthetics.* Seattle: University of Washington Press, 1961. This is a helpful book for an understanding of not only Thoreau and Whitman, but Emerson and the intellectual climate in which they all worked.

Selected Bibliography

Miller, James E., Jr. *A Critical Guide to Leaves of Grass*. Chicago: University of Chicago Press, 1957. With Allen's *Walt Whitman Handbook*, this is a valuable guide to Whitman's work.

Miller, Perry. *The American Puritans: Their Prose and Poetry*. Garden City, N.Y.: Doubleday & Co., 1956. This is a useful, compact anthology.

————. *The New England Mind from Colony to Province*. Cambridge, Mass.: Harvard University Press, 1939. This is an excellent standard work on Puritan thought and its evolution in New England.

————. *The Transcendentalists: An Anthology*. Cambridge, Mass.: Harvard University Press, 1950. Miller brought his usual perspicacity to the making of this anthology; to read it thoroughly is to acquire a good working knowledge of American Transcendentalism.

Ong, Walter J., S. J., *Ramus: Method and the Decay of Dialogue*. Cambridge, Mass.: Harvard University Press, 1958. Ong carefully explains the nature of Ramist logic and its importance to Puritan thought.

Paul, Sherman. *The Shores of America: Thoreau's Inward Exploration*. Urbana: University of Illinois Press, 1958. Paul's discussion is excellent, particularly for its examination of the causes and artistic effects of Thoreau's relative isolation.

Pearce, Roy Harvey. *The Continuity of American Poetry*. Princeton: Princeton University Press, 1961. Although Pearce's study can occasionally get a bit cranky, it is still the best—a benchmark against which other examinations of American poetry must be measured.

Perkins, George, editor *American Poetic Theory*. New York: Holt, Rinehart & Winston, 1972. The collection of important statements on poetics, by Americans from Freneau to James Dickey, is broad, and Perkins's introduction to the book is perceptive.

Perlman, Jim, Ed Folsom, and Dan Campion, editors. *Walt Whitman: The Measure of His Song*. Minneapolis: Holy Cow! Press, 1981. This is a wonderful compilation of reactions to Whitman, from his own time to the present, from America and from abroad.

Quinn, Patrick F. *The French Face of Edgar Poe*. Carbondale: Southern Illinois University Press, 1957. This study is especially good on the affinity between Poe and the French poets who have admired his work.

Richmond, M. A. *Bid the Vassal Soar: Interpretive Essays on the Life and Poetry of Phillis Wheatley and George Moses Horton*. Washington, D.C.: Howard University Press, 1974. This is a good, thorough study of the two early Afro-American poets Wheatley and Horton.

Robinson, William H., Jr. *Early Black American Poets: Selections with Biographical and Critical Introductions*. Dubuque, Iowa: William C. Brown, 1969. This may still be the most useful anthology of early Afro-American poetry available. The introductions are helpful.

Selected Bibliography

Rubin, Joseph Jay, and Charles H. Brown, eds. *Walt Whitman of the New York "Aurora."* State College, Pa.: Bald Eagle Press, 1950. Seeing examples of the work of the early and transitional Whitman is helpful to an understanding of his accomplishment.

Rusk, R. L. *The Life of Ralph Waldo Emerson.* New York: Charles Scribner's Sons, 1949. This biography has long been widely regarded as standard.

Shurr, William H. *The Mystery of Iniquity: Melville as Poet, 1857–1891.* Lexington, Ky.: University Press of Kentucky, 1972. Shurr's treatment of Melville's poetry, which focuses on Melville's relentless inquiry into the relationship of good and evil, sheds more light on Melville as poet than any other examination of the poetry. The book is ambitious, even including *Billy Budd* with the poetry, and it fulfills its ambition. The student of Melville's prose as well as his poetry comes away from this study with firmer understanding of Melville's worldview.

Silverman, Kenneth, editor *Colonial American Poetry.* New York and London: Hafner Publishing Co., 1968. This is a treasure chest of an anthology, with broad selections and informative introductions.

Stanford, Donald E. "Edward Taylor's 'Spiritual Relation.' " *American Literature* 35 (1964):467–75. Stanford's essay is a good basic one on Taylor's work.

Stauffer, Donald Barlow. *A Short History of American Poetry.* New York: E. P. Dutton & Co., 1974. Stauffer's is one of the few good comprehensive histories of American poetry.

Stein, William Bysshe. *The Poetry of Melville's Late Years: Time, History, Myth, and Religion.* Albany: State University of New York Press, 1970. The study is valuable as far as it goes, though for greater depth and breadth, one would go to Shurr's *The Mystery of Iniquity,* which includes fine essays on works not covered by Stein (notably *Battle Pieces* and *Clarel*).

Stovall, Floyd. *The Foreground of "Leaves of Grass."* Charlottesville: University Press of Virginia, 1974. Stovall's book is important for its treatment of Whitman's emotional and intellectual preparation for the composition of *Leaves of Grass.*

Sutton, Walter. *American Free Verse: The Modern Revolution in Poetry.* New York: New Directions, 1973. Sutton's chapter "The Romantic Revolution" nicely places Whitman and the free-verse revolution in context, and his examination of facets of Whitman's technique is well done.

Traubel, Horace. *With Walt Whitman in Camden,* 5 vols. (1906–64). Vol. 1, Boston, 1906; 2, Boston, 1908; 3, Boston, 1914; 4, Philadelphia,

1953; 5, Carbondale, 1964. The account, by one of Whitman's closest friends, is fascinating.

Van Doren, Mark. *Thoreau: A Critical Study.* New York: Houghton Mifflin & Co., 1916. Van Doren weathers very well; the volume is still important.

Waggoner, Hyatt H. *American Poets from the Puritans to the Present.* New York: Dell Publishing Co., 1968. Waggoner's is one of the few excellent studies of American poetry. Some of his value judgments may be debated, but they are well argued and must be respected.

———. *Emerson as Poet.* Princeton, N.J.: Princeton University Press, 1974. This work by one of the outstanding critics of American literature must be regarded as basic to an understanding of Emerson's work.

Warren, Robert Penn. "Melville the Poet." *Kenyon Review* 8 (1946):208–23. This is a sensitive, perceptive essay by another poet.

Whicher, Stephen E. *Freedom and Fate: An Inner Life of Ralph Waldo Emerson.* Philadelphia: University of Pennsylvania Press, 1953. Whicher's is a fine examination of Emerson's great complexity.

Winslow, Ola E. *American Broadside Verse.* New Haven, Conn.: Yale University Press, 1930. This is a landmark work, important for an understanding of the omnipresence of broadside verse in seventeenth- and eighteenth-century America.

Woodbury, Charles J. *Talks with Emerson.* New York: Horizon Press, 1970. The book presents Emerson secondhand by a worshipper, but it contains valuable reports on Emerson's opinions concerning a variety of matters.

Zweig, Paul. *Walt Whitman: The Making of the Poet.* New York: Basic Books, 1984. Zweig's is the most fascinating account of the transmogrification of Walt Whitman into the poet of *Leaves of Grass.* It is one of the most important studies of Whitman and is eminently readable.

· *Index* ·

Index

Mother of a Mighty Race," 79;
"The Poet," 79; "On Poetry in
Relation to Our Age and Country"
[essay], 79–80; "The Prairies,"
78–79; "Thanatopsis," 76–77; "To a
Waterfowl," 77; "To Cole, The
Painter Departing for Europe," 78
Bucke, R. M., 172
Burns, Robert, 90
Burton's Gentleman's Magazine, 111
Butler, Samuel, 64
Byles, Mather, 38–39, 60
Bynner, Witter, 94
Byrd, William: "Upon a Fart," 48
Byron, Lord, 75–76, 80

Calvinism, 2, 22, 26, 33–34, 41, 46,
49, 68, 133
Campion, Thomas, 10
Carlyle, Thomas, 152
Channing, W. H., 129, 143
Charles I, 3
Charles II, 28
Chaucer, Geoffrey, 85
Chauncy, Charles, 28
Chukovski, Kornei, 179
Church, Benjamin, 38
Church of England, 3, 28
Civil War, American, 74–75, 89, 90,
92, 97–98, 102–7, 147, 172, 175
Cole, Thomas, 78
Coleridge, Samuel Taylor, 75–76, 80,
82, 118, 130
College of Philadelphia, 43–45, 49
College of William and Mary, 49
Connecticut Wits. *See* Timothy
Dwight, Joel Barlow, and John
Trumbull
Conrad, Joseph: *Heart of Darkness*, 105
Cooke, Ebenezer: "The Sot-Weed
Factor," 48
Cooper, James Fenimore, 82, 88
Cotton, John, 3, 36
Cowley, Abraham, 10
Cranch, Christopher Pearce, 145,
146–48
Crane, Hart, 178
Creeley, Robert, 178
Cromwell, Oliver, 28
Cullen, Countee, 44

Daniel, Samuel, 10
Dante, 85, 133

Darwin, Charles, 90, 92, 103, 168
Democratic Review, the, 153
Dial, The, 143, 144, 147, 148, 149
Dickens, Charles: *Barnaby Rudge*, 120
Dickinson, Emily, 4–5, 19, 23, 28, 76,
93, 97, 124, 126, 146, 150; "Further
in Summer than the Birds" (J 1068),
95, 124
Donne, John, 10, 20
Doyle, Peter, 173
Drake, Joseph Rodman, 80–82
Drayton, Michael, 10
Dryden, John, 38
DuBartas, Guillaume de Salluste Sieur,
9–10, 21
Dudley, Thomas, 3
Dumbleton, Joseph, 60
Dunbar, Paul Laurence, 72
Dwight, Timothy: "America or a
Poem on the Settlement of the
British Colonies," 61–62; "The
Conquest of Canaan," 61–62;
"Greenfield Hill," 62

Eakins, Thomas, 179
Eaton, W. P., 94
Edwards, Jonathan, 33, 38
Elegiac poetry, 14–15, 39–42, 54,
57–58
Eliot, T. S., 19, 124, 178
Emerson, Ralph Waldo, 1, 4, 18–19,
66, 67, 74–75, 79, 80, 82, 95, 97,
99, 106, 124, 126–42, 143, 144, 145,
147, 149, 150–51, 152, 153, 154,
156–71, 175, 177–78, 179;
"Bacchus," 133, 136; "Brahma,"
133, 142; "Compensation" [essay;
poem], 139; "Concord Hymn," 135;
"Each and All," 141; "Hamatreya,"
135, 141; "The Humble Bee," 141;
May-Day and Other Pieces, 139;
"Merlin," 127, 133, 134, 135, 136,
137, 138; "Mithridates," 133;
"Musketaquid," 135; "The Ode
Inscribed to W. H. Channing," 135,
141; *Poems*, 139; "The Poet" [essay],
124, 127, 130–35, 139, 142, 150–51;
"The Poet" [poem], 139; "The
Problem," 141, 147–48, 156–57;
"The River," 141; "The Rhodora,"
141; "Saadi," 133, 134, 136, 137;
"Self-Reliance" [essay], 140; "Self-
Reliance" [poem], 141; "The

Index

Locke, John, 35–36
Longfellow, Henry Wadsworth, 82–85, 88, 175; "The Arsenal of Springfield," 84; "The Defence of Poetry" [essay], 85; "Divina Commedia" cycle, 85; "The Harvest Moon," 85; "Hiawatha," 84; "Hymn to the Night," 84; "The Jewish Cemetery at Newport," 85; "My Lost Youth," 85; "Nature," 84
Lorca, Garcia, 179
Lowell, Amy, 178
Lowell, James Russell, 83, 85, 87–90, 146; "The Cathedral," 89; *The Bigelow Papers*, 88–89; *A Fable for Critics*, 88, 125; "Ode Recited at the Harvard Commemoration, July 21, 1865," 89–90; *The Vision of Sir Launfal*, 89

Mallarmè, Stephane, 124
Maryland Gazette, 50
Massachusetts Bay Colony, 2–8, 22, 28
Massachusetts Bay Company, 3–4
Massachusetts Magazine, 53
Masters, Edgar Lee, 178
Mather, Cotton, 10, 32–33, 36, 45, 54; *Magnalia Christi Americana*, 63; *Manductio ad Ministerium*, 32–33
Mather, Increase, 28, 36
Mayakovski, Vladimir, 179
Mayflower, The, 2, 3
Melville, Herman, 18–19, 75, 76, 99–107, 141; "Bartleby the Scrivener," 99; *Battle-Pieces and Aspects of the War*, 100; *Billy Budd*, 99, 102; "Billy in the Darbies," 102; *Clarel*, 100–2; "The Conflict of Convictions," 104; "Donelson," 104; "The House-Top: A Night Piece (July, 1863)," 105; *John Marr and Other Sailors*, 102; "The Maldive Shark," 102–4; "Malverne Hill," 104; "The March into Virginia: Ending in the First Manassas (July, 1861)," 104–5; "Shiloh," 104; "A Utilitarian View of the *Monitor's* Fight," 105
Metaphysical poetry, 10, 20, 24
Mexican War, 89, 137
Middle Colonies, 33–34
Miller, Perry, 4

Milton, John, 80, 85, 122, 133, 175
Morton, Sarah, 51, 52, 53
Murray, Judith Sargent, 52, 53

New York, 33–34, 75, 80–81, 83, 105, 150, 152, 155
Newton, Sir Isaac, 35–36
North American Review, 83, 88
Noyles, Nicholas, 14

Oakes, Urian, 15, 54
Olson, Charles, 80, 178
Over-Soul, 128, 131, 133, 135, 153

Paine, Thomas, 67
Parker, Reverend Thomas, 51
Parks, William, 50
Pastorius, Francis Daniel, 8–9, 34
Paulding, James Kirke, 80, 82
Penn, William, 34
Pennsylvania Chronicle, 53
Pennsylvania Wits. *See* Junto.
Philadelphia, 40–46, 83
Plath, Sylvia, 178
Poe, Edgar Allan, 6, 75, 83, 95–96, 97, 99, 108–25, 126–30, 131, 136, 137, 142, 150, 151; biography, 108–14; "Al Aaraaf," 122–23; "Annabel Lee," 115, 118; "The City in the Sea," 116; "A Dream Within a Dream," 116; "Dream-Land," 116; "The Fall of the House of Usher," 121; "For Annie," 115, 118–19; "The Haunted Palace," 116, 121; "Israfel," 114, 136; "Lenore," 115; "The Poe, Philosophy of Composition," 120–25; "The Poetic Principle," 122–25; "The Purloined Letter," 117; "The Rationale of Verse," 97; *The Raven and Other Poems*, 112, 120; "The Raven," 115, 119–23, 126; "The Sleeper," 115; "Sonnet—To Science," 116, 117–18; *Tamerlane and Other Poems*, 110; "Tamerlane," 114; "To Helen," 114; "To One in Paradise," 115; "Ulalume—A Ballad," 115, 116–17, 129; "The Valley of Unrest," 116
Pope, Alexander, 36, 38, 45, 64, 69, 75
Pound, Ezra, 127, 178
Puritans, 1–34, 35, 37, 39, 46, 47, 49, 53, 54, 61–62, 68, 75, 76, 77,

Index

80–81, 103, 128, 141, 144, 179;
aesthetics, 2–3, 5–9, 41; classical
training, 9; legacy, 15–19; sources of
poetry, 9–15; theology, 2–8, 14–15,
21–22
Puttenham, George, 29

Quakers, 12, 34, 40, 90
Quarles, 10

Ramist logic. *See* Ramus, Peter
Ramus, Peter, 5, 7, 40, 77
Reed, Sampson, 147
Robinson, Edwin Arlington, 19, 88
Roethke, Theodore, 127
Rogers, John, 20
Romanticism, 74–107
Russell's Magazine, 97

Saffin, John, 7, 11, 32
Sandburg, Carl, 178
Saturday Club, 91
Schoolroom poets. *See* Fireside poets.
Scott, Sir Walter, 152
Scull, Nicholas, 42
Seagood, George, 47
Selijns, Henricus, 33
Sewall, Samuel, 5–6
Shakespeare, William, 10, 80, 134
Shelley, Percy Bysshe, 161
Sidney, Sir Philip, 10
Sigourney, Lydia, 83
Simms, William Gilmore, 75, 98–99
Smith, Anna Young, 53
Smith, William, 43–45, 47
South Carolina Gazette, 50
Southern Colonies, 46–49
Southern Literary Messenger, 97, 111
Steere, Richard, 8, 10, 34
Stevens, Wallace, 78, 81, 124, 178
Stockton, Annis, 52, 53
Sturgis, Caroline, 140, 144
Sturgis, Ellen, 144
Stylus, The, 113
Swains of the Schuylkil, 43–46, 59
Swedenborg, Emanuel, 141, 147
Swinburne, Charles, 96, 124
Sylvester, Joshua, 9

Tappan, Caroline Sturgis. *See* Sturgis,
Caroline
Taylor, Edward, 5, 7, 19, 28–33, 35,
38, 53, 128, 131, 145, 146;

"Prologue" to *Preparatory
Meditations, Second Series*, 7;
Preparatory Meditations, 29–31;
"Upon a Spider Catching a Fly," 5
Taylor, Jacob, 43
Tennyson, Alfred Lord, 89–90, 175
Thoreau, Henry David, 74–75, 129,
137, 141, 143, 148–49, 177
Timrod, Henry, 75; 97–98;
"Ethnogenesis," 98; "Ode Sung on
the Occasion of Decorating the
Graves of the Confederate Dead, at
Magnolia Cemetary, Charleston,
S.C., 1867," 98; "Spring," 98; "The
Unknown Dead," 98
Tompson, Benjamin, 12–13
Transcendentalism, 21, 127–30, 135,
141, 143, 145, 146–47, 162
Translation, The, 44–45, 47–48, 59–61
Traubel, Horace, 172
Trumbull, John: M'Fingal, 63–65; The
Progress of Dulness, 63, 64
Tuckerman, Frederick Goddard, 93–95;
"The Cricket," 93, 94–95; "Sonnets:
Second Series," 94
Tulley, John, 13
Turell, Jane Coleman, 50, 52, 53
Twain, Mark, 88, 92

Unitarianism, 76–77, 128
University of Pennsylvania. *See*
College of Philadelphia

Verlaine, Paul, 124
Very, Jones, 92, 129, 145–46
Virginia Gazette, 50

Walpole, Horace: *Reminiscences*, 120
Ward, Nathaniel, 51
Warren, Mercy Otis, 50, 52, 53
Warren, Robert Penn, 100
Wheatley, Phillis, 50, 53, 69–72; "On
Being Brought from Africa to
America," 70–71; "To His
Excellency George Washington," 71;
"To the Right Honorable William,
Earl of Dartmouth, His Majesty's
Principal Secretary of State for
North-America, & C.," 71–72
Whitman, Walt, 1, 4, 18–19, 23, 66,
67, 75, 79, 80, 82, 93, 95, 98, 99,
103, 106, 124, 126–27, 131, 132,
139, 142, 144, 146, 149, 150–79;

· *About the Author* ·

Alan Shucard is the author of *Countee Cullen* (1984) in Twayne's United States Authors series and of two volumes of poems, *The Gorgon Bag* (1970) and *The Louse on the Head of a Yawning Lord* (1972). In addition, he has published numerous essays, review articles, and reviews on American, Afro-American, and Canadian and Commonwealth literatures. He received his Ph.D. from the University of Arizona in 1971 and has taught there and at the universities of Connecticut and British Columbia. In 1980–81 he was Fulbright Lecturer at the University of the West Indies, Cave Hill, Barbados, where he lectured in American and Afro-American literatures. He is currently Professor of English at the University of Wisconsin-Parkside.